Return of the Barbarians

Barbarians are back. These small, highly mobile, and stateless groups are no longer confined to the pages of history; they are a contemporary reality in groups such as the Taliban, Al-Qaeda, and ISIL. *Return of the Barbarians* reexamines the threat of violent non-state actors throughout history, revealing key lessons that are applicable today. From the Roman Empire and its barbarian challenge on the Danube and Rhine, Russia and the steppes to the nineteenth-century Comanches, Jakub J. Grygiel shows how these groups have presented peculiar, long-term problems that could rarely be solved with a finite war or clearly demarcated diplomacy. To succeed and survive, states were often forced to alter their own internal structure, giving greater power and responsibility to the communities most directly affected by the barbarian menace. Understanding the barbarian challenge, and strategies employed to confront it, offers new insights into the contemporary security threats facing the Western world.

Jakub J. Grygiel was a senior fellow at the Center for European Policy Analysis (Washington, DC) and an associate professor at the Paul H. Nitze School of Advanced International Studies of The Johns Hopkins University (Washington, DC). He is currently serving on the policy planning staff at the US Department of State.

Return of the Barbarians
Confronting Non-State Actors from Ancient Rome to the Present

Jakub J. Grygiel
US Department of State

CAMBRIDGE
UNIVERSITY PRESS

CAMBRIDGE
UNIVERSITY PRESS

University Printing House, Cambridge CB2 8BS, United Kingdom

One Liberty Plaza, 20th Floor, New York, NY 10006, USA

477 Williamstown Road, Port Melbourne, VIC 3207, Australia

314–321, 3rd Floor, Plot 3, Splendor Forum, Jasola District Centre, New Delhi – 110025, India

79 Anson Road, #06–04/06, Singapore 079906

Cambridge University Press is part of the University of Cambridge.

It furthers the University's mission by disseminating knowledge in the pursuit of education, learning, and research at the highest international levels of excellence.

www.cambridge.org
Information on this title: www.cambridge.org/9781107158573
DOI: 10.1017/9781316665909

© Jakub J. Grygiel 2018

This publication is in copyright. Subject to statutory exception and to the provisions of relevant collective licensing agreements, no reproduction of any part may take place without the written permission of Cambridge University Press.

First published 2018

Printed in the United Kingdom by Clays, St Ives plc

A catalogue record for this publication is available from the British Library.

ISBN 978-1-107-15857-3 Hardback
ISBN 978-1-316-61124-1 Paperback

Cambridge University Press has no responsibility for the persistence or accuracy of URLs for external or third-party internet websites referred to in this publication and does not guarantee that any content on such websites is, or will remain, accurate or appropriate.

To Tobias, Nina, and Sybil

Contents

Acknowledgments		*page* viii
	Introduction	1
1	The Nature of the Premodern Strategic Environment	12
2	Barbarians and the Character of the Competition	48
3	The Return of Premodern History?	86
4	Altering the State: Decentralization	122
5	Three Saints and the Barbarian Threat	154
6	Settlements, Local Forces, Fortifications, and Altering the Environment	184
7	Conclusion: Sidewalks and Two Fronts	210
Index		219

Acknowledgments

This book took many years to complete. Consequently, the list of individuals who have made comments, observations, and critiques – or who simply listened with great patience to various snippets of this topic – is long. The germ of the idea began with a presentation at a small seminar hosted by the late Dr. Zbigniew Brzezinski. It then turned into a short essay, encouraged and chiseled by Adam Garfinkle, the editor of *The American Interest*, who was present at that seminar. From then on, several small or large aspects of the argument in this book have appeared in *Orbis, Security Studies, Policy Review, Infinity Journal*, and, again, *The American Interest*. I am grateful to the editors, the anonymous reviewers, and the readers who commented on these pieces. I have also presented parts of these arguments in many places (Princeton, Johns Hopkins, Naval Postgraduate School, Foreign Policy Research Institute, and the SGRI meeting in Trento, among others) and benefited from the discussions and the criticism offered at these events. The list of people to thank would be too long here.

I wrote the original draft while on the faculty at the Paul H. Nitze School of Advanced International Studies of The Johns Hopkins University. I benefited there from my frequent interactions with some great colleagues, in particular Charles Doran, Eliot Cohen, Riordan Roett, Marco Cesa, and Daniel Markey. My fabulous assistant, Starline Lee, helped with the daily tasks with great cheer. The SAIS librarians – Sheila Thalhimer, Susan High, Stephen Sears, and others – fulfilled every request I sent their way, giving me access to otherwise difficult-to-find books and articles.

I put the finishing touches on the manuscript as a senior fellow at the Center for European Policy Analysis. Conversations with its then president, Wess Mitchell, strengthened several arguments in this book – not to mention that they also led to another book we coauthored in the meantime. Larry Hirsch supported me for years, and my stay at CEPA would not have been possible without him. The rest of the cheerful CEPA

Acknowledgments

team were supportive in all my other tasks, allowing me to find time to edit the book, and are an incredibly friendly bunch.

Several research assistants helped me throughout the years on a variety of topics and among them are Philip Reiner, Carsten Schmiedl, and Alexander Bellah. Dianne Sehler from the Bradley Foundation, and Nadia Schadlow and Marin Strmecki from the Smith Richardson Foundation supported various projects that, while not directly related to this book, touched upon themes that make an appearance in it. Dr. Schadlow, in particular, has always been a font of encouragement and has often commented on early drafts of several of my writings.

Michael Watson at Cambridge University Press patiently combed through the manuscript, and even more patiently waited for my ruminations and final edits. Lisa Carter has helped with the preparation and publicity of the book.

Last but obviously not least, my wife and kids have kept me busy, stepping over the piles of books on barbarians strewn on my floor. The children have been lobbying, individually of course, to have the book dedicated to them. As always, they win, even though they will have to share the dedication with each other.

Introduction

Barbarians are back. Small groups, even individuals, administering little or no territory, with minimal resources but with a long reach, are unfortunately on the front pages of newspapers because of their destructive fury. They harass and attack states from the streets of London, Paris, and Barcelona to wider areas in the Middle East and elsewhere. They are not merely tragic and bloody nuisances but strategic actors that compete with existing states, forcing them to alter their behavior, their military postures, and even their domestic lifestyles. The various Islamist groups and individuals who over the past decade have presented in different ways a persistent threat to the United States and the West, as well as to states in other regions of the world, come immediately to mind. It would be certainly wrong to ignore the religious connotations of these groups, arising from the Islamic world, but it is equally dangerous to think that the conditions that are making these murderous groups possible are rooted exclusively in Islam. Barbarians are back because there are deep trends that bestow lethality, and thus a strategic role, to groups that do not need the vast administrative apparatus, the territory, and the skilled and rule-abiding citizenry of modern states.

Barbarians – small, highly mobile groups that often were not settled in a fixed place – are a recurrent reality in history. In the modern era, the nation state proved to be the most effective strategic actor, with barbarians receding from the geopolitical landscape. But the trends that made the modern state the preeminent actor may be changing, favoring a return of barbarians. The wide availability of lethal technology, inaccessible spaces that make state governance more arduous, and the appeal of nonmaterial objectives are some of these trends. The modern state will not disappear but will have to compete with peer rivals as well as with barbarians, a geostrategic conundrum that was well known to premodern polities such as ancient Rome.

The particular barbarian groups we face at this moment may be defeated but the trends that made them possible are harder, perhaps impossible, to control. Barbarians are likely to be at our gates for a while. They will assault territorial polities and create conditions of such insecurity as to force the targeted states to alter their foreign policies and, in the long term, also their internal structure. For example, if the barbarian threat is decentralized, striking in surprising places but with a level of violence that affects only the immediate target (the street, the neighborhood or the small city rather than the entire state), the result may be that in order to be most effective security provision will have to become more decentralized. Competition and conflict are powerful forces that alter the way we organize ourselves, and thus the way states function.

If a return of barbarians proves to be enduring, studying premodern history and the security challenges it presented is too important to be left to historians. Students of security and politics should take a vigorous look at it. It is there, in fact, in that long period preceding the rise of the modern nation state, that barbarians in all their different permutations played important roles, competing with settled communities, assaulting empires, defeating legions, and altering how polities organized themselves to defend their own populations. There is a lot of value, therefore, in studying premodern history – and this book is driven by the premise that premodern history is an underexplored field for students of national security and international relations. We have secondhand experience of ancient history through thinkers such as Niccoló Machiavelli, who was well versed in Roman history and wrote for an audience that knew the difference between Lucius Junius Brutus and Marcus Junius Brutus. We have some sense of the Middle Ages through concepts such as "neo-medievalism." And we receive an inkling of the violence of premodern times through frequent citations of Thucydides' "Melian Dialogue." But we rarely go back to these sources themselves, and with occasional exceptions, do not venture much past the intellectual safety of the nineteenth or twentieth century. We read Florentine commentaries on Titus Livius, but not Titus Livius himself; we are more familiar with Bismarck and Gorchakov than Julius Caesar and Vercingetorix.

I exaggerate perhaps, but not extravagantly. Studies on international relations are imbued with modern history, while the Middle Ages, Republican or Imperial Rome, or Ancient Greece usually serve only as vignettes to underline a continuity (for instance, the eternal quest for power) or divergence (such as, perhaps, the decrease in violence) with present times. It may certainly be that this lacuna is justified and appropriate. The state is seen as the main and often only actor on the world scene because it is the only one capable of mustering sufficient resources to provide security for its members and defend its interests. There are certainly good reasons to place such emphasis on the role of the state.

The history of the twentieth century is after all a prime example of a world characterized by conflicts between states (the two world wars, but also the wars in Korea, between Iran and Iraq, and most recently the US invasion of Iraq come to mind). Moreover, as the various wars of decolonization in the second half of the twentieth century indicate, control over the state was the objective of the parties involved in these conflicts, and state-creation has been one of the main causes of war since 1945.[1] This argument can also be extended to the nineteenth century when Europe frequently witnessed national uprisings aimed at freeing ethnic groups from the political control of empires. Some, notably Germany and Italy, succeeded in establishing their own unified state in the second half of the nineteenth century, while most of the others had to wait until the end of World War I when the collapse of the Ottoman and Austro-Hungarian empires resulted in the creation of several new states in Central and Southeastern Europe. In brief, the state was the main tool of survival of groups and therefore also their primary political objective.

This focus on the role of states permeates also international relations theory, which is grounded in the study of the nineteenth and twentieth centuries.[2] Broadly speaking, there are two, quite different in their origins but complementary in their outcome, arguments in favor of focusing on modern history. The first, roughly overlapping with liberal theories, is that the world today is so fundamentally different that the more distant past is even less relevant than the eighteenth or nineteenth centuries. The strategic actors, the norms of behavior, and the domestic and international institutional settings have few parallels in history, and in fact, are the result of a progressive improvement in how we behave in politics. Hence, the argument continues, the twenty-first century has rules of behavior that will find few similarities with those of the nineteenth century and even fewer with those of more distant periods. History is characterized after all by progress, and the farther back in history one peers, the less relevant that observation becomes. In fact, one of the most famous findings stemming from liberal theories, the "democratic peace argument,"

---

[1] Kalevi J. Holsti, *The State, War, and the State of War* (New York, NY: Cambridge University Press, 1996), 61–81.

[2] Neorealist theory, in particular, stresses the state as the key, if not only, actor in the anarchical international system. Its arguments are often based on the post-1648 period, and the claim is that the theory should work particularly well in explaining the modern era. For a very critical perspective, see Paul Schroeder, "Historical Reality vs. Neo-Realist Theory," *International Security*, Vol. 19, No. 1 (Summer 1994), 108–148. See also Yale H. Ferguson and Richard W. Mansbach, "Polities Past and Present," *Millennium*, Vol. 37, No. 2 (2008), 365–379. On the links between diplomatic history and international relations theory, see also Stephen H. Haber, David M. Kennedy and Stephen D. Krasner, "Brothers under the Skin: Diplomatic History and International Relations," *International Security*, Vol. 22, No. 1 (Summer 1997), 34–43.

focuses on the past two centuries, based on the underlying premise that the novelty of domestic institutional arrangements – democracies, that is – has fundamentally altered international relations.[3] Progress, in brief, makes premodern history a not very useful source of strategic experience and political knowledge. The past is only a description of how things were, and not of how they are or will be.

The other argument, arising from within the Realist school of thought, begins from a very different assumption. History in this worldview is characterized by certain timeless, constant realities, and there is nothing fundamentally new in the political life of men.[4] Because of this continuity, studying ancient Rome, 1914, or the Cold War makes little difference from a practical point of view. All of these moments in history convey some eternal truths about strategic behavior and human motivations. As Hans Morgenthau put it, "human nature, in which the laws of politics have their roots, has not changed since the classical philosophies of China, India, and Greece have endeavored to discover these laws."[5] But reference to ancient authors (often limited to Thucydides and his "Melian Dialogue" in particular) is by and large only a search for some sort of recognition of intellectual *gravitas*, rather than appreciation for the complexity of political realities and for the profound difference of international relations throughout history.[6] Albeit we can learn from all of these, the argument goes, we might as well choose the most approachable and the most vivid historical example. From a didactic point of view, more recent history is thus preferable.

These two arguments have some validity, even though they are based on different assumptions about history and the possibility of mankind's

---

[3] Michael Doyle, "Kant, Liberal Legacies, and Foreign Affairs," Parts I and II, *Philosophy and Public Affairs*, Vol. 12, No. 3 (Summer 1983), 205–235, and No. 4 (Fall 1983), 323–353; Michael Doyle, "Liberalism and World Politics," *American Political Science Review*, Vol. 80, No. 4 (December 1986), 1151–1169.

[4] See Hans Morgenthau, *Politics among Nations* (New York, NY: McGraw Hill, 1993), 10. See also Markus Fischer, "Feudal Europe, 800–1300: Communal Discourse and Conflictual Practices," *International Organization*, Vol. 46, No. 2 (Spring 1992), 427–466; Stuart J. Kaufman, "The Fragmentation and Consolidation of International Systems," *International Organization*, Vol. 51, No. 2 (Spring 1997), 173–208.

[5] Hans Morgenthau, *Politics among Nations*, 4.

[6] An interesting exception is Arthur M. Eckstein, *Mediterranean, Anarchy, Interstate War, and the Rise of Rome* (Berkeley, CA: University of California Press, 2006). In this book, Eckstein uses Realist theory to explain the rise of Rome and the establishment of a "unipolar" or hegemonic system in the Mediterranean. It is worth noting that the author is a historian, not a political scientist, and one is left to wonder whether a book like his could have been written by an international relations theorist. Another exception, on the use of Thucydides, is Richard Ned Lebow, "Thucydides and Deterrence," *Security Studies*, Vol. 16, No. 2 (April–June 2007), 163–188.

progress. The reason why the incorporation of premodern history into the study of international relations is so parsimonious may be that there is little advantage in dwelling on eras that are distant from us in time and sensibility. Studying premodern history may be appealing only because it is a trove of evidence unexplored by international relations and security studies scholars, presenting a vast open field for testing existing theories and arguments. There is abundant historical literature on premodern history, from Classical Greece to the Middle Ages, and one can fill an intellectual niche by mining it from an international relations perspective. This alone may be a solid reason to study premodern history, that long stretch of time before the seventeenth (or, as I will explain later, fifteenth) century.[7]

But there is more. Both views sketched above are correct, at least in part: There is both change and continuity in history. Premodern history is different from modern times (as the liberal view has it, stressing change in history), but its peculiar characteristics are recurrent and are again becoming more visible (as, at least in part, the realist view has it, stressing continuity in history). This, in a nutshell, is the underlying argument of this book and I will explain it in greater detail in the chapters to come. Here, I want to point out a reason for studying premodern history, stemming from this pithy statement of my argument. If correct, this argument points to the possibility that some strategic realities and actors, which are particular to premodern history, may be making a resurgence. But we are intellectually handicapped because our perspective is thoroughly molded by modern history. For instance, international relations theories have a hard time explaining, among others, the "Achaean League, the Hanseatic League, the Swiss Confederation, the Holy Roman Empire, the Iroquois Confederation, the Concert of Europe,

---

[7] An exception to this avoidance of ancient history is the literature on "new medievalism," started in part by Hedley Bull. The core argument is that the sovereignty of states is being challenged by multiple actors, from larger ones (e.g. the European Union) to smaller ones (e.g. cities and private companies), resulting in overlapping authorities and diluted sovereignty. This leads to a gradual return to the "new Middle Ages," where the particular, exclusive, and often national identities and authorities compete with several other sources of authority and power. The argument I present in this book is slightly different, however. The decline of the modern state is often portrayed in the "new medievalism" literature as the result of globalization and economic forces, which weaken the power of the state to influence its political and economic fate within its borders. As I see it, the state is not necessarily weakening – indeed, in many aspects it is strengthening and its authority becoming more centralized, even economically in light of the current recession – but is being challenged and attacked by non-state groups. Moreover, the rise of these groups is only in part due to economic trends of globalization. It is also caused, as I will discuss later, by the expansion of uncontrolled spaces, the revival of religious extremism, and the diffusion of technology. See Hedley Bull, *The Anarchical Society* (New York, NY: Columbia University Press, 1995).

and the early United States."[8] Barbarians are another reality to add to this list. We think by analogies and our analyses of, as well as responses to, security challenges are informed by our knowledge of the past. Faced by an array of new strategic actors, we lack analogies to many current strategic challenges that have been rare in the past two or three centuries.

Our approach to international relations is a modern one: a modern theory about modern strategic realities. At the basis of this modern theory, or schools of thoughts as there is clearly no single theory of international relations, is the belief that the state – the modern nation state, territorially delimited, hierarchically organized, and in possession of the legitimate and monopolistic use of force – is the principal actor. This belief is an outcome of a deeper intellectual revolution that separates premodern from modern political thought, a break characterized in large measure by a different understanding of the origins of political order. In a very brief and necessarily imperfect summation, it can be said that the modern view puts political order as a willful and forceful creation of man. This order arises within or through a state that organizes under a common power an otherwise clashing rabble of individuals. Hobbes and his Leviathan are a case in point. The premodern, classical view of political order is less state-centric, and political order is an outcome of long, natural developments of which politics and the state are only a reflection. There are many different sources of political order, starting from the family and friendship, that precede the state, and upon which the state is founded. In fact, the collapse or degeneration of these primary societal groups leads to state failure: "sons killed their fathers," as Thucydides recounts in this description of Corcyra's Civil War, and this was a clear symptom that the city in question was politically dead.[9] For premodern thought the state is the outcome, not the cause, of social order. This passage from premodern to modern thought marks a big intellectual break, a revolution of thought, that cannot but have also an impact on how we understand international relations. In the passage to modernity we gained a certain elegance and parsimony by focusing on the state, but we lost also an appreciation for the multiplicity of political actors that provide social cohesion (or disruption) and are strategic actors in international relations.

---

[8] Daniel H. Deudney, "The Philadelphian System: Sovereignty, Arms Control, and Balance of Power in the American States-Union, Circa 1787–1861," *International Organization*, Vol. 49, No. 2 (Spring, 1995), 193. See also, William Wohlforth et al., "Testing Balance-of-Power Theory in World History," *European Journal of International Relations*, Vol. 31, No. 2 (2007), 155–185; S. Kaufman, R. Little and W. Wohlforth, eds., *Balance of Power in World History* (New York, NY: Palgrave, 2007).

[9] Thucydides, *The Landmark Thucydides*, ed. by Robert B. Strassler (New York: The Free Press, 1996), 3.81, 199.

The rise of the modern state as the most effective provider of security and unity, and its gradual and apparently relentless expansion to every corner of the world, are good reasons why we favor this modern approach to international relations. But what if the security conditions were changing and the modern state were only one of the many methods of societal organization and strategic behavior? I do not argue that the modern state is in decline, as it has been suggested with some recurrence from a variety of perspectives over the past few decades, but only that it may no longer be the only strategic actor on the world scene. And even more narrowly, here I simply want to point out that it behooves us to study premodern history as a long period in human history in which there were multiple, often overlapping, sources of political order and, consequently, a multilayered nature of international politics.

The problem with ignoring ancient history is that if we look at the past three hundred years or so, characterized by competition between well-formed and clearly defined states, it is difficult to find analogies that are appropriate to describe the situation currently facing the United States. There are several large trends – namely, the growing separation between industrial resources and military capability, the diminishing importance of exclusive territorial control necessary to be a strategic actor in international relations, the rise of sources of authority and allegiance alternative to the state, and the reemergence of nonnegotiable objectives – that are altering the strategic landscape of the world, making it under certain aspects similar to that of ancient history. These are only trends and not outcomes, and thus may not result in lasting and comprehensive changes. But they are also outside the control of individual states or great powers, and as such they cannot be stopped or diverted.

At a minimum, these "ancient" traits will coexist with more "modern" features of international relations (e.g. the territorial nature of states, the unmatched power of states to muster resources, and the ability of states to engage in diplomacy) resulting in an added layer of complexity to international relations. While obviously the world will not revert to the Middle Ages or ancient Roman times, some of its features will resemble those periods.

The results of these trends are by no means certain, but broadly speaking there are two sets of challenges that we will continue to face in the future – challenges that are more common in ancient than modern history. First, there is a growing array of strategic actors, other than states, that will continue to oppose US interests. Second, the objectives pursued by them will not be easily amenable to political settlements, increasing the level of violence and instability in the world. Thus, our perspective and our strategies are thoroughly modern but the realities that confront us are increasingly less so.[10] It is important to dust off our knowledge of ancient history because it may give us a better sense of the nature of the threats and the most effective strategies to deal with them.

To be clear, this book cannot fill the lacuna of historical knowledge, nor does it propose a grand new model of international relations. It is not a history of barbarians, nor does it aspire to offer a theory of barbarian tribes and their interactions with settled communities. I do not recount every, or even a few in-depth cases, of interactions and conflicts between barbarians and empires. This is the proper role of historians, who have much greater knowledge and skills to embark, as many have done and to whom we are indebted, on this intellectual pursuit. The catalogue of the violence, and of the moments of cooperation and even peace, between these two sets of strategic actors – the nomadic and the settled, the uncivilized and the civilized, the mobile tribe and the sedentary cities, the barbarians and the empire – is long, and it has seen a pause only in more recent, modern times.

Rather, the book suggests that premodern history can be of use to those who study national security and describes the conditions that lead to the rise of barbarians, the challenges they present, and the effect they may have on the targeted states.

Barbarians

To justify the study of premodern history may be less necessary than a preventive defense of the term "barbarian," a term that can raise criticism from many fronts. One reproach is that it carries denigrating connotations of cultural inferiority and barbaric behavior, traits that after all are not unique to non-state groupings. Consequently, it is seen less as an analytical concept than as a slur. But in its simplest usage, "barbarian" referred to groups that spoke a different, incomprehensible language. It was not necessarily an insult but an all-encompassing description of foreign groups. And the word "barbarian" points more to the user of this term, rather than the subject defined by it: It shows the inability to understand the groups in question. First and foremost, therefore, it is a term of intellectual frustration, of the difficulty of comprehending the

---

[10] There are, of course, some exceptions. See, for instance, John Gerard Ruggie, "Continuity and Transformation in the World Polity: Toward a Neorealist Synthesis," *World Politics*, Vol. 31, No. 2 (January 1983), 261–285; Myron Weiner, "Security, Stability, and International Migration," *International Security*, Vol. 17, No. 3 (Winter 1993), 91–126; Rey Koslowski, "Human Migration and the Conceptualization of Pre-Modern World Politics," *International Studies Quarterly*, 46 (2002), 375–399. There are also more recent studies that use ancient history to shed light on current security challenges. See, for example, Kimberly Marten, "Warlordism in Comparative Perspective," *International Security*, Vol. 31, No. 3 (Winter 2006/07), 41–73.

rival. While in Ancient Greece this inability may have been limited to the linguistic realm, now it points to a larger incomprehension: The groups may be quite understandable linguistically, but their motivations, their goals, the foundations of their strength and weakness, and their very reason to exist remain somewhat incomprehensible. They are barbarians because they remain poorly understood and represent an intellectual challenge; we are baffled by them and we do not understand them. In strategy one must understand the interlocutor, the rival who through actions and words is communicating something that calls for a response. The term "barbarian" meant that the user of it did not fully understand his strategic interlocutor, the enemy.

A related criticism of the term "barbarian" is that it is too broad, encompassing a wide variety of groups ranging from small nomadic tribes to large and semi-settled groups that overran empires. Throughout premodern history, some barbarians merely harassed imperial armies or preyed on commerce along poorly defended roads, while others fielded large armies that in some cases trampled over the forces of well-established states or empires. The catchall nature of the term, in other words, seems to glaze over crucial differences and consequently could be considered as of little analytical use. But there are also important commonalities among these groups, such as high mobility and less hierarchical structures, that merit a single term. More recently, there have been several terms struggling to define these strategic actors – from "terrorists" and "non-state violent groups" to "networks" or "acephalic groups." All of these descriptive phrases have their own benefits, but there is no single term that embraces all of these groups or the broad challenges they produce. Using the old word of "barbarians" is appropriate. It is akin to the word "polity," which does not take into account wide differences in geographic size, domestic regime, economic independence, military power, or tactical preferences among territorial polities, but which nevertheless is useful in identifying a particular category of strategic actors.

A critic may point out that "barbarians" may apply to ancient groups, but modern stateless terrorist organizations are different: The latter often are inside targeted states, living in the *banlieus* and not on the other side of an imperial frontier. Other differences also are visible, such as the greater lethality of today's small groups. Differences abound, of course. But there are also parallels, in particular in the nature of the threat ancient and modern barbarians present: The threat is localized, individually small, and geographically diffused, unlike that of mass armies of other industrial states marching across borders. Barbarians raid but rarely invade; they plunder, rather than control territory; they terrorize, rather than administer populations.

I do not want to suggest that, say, modern Islamist terrorists are exactly like the Huns or the Comanches. There are indeed many differences among all of these groups, and scholars ought to focus on the characteristics particular to these groups. And academic efforts to comprehend today's strategic landscape are very vibrant, using a range of methods from quantitative to in-depth studies of modern-day cases, and for the most part do not rely on the study of ancient history.[11] The fact that few security studies students look at ancient history may be, therefore, quite justified.[12] But I think that we lose a lot of richness by ignoring parallels with premodern history. By itself, the study of ancient history will not generate revolutionary new theories of asymmetric conflicts, balance of power, or deterrence in a polynuclear world. However, it can help us understand current strategic challenges by underlying certain characteristics of international relations, such as a decreased effectiveness of diplomacy and deterrence, that were salient in premodern times and that may recur in the future.

Finally, I use the term "barbarians" with full cognizance that these groups in the past, as today, were violent and destructive. They destroyed more than they built. They plundered more than they cultivated. They were more interested in blood than law. Barbarians were barbaric. Nothing indicates that the future will be different.

The book begins with an analysis of the conditions, such as wide availability of lethal technology and the existence of difficult-to-reach geographic spaces, under which barbarians prosper. Chapter 2 then describes the challenges of competing and fighting with barbarians, focusing on the difficulties of diplomacy and deterrence as well as on the effectiveness of using military force against them. I then move in Chapter 3 to consider the possibility of a return of barbarians and of features that characterized premodern history. In the rest of the book

---

[11] For instance, the literature on radical Islamic terrorism has been growing. See Oliver Roy, *Globalized Islam: The Search for a New Umma* (New York, NY: Columbia University Press, 2006); Mary Habeck, *Knowing the Enemy: Jihadist Ideology and the War on Terror* (New Haven, CT: Yale University Press, 2006); Giles Keppel, *Jihad: The Trail of Political Islam* (Cambridge, MA: Belknap Press, 2003); Fawaz Gerges, *The Far Enemy* (New York, NY: Cambridge University Press, 2005); Lawrence Wright, *The Looming Tower* (New York, NY: Knopf, 2006). There is also a vast literature studying the motivations of terrorists writ large, not limited to the jihadist kind. See, for instance, Robert Pape, *Dying to Win: The Strategic Logic of Suicide Terrorism* (New York, NY: Random House, 2006); Alan Krueger, *What Makes a Terrorist* (Princeton, NJ: Princeton University Press, 2007).

[12] There are, of course, exceptions. See Ruggie, "Continuity and Transformation in the World Polity"; Weiner, "Security, Stability, and International Migration"; Koslowski, "Human Migration"; Marten, "Warlordism in Comparative Perspective"; Victor Davis Hanson, ed., *Makers of Ancient History* (Princeton, NJ: Princeton University Press, 2010), in particular the introduction.

I examine the effect that rivalry with barbarians has on the targeted polity and how that polity may respond to the threat. In Chapter 4 I examine how ancient polities, the Roman Empire in particular, have experienced a process of decentralization when the barbarians were assaulting on the frontier. I continue the description in Chapter 5 by looking at how three Roman individuals dealt with the barbarian menace and how they related to the central authorities of the empire. Finally, in Chapter 6 I examine a few other strategies adopted by states that were threatened by barbarian groups.

1 The Nature of the Premodern Strategic Environment

> *In Asia as in Europe, the inhospitable north has always been ready to disgorge its predatory hordes on lands more favored by the sun.*[1]

Barbarians are a recurrent but not constant reality in history. For centuries, they appeared on the frontiers of established polities, surprising their victims, bringing violence and devastation, and then vanishing back into uncharted territories. In some cases, they turned out to be more than a momentary menace and contributed to the weakening of the targeted empire. And, like individual great powers, over the course of history specific barbarian groups rose to prominence and disappeared from the map. Interestingly, however, not every age has been characterized by the presence of barbarians as sources of fear, threat, and instability, and the main strategic preoccupation of statesmen was the jousting among similarly organized states. The past two or three centuries, in particular, have seen a marked decline in the strategic relevance of barbarian groups. Some of the last examples, such as the Comanches in nineteenth-century North America, were more of a nuisance to solitary outposts of the growing US power than a danger attracting the attention of the federal government. The international relations of the past few centuries have been marked by competing states, fighting for territory and resources even when seeking the victory of their own political ideas, while barbarian groups were becoming extinct.

Given the fluctuation in, and the more recent steady decline of, the strategic relevance of barbarians, it is important to consider the conditions under which they arise. Their rise and decline may certainly be a result of their victories and defeats, that is, they may have vanished as political actors simply because they had been vanquished on the battlefield. But their disappearance from the strategic chessboard of the world is not only an outcome of tactical victories of modern industrial states. There are other, deeper reasons why a fourth-

[1] W. A. P. Martin, "The Northern Barbarians in Ancient China," *Journal of the American Oriental Society*, Vol. 11 (1885), 362.

century AD Roman emperor was preoccupied with barbarians more than a German Kaiser in the 1890s or a US president in the 1950s. Some conditions endemic to the international environment allowed these groups to prosper, making them serious challengers to the security of territorial states.

This chapter will examine the reasons behind the rise of barbarian groups. What are the circumstances that make barbarians possible, and more precisely, that make them into threats requiring a concerted response? Why are barbarians more dangerous in premodern history? Even a cursory reading of premodern history, spanning from ancient Rome and beyond to the Middle Ages, shows that barbarians frequently presented serious problems to settled communities, cities, and empires alike. The questions examined here concern, therefore, the reasons why that is the case. Prior to the fifteenth or sixteenth centuries, the world was marked by several common features – such as the existence of ungoverned spaces, the availability and ease of use of weapons, and the relatively low importance of controlling territory – that allowed barbarians to arise and challenge civilized polities.

This is not simply an exercise in historical analysis. As Chapter 3 will describe, it is plausible to argue that some of these premodern features are reappearing in the present day. Over the past several years, many authors have described the changing landscape of the international arena, with symptoms such as an uptick in intrastate wars and the rise of non-state actors. The symptoms point to the existence of conditions that are analogous to those present in premodern times. If that is the case, then a likely outcome will be the resurgence of barbarian groups, of which the conflicts with various Islamist groups of the past decade may only be the first flare-up.

1.1 How to Define Premodern History?

The premise of this chapter, and indeed of the entire book, is that international relations in premodern history are in some ways different from those of modern times – and that we are moving toward a strategic landscape that may be more analogous to the former than the latter. For instance, as I will discuss in a later chapter, diplomacy and deterrence were not as effective in ancient history as in the modern age. Moreover, wars were often less defined, with no clear beginnings and ends and with a diffuse geographic theater. As a result, violence in ancient history was more pervasive and common, both between and within polities. The question is why.

14   The Nature of the Premodern Strategic Environment

Before we dwell on the reasons for these differences, it is necessary to define premodern history, a difficult and imprecise endeavor, in which historians are rightly reluctant to engage.[2] History does not move neatly from period to period, the differences between which are often visible only years and perhaps generations afterward. Marking historical periods occurs necessarily *post hoc*. Nonetheless, it is important for strategists to think in terms of historical periods because this allows them to delineate the particular contours of the security environment they face in a given moment in time. For instance, a crucial political characteristic of any historical period is the nature of the predominant strategic actors, whether they are city-states, empires, tribes, or nation states. Changes in their nature and composition will shape international relations, determining what the most effective strategic posture will be for a polity. More narrowly, the rise of a new great power or the decline of an existing one also mark the passage from one period to another (e.g. the end of the Cold War). Drawing a map of the principal rivals, whether specific powers or broad types of strategic actors, is the starting point of any strategy, as well as one way of separating history into different periods. Hence, there is a natural professional divide that arises: Historians may resist periodization, but strategists must engage in it as the foundation of their intellectual pursuit.

It is difficult to draw a clear line separating modern from premodern history, but a commonly accepted marker for the beginning of the latter, and, as a result, for our understanding of international relations, is the seventeenth century, namely the Peace of Westphalia (1648). The treaties that ended the wars of the early seventeenth century established the modern state as a political entity with full and exclusive sovereignty.[3]

---

[2] The difficulty of drawing clear boundaries between different historical periods is clearly shown in two classic books: Johan Huizinga, *The Waning of the Middle Ages* (New York, NY: Dover Publications, 1998) and Theodore K. Rabb, *The Last Days of the Renaissance and the March to Modernity* (New York, NY: Perseus Books, 2007). See also William Green, "Periodization in European and World History," *Journal of World History*, Vol. 3, No. 1 (Spring 1992), 13–53; Jerry H. Bentley, "Cross-Cultural Interaction and Periodization in World history," *The American Historical Review*, Vol. 101, No. 3 (June 1996), 749–770; Nicola Di Cosmo, "State Formation and Periodization in Inner Asian History," *Journal of World History*, Vol. 10, No. 1 (Spring 1999), 1–40. On the distinction between ancient and medieval history, H. M. Gwatkin, "Constantine and His City," in J. B. Bury, H. M. Gwatkin and J. P. Whitney, eds., *Cambridge Medieval History* (New York, NY: Macmillan Company, 1911), Vol. I, 1.

[3] Leo Gross, "The Peace of Westphalia, 1648–1948," *American Journal of International Law*, Vol. 42, No. 1 (January 1948), 20–41; Daniel Philpott, "The Religious Roots of Modern International Relations," *World Politics*, Vol. 52 (January 2000), 206–245; Stephen Krasner, *Sovereignty: Organized Hypocrisy* (Princeton, NJ: Princeton University Press, 1999); Stephen Krasner, "Westphalia and All That," in Judith Goldstein and Robert O. Keohane, eds., *Ideas and Foreign Policy: Beliefs, Institutions, and Political Change* (Ithaca, NY: Cornell University Press, 1993); Stephen Krasner, "Compromising Westphalia," *International Security*, Vol. 20, No. 3 (Winter 1995/96),

Imperial and church institutions gradually lost their sway over the legal and political life of states, and states slowly consolidated their territorial holdings. At least in principle, from then on states were legally equal and claimed the right of nonintervention in their internal affairs, becoming thus the main, if not only, strategic actors on the international scene.

Another marker, with a less precise date but therefore more appropriate, is the growing need of states to garner massive assets in order to defend themselves as well as to wage offensive wars – in other words, the rise of the modern centralized state that acquires and manages resources to maintain its security. The state needed to control both capital and coercion – the latter necessary to generate military force, and the former to extract and defend capital. This process was completed only in the aftermath of the post-World War II decolonization that left the world map cleanly demarcated, even though it never fully eradicated premodern actors.[4]

The beginning of this process is even more difficult to date because it was a long trend, but it can perhaps be limited to the period between the end of the fifteenth century (with the battering down of Italian city-states by French and Spanish artillery)[5] and the mid-nineteenth century when the ability to muster industrial power became indispensable to be an international actor.[6] Martin Wight, for instance, places the beginning of modern international relations in the year 1494, which "marks the point from which the European powers at large begin to adopt the habits of Italian power politics" characterized by the "efficient, self-sufficient, secular state."[7] For him, the modern era begins with the extension of Italian-style politics to the rest of the European continent, whereas for the sixteenth-century Florentine historian Francesco Guicciardini political modernity begins with the arrival in Italy of Europe's Atlantic powers, armed with artillery and supported by a large administrative apparatus. As Guicciardini famously put it, "wars before 1494 were long, bloodless

---

115–151; and for a review of some arguments critical of establishing Westphalia as a marker, see Daniel Philpott, "Review: Usurping the Sovereignty of Sovereignty?", *World Politics*, Vol. 53, No. 2 (January 2001), 297–324.

[4] Charles Tilly, *Coercion, Capital, and European States* (Cambridge, MA: Blackwell, 1992), 3.

[5] On the role of artillery (the "plague of artillery") in the 1494 invasion of Italy, see also Francesco Guicciardini, *The History of Italy* (Princeton, NJ: Princeton University Press, 1984), 50–51, 56; Bert S. Hall, *Weapons and Warfare in Renaissance Europe* (Baltimore, MD: The Johns Hopkins University Press, 1997), 157–176; Geoffrey Parker, *The Military Revolution* (Cambridge: Cambridge University Press, 1988), 10.

[6] Raymond Aron, *The Century of Total War* (Boston, MA: The Beacon Press, 1955), 74–92; Bernard and Fawn M. Brodie, *From Crossbow to H-Bomb* (Bloomington, IN: Indiana University Press, 1973), 75.

[7] Martin Wight, *Power Politics* (London: Continuum, 2002), 30.

16 The Nature of the Premodern Strategic Environment

battles, and the methods used to conquer lands slow and difficult; and although artillery was already present, it was used in such an inefficient way that it did not do much damage, so that if you had a state, it was almost impossible to lose it."[8] We can also add Russia's conquest of the steppes, in particular with the 1552 siege of Kazan, as evidence of parallel, slightly delayed developments on Europe's eastern frontiers.[9] Ivan IV had in fact introduced firearms and artillery into the Russian army, increasing its ability to overwhelm nomadic tribes. In the 1552 campaign, Russia fielded about 150 medium and heavy cannons; twenty years later the Russian army had more than 2,000 pieces of artillery.[10]

Guicciardini and Wight agree on the year 1494 as the beginning of the modern period of history, and differ slightly on the primary feature ("artillery" or "power politics"), or geographic direction (from the Atlantic shores to the Italian peninsula or the other way around), that characterized the dramatic political change. But they fundamentally agree that the main requirement of political modernity was the ability to compete with each other, and to compete it was necessary to generate large amounts of material power. If a state wanted to survive, it needed to field well-trained mass armies with vast quantities of armor, artillery, and corresponding logistical supplies.[11] The competitive nature of the

---

[8] Francesco Guicciardini, *Ricordi – Storie Fiorentine* (Milan: TEA, 1991), #64, 24.

[9] The delay in Russia's adoption of gunpowder and the resulting changes in military formations and tactics, as well as state growth, were due to a variety of factors: epidemics that affected demographic growth, economic and social backwardness, and the need to import technological knowhow. But the security environment faced by Russia up until the sixteenth to seventeenth centuries was perhaps the most important factor in the delayed adoption of modern Western warfare and organization. Unlike Western Europe, Muscovy did not have to compete with other large states, with the exception of occasional wars with Lithuania, Poland, and Sweden. Instead, until the late sixteenth and early seventeenth centuries, steppe warfare was its principal preoccupation and the military forces were designed for it. The great distances of the steppes meant that the army had to be very mobile, and thus could not maintain a large logistical tail that was vulnerable to harassment as well as fire (a common tactic of the Tatars was to ignite the steppe grass). Failure to field forces organized expressly for steppe warfare was disastrous. For instance, toward the end of the seventeenth century, "two large Russian armies, organized more or less along Western lines, completely failed to strike at the Tatars' home base in the Crimea because they could not cross the hundreds of miles of steppe and arrive at their destination in a condition to do battle." Thomas Esper, "Military Self-Sufficiency and Weapons Technology in Muscovite Russia," *Slavic Review*, Vol. 28, No. 2 (June 1969), 192. Also, Carol B. Stevens, *Soldiers of the Steppe* (DeKalb, IL: Northern Illinois University Press, 1995). For a detailed analysis of the logistical challenges facing Russia, see Dianne L. Smith, "Muscovite Logistics, 1462–1598," *The Slavonic and East European Review*, Vol. 71, No. 1 (January 1993), 35–65.

[10] Michael C. Paul, "The Military Revolution in Russia, 1550–1682," *The Journal of Military History*, Vol. 68, No. 1 (January 2004), 29.

[11] See MacGregor Knox, "Mass Politics and Nationalism as Military Revolution: The French Revolution and after," in Macgregor Knox and Williamson Murray, eds., *The Dynamics of Military Revolutions, 1300–2050* (New York, NY: Cambridge University

international system forced all political actors to adapt and imitate the most successful among them, the modern nation state, which gradually eliminated other, less capable polities, such as the Italian city-states or, in Asia, nomadic steppe groups.[12]

In brief, it took a state to defeat another state. It is not surprising, therefore, that the colorful political map of Italy, composed of many city-states, small potentates, and *condottieri*-led mercenaries, would gradually be overtaken by the fewer and geographically larger states such as France and Spain. Geopolitical diversity has declined since then, leaving the modern state as the principal strategic actor in international relations.[13]

By premodern history, I refer therefore to that long period of time that precedes the seventeenth, and perhaps even the late fifteenth, century. It is undoubtedly problematic to put hundreds of years under a single rubric of "premodern history," which may suggest a uniformity that did not exist as well as a distinction with modern times that may not be quite so dramatic. There are important differences, for instance, between the Roman Republic and medieval Europe, starting from the distribution of power in the system and ending in the types of war waged by the various actors. There are also some commonalities between premodern and modern history, as the latter period carries certain traces from the preceding centuries; for instance, premodern actors continue to appear in the nineteenth century, notably with the fierce and yet futile opposition of Comanche tribes to the expansion of US power. Another similarity between premodern and modern times is the reality of territorially fixed and hierarchically organized polities. Stephen Krasner has consistently argued that many "modern" traits were present in the Middle Ages, and that many "medieval" features (e.g. compromises of sovereignty) continued after Westphalia.[14] Furthermore, the existence of transnational

---

Press, 2001), chapter 4, 57–73. On the spread of nationalism, and of the mass army, see Barry R. Posen, "Nationalism, the Mass Army, and Military Power," *International Security*, Vol. 18, No. 2 (Autumn 1993), 80–124. On the increase of logistical needs, see Martin Van Creveld, *Supplying War* (New York, NY: Cambridge University Press, 2004).

[12] Hendrik Spruyt, *The Sovereign State and Its Competitors* (Princeton, NJ: Princeton University Press, 1994), chapter 8, 153–180; Hans Delbrück, *The Dawn of Modern Warfare: History of the Art of War*, Vol. IV (Lincoln, NE: University of Nebraska Press, 1990).

[13] State-building was different in other regions, notably Africa and Asia, where the nation state is not as strong or prevalent as in Europe. See, for instance, Jeffrey Herbst, "War and State in Africa," *International Security*, Vol. 14, No. 4 (Spring 1990), 117–139; Victoria Tin-bor Hui, *War and State Formation in Ancient China and Early Modern Europe* (New York, NY: Cambridge University Press, 2005).

[14] See Krasner, "Compromising Westphalia," in footnote 2.

groups, whose unity was built upon ideological affinity rather than contiguous shared territory, created conditions for international instability and protracted conflicts even well after the modern state became preeminent.[15] In brief, between premodern and modern history there is continuity as much as there are differences. But the differences outweigh the continuity because they created distinctive strategic landscapes that differed in terms of the strategic actors involved, the objectives pursued by them, and, in the end, in the effectiveness of tools of statecraft (use of force and diplomacy, among others). There are good reasons, therefore, why most historical studies of modern international relations start from the Peace of Westphalia.

When looking at the differences between premodern and modern international relations, there are at least two possible analytical approaches. One is to consider the systemic aspects of international relations, which are, as always, anarchic, but in premodern history they remain unmitigated by international law, institutional arrangements, and standing international organizations. As Arthur Eckstein observes, the ancient international system presented an extremely harsh environment that, untamed by agreed-upon conventions, put a premium on ferocity and bellicosity.[16] States, whether Greek cities or the Roman Republic, had to adapt to such system and, in order to avoid paying the very cruel price of defeat that often meant annihilation or enslavement, assumed a very aggressive military and diplomatic posture. They were violent and aggressive because the system gave them no other option, quickly socializing them into a pattern of belligerent behavior. The modern period has certainly not shed its anarchic nature but has perhaps developed ways of coping with it through international institutions, deeper commercial interdependence, norms of international behavior, and the development of liberal democratic domestic regimes, all mitigating some of the worst effects of the international system. The system has not changed and thus there is constancy; the difference is in the mechanisms devised to alleviate the ferociousness and bellicosity that stem from anarchy.[17] This is an appealing explanation because it combines change and continuity in an

---

[15] John Owen, *The Clash of Ideas in World Politics: Transnational Networks, States, and Regimes, 1510–2010* (Princeton, NJ: Princeton University Press, 2010).

[16] Arthur M. Eckstein, *Mediterranean Anarchy, Interstate War, and the Rise of Rome* (Berkeley, CA: University of California Press, 2006); Arthur M. Eckstein, "Review: Brigands, Emperors, and Anarchy," *The International History Review*, Vol. 22, No. 4 (December 2000), 862–879.

[17] For a cogent analysis of the factors mitigating anarchy and lowering the prospects of conflict applied to the Asian theater but with wider implications, see Aaron Friedberg, "Ripe for Rivalry: Prospects for Peace in a Multipolar Asia," *International Security*, Vol. 18, No. 3 (Winter 1993–94), 5–33.

The Proliferation of Strategic Actors 19

elegant framework, leaving also ample space for policy. Statesmen can improve international conditions by establishing political institutions or economic linkages among countries, constraining the ferocity instilled in them by the system.

The systemic explanation of the difference between modern and premodern history is not necessarily exclusive of the second approach, which focuses on the nature and objectives of the actors and the resulting character of conflict. The point of departure is different: the former starts from an analysis of the international system, the latter from the existence of different strategic actors and their behavior. The conclusion, namely that international relations in the premodern past were characterized by less diplomacy, weaker deterrence, and more violence, is similar in both approaches. The advantage of focusing on the actors is that such an approach may be more relevant to the current strategic environment: the current systemic features are unlike those of premodern times because they are characterized by growing involvement of international organizations, by more attention paid at least rhetorically to international law, and by multilateral agreements on a variety of issues. But some of the strategic actors may be becoming more akin to those of premodern times. The international system and its mitigating factors are modern, but the actors jousting within it are not.

This book tilts toward the latter approach even though there is enormous validity in the argument pointing to the systemic sources of strategic behavior. There were certain key features of ancient international relations, some of them arguably systemic (e.g. "ungoverned territories" or "empty spaces") but some less so (e.g. military technology), that created the conditions for barbarian groups to arise and prosper. But the anarchic system alone did not make barbarians.

The next question, then, is: What are the factors that allow the rise of barbarian groups?

1.2 The Proliferation of Strategic Actors

To the modern eye the most striking characteristic of premodern history is the diversity and multiplicity of international actors. We are used to international relations conducted by states, sometimes in polite conversation at high-level meetings and sometimes locked in deadly struggles fought with ever more elaborate weapons. Since the late seventeenth century, the state – the modern, nation state – has been growing in political importance and increasing in numbers. At least on a map, the post-World War II decolonization process completed the division of the world into clearly demarcated polities. As Charles Tilly writes, "[o]nly since World War II has almost the entire world come to be occupied by nominally independent states whose rulers recognize, more or less, each other's existence and right to exist."[18] Modern history can be seen therefore as a gradual and relentless, but never completely finished, process of eliminating from the world scene actors other than nation states.[19]

This story is in noticeable contrast to premodern history. It is virtually impossible to describe premodern international relations without considering the vast array of political entities that were part of it. Multiple and diverse, often geographically overlapping, actors competed among each other. The spectrum of sovereignty was wider, and in various moments in history empires coexisted and competed with cities, small commercial republics, tribal forces, and other armed groups. The latter category was particularly premodern, and the growth of the modern state made tribes and other groups gradually irrelevant as strategic actors.[20] During most of premodern history, the world was replete with small bands of people, such as pirates or nomadic tribes, leading a predatory lifestyle with very limited territorial possessions but with sometimes dramatic impact on the political fate of geographically fixed states.[21] Barbarians were a recurrent and serious security problem.

For empires, the barbarian challenge was both internal and external. It was very difficult for premodern states to establish an internal monopoly of force as well as to protect their borders.[22] Internally, even the strongest state or empire had to deal with the presence of a constant level of violence, albeit often of low-intensity. Most polities had a perennial domestic problem of brigands, unruly local leaders, and roaming bands of mercenaries. Internal instability increased in moments of weakness of the central authority, whether during the last centuries of the Roman Empire or in cases of failed states in the present day. Yet, even at the peak of their power, many premodern empires had a tenuous hold over much of their territory. In the first century AD, when Rome was unquestionably a powerful empire, it was considered to be dangerous to travel without military escort even in northern Italy because of the uncertain affiliation of local settlements and of their forces. A telling anecdote is the story of Tiberius rushing to his brother's camp in Gaul, a trip that was remarkable because he traveled alone, risking his life in a territory that, albeit

---

[18] Tilly, 3.
[19] See, for instance, the case of the duchy of Burgundy, the "nonterritorial alternative" of the fourteenth and fifteenth centuries in Mann, Vol. I, 438–440.
[20] Joseph Strayer, *On the Medieval Origins of the Modern State* (Princeton, NJ: Princeton University Press, 2005), 3–4.
[21] Aldo A. Settia, *Rapine, assedi, battaglie* (Bari: Editori Laterza, 2009), Part I, 3–76.
[22] Karen Barkey, *Bandits and Bureaucrats: The Ottoman Route to State Centralization* (Ithaca, NY: Cornell University Press, 1994); Susan Mattern, *Rome and the Enemy* (Berkeley, CA: University of California Press, 2002), 103.

nominally under Roman control, was not fully settled and pacified.[23] In fact, Roman authorities could never rest because "most places had to be conquered not just once, but more than once, sometimes several times; and the Romans seem to have known and expected this."[24] An analogous story can be told about the Ottoman empire that struggled to incorporate various armed groups into state structures, and at times had to deal with highly disruptive bands roaming in the countryside.[25]

The situation on the frontiers was even more unstable. With great persistence but with mixed results, empires from Rome to Ming China held the line. Yet, in effect, they had to manage the insecurity of a tenuously held porous region that separated them from untamed groups. Small groups, with no territorial possessions and limited technical skills, could assault and often win against the armies of well-established states or empires. As French historian Fernand Braudel put it in colorful terms, nomads, "comparable to the biblical plagues of Egypt," were "hordes of violent, cruel, pillaging horsemen full of daredevil courage" and remained a constant source of danger until they declined in the mid-seventeenth century.[26] The waning days of the Western Roman Empire in the fifth century, when highly mobile armies of nomads (the Huns) or migrants (the Goths) won several dramatic military victories against Roman legions, serve as another powerful example of this situation.[27] A few centuries later, as Richard Bean observes, the "spectacular conquests of the Middle Ages – Saxon England, Sicily, and the Levant – were not carried out by feudal armies. Instead, the conquerors were bands of adventurers who expected to be paid by their share of the loot, and most of that loot was land and serfs."[28] Such "bands" were worthy antagonists

---

[23] Anthony Everitt, *Augustus* (New York, NY: Random House, 2006), 274.
[24] Mattern, *Rome and the Enemy*, 103.
[25] Barkey, *Bandits and Bureaucrats: The Ottoman Route to State Centralization*.
[26] Fernand Braudel, *A History of Civilization* (New York, NY: Penguin, 1994), 164.
[27] For a history of the "barbarian" attacks on the Roman Empire, see Guy Halsall, *Barbarian Migrations and the Roman West, 376–568* (New York, NY: Cambridge University Press, 2007); J. B. Bury, *The Invasions of Europe by the Barbarians* (New York, NY: W. W. Norton & Co., 1967); Peter Heather, *The Fall of the Roman Empire* (London: Pan Macmillan, 2006); Bryan Ward-Perkins, *The Fall of Rome* (New York, NY: Oxford University Press, 2006); Adrian Goldsworthy, *How Rome Fell* (New Haven, CT: Yale University Press, 2009).
[28] Richard Bean, "War and the Birth of the Nation State," *Journal of Economic History*, Vol. 33, No. 1 (March 1973), 218–219. See also Georges Duby, *The Early Growth of the European Economy* (Ithaca, NY: Cornell University Press, 1978), 166–167; Georges Duby, *The Chivalrous Society* (Berkeley, CA: University of California Press, 1980), especially chapter 11, 158–170. Piracy was another recurrent problem in pre-modern history. See Janice E. Thompson, *Mercenaries, Pirates, and Sovereigns* (Princeton, NJ: Princeton University Press, 1994); Gunther E. Rothenberg, "Venice and the Uskoks of Senji: 1537–1618," *The Journal of Modern History*, Vol. 33, No. 2 (June 1961), 148–156.

of existing kingdoms and empires throughout much of premodern history.

There are three broad factors that allowed the proliferation of actors, and in particular of barbarian groups, in premodern history. First, military technology was widely available, relatively inexpensive, and easy to use. Second, as a result, the key source of power was control over men, rather than arms or technology. Third, vast regions were characterized by absence of effective political control, allowing various societal organizations, especially stateless groups, to develop and prosper.

a. Military technology: The first reason for the multiplicity of strategic actors in ancient history was the relative cheapness, availability, and ease-of-use of military technology. The exercise of violence was not prohibitively expensive because military technology remained relatively primitive in most theaters of combat until the fifteenth to sixteenth centuries when the effective use of gunpowder began to change armed forces as well as societal organization. Until then, however, military technology was cheap and widely available, and made monopoly of violence difficult.

Lethality, and the ability to be a strategic actor, was not dependent on the possession of a state. A small tribal group could acquire and employ weapons that were as effective as those fielded by well-trained and well-supplied imperial armies. It is true that barbarian forces lacked the capacity to produce standardized weaponry that could be adopted *en masse* by the various tribes. This shortcoming was particularly relevant when there was a need to mobilize rapidly for large-scale combat, for instance to defend against a military foray of imperial forces.[29] Most of such tribal groups could not match in a frontal battle well-trained, consistently armed, and abundantly supplied imperial armies. But this did not mean that such armies could defeat these tribes, who preferred a "skulking way of war" to set piece confrontations.[30] The adoption of guerilla warfare in response to a tactical disadvantage is obviously not an exclusively premodern option, and has characterized many conflicts between rivals with large military differentials.

But this relative weakness in the production of standardized mass weaponry was insufficient to prevent barbarians from being lethal and from creating serious and often intractable security challenges. Various cases from Roman times to the Comanches point to three sources of lethality for barbarians: battlefield spoils, trade, and indigenous

---

[29] E. A. Thompson, "Early Germanic Warfare," *Past and Present*, No. 14 (November 1958), 7.

[30] Patrick M. Malone, *The Skulking Way of War* (Baltimore, MD: The Johns Hopkins University Press, 1993).

technological innovation and adaptation. All were possible because of the overarching point mentioned earlier, namely the simplicity of use of many weapons that did not require complex technical knowledge to build and use them, and vast administrative apparatuses to manage necessary resources.

The first source of weaponry was the least reliable but not inconsequential: battlefield spoils. The detritus of battles provided a symbol of glory but also of weapons, and in some famous cases (such as the 378 AD battle of Adrianople), the barbarian groups acquired the bulk of their weapons that they then used to continue their assault.[31] The uncertainty of such a method of acquiring weapons gave barbarians occasional jolts of capabilities, but it certainly does not explain the persistence of the military threat posed by them. It also was made possible because of a lucky moment for the barbarian group and a surprising defeat, or perhaps a hasty retreat, of the well-armed opposing forces.

A critical, and more reliable, source of military technology for barbarians was trade with the neighboring settled communities or empires. The fact that trade could diminish the relative strength of the imperial armies was clearly recognized by many states, which tried to ban arms transfers to foreigners and in particular to nearby barbarians. The possession and transfer of swords in the Roman Empire was heavily regulated, by threatening harsh punishments on soldiers who lost their weapon.[32] It also appears that Roman soldiers could not keep their weapons once they finished their military service.[33] And civilians were prohibited to carry arms, except in some extreme circumstances when, for instance, Goths invaded the Italian peninsula in the early fifth century AD.[34] The transfer of technical knowhow was also prohibited. The fifth century Code of Theodosius has a law prescribing the "death penalty for anyone caught teaching shipbuilding techniques to barbarians."[35] Charlemagne tried and failed to prevent arms manufacturers from selling weapons to foreigners.[36] Similarly, in the seventeenth century, Spanish authorities prohibited the sale of firearms to Indians in

---

[31] Ammianus Marcellinus, *The Later Roman Empire* (New York, NY: Penguin, 2004), 420–421 (book 31); Antonio Barbero, *9 Agosto 378: Il Giorno dei Barbari* (Rome: La Terza, 2005).
[32] Janet Lang, "Study of Metallography of Some Roman Swords," *Britannia*, Vol. 19 (1988), 202.
[33] Ramsay MacMullen, "Inscriptions on Armor and the Supply of Arms in the Roman Empire," *American Journal of Archeology*, Vol. 61, No. 1 (January 1960), 24.
[34] A. H. M. Jones, *The Later Roman Empire, 284–602* (Baltimore, MD: The Johns Hopkins University Press, 1986, reprint 1964), Vol. 2, 1062.
[35] Giusto Traina, *428 AD* (Princeton, NJ: Princeton University Press, 2009), 68.
[36] Kelly DeVries, *Medieval Military Technology* (Lewinston, NY: Broadview Press, 1992), 48.

New Mexico.[37] The imperial authorities clearly wanted to maintain an edge in military capabilities by controlling trade with barbarians and limiting it to nonlethal goods.

But it was virtually impossible to prevent technological diffusion through trade. Today's term "globalization," describing intense and far-reaching contacts among geographically disparate entities and individuals, is applicable also to premodern times. The geographic reach of trade in premodern history united vast regions and allowed the diffusion of products and knowhow well outside the borders of empires. In both Greek and Roman times, the Mediterranean was characterized by a political and economic unity that favored technology transfer.[38] This unity was interrupted perhaps only, as Henri Pirenne argued, by the seventh- and eighth-century Islamic conquests.[39] Commercial exchanges were not limited, however, to this region, and the Roman Empire had commercial interactions with groups east of the Rhine and as far as Asia, where several Roman goods, including metal products, had been found.[40] In the end, archeological evidence seems to indicate that there were more Roman swords outside the empire than inside it.[41] This, of course, could mean that Roman soldiers died in greater numbers in foreign wars outside the *limes* rather than in civil conflicts or police operations inside the empire. But it also indicates that the diffusion of a weapon such as the Roman *gladius* could not be prevented by legal decree, and either through battle losses or trade arms spread in vast numbers outside of the exclusive control of imperial forces.

Similarly, throughout the centuries, the Central Asian steppes were avenues for extensive trading, creating a region – the "Silk Road" – characterized by a unified "socio-economic-political-cultural system" that permitted rapid technological diffusion.[42] Premodern history,

---

[37] Thomas Frank Schilz and Donald E. Worcester, "The Spread of Firearms among the Indian Tribes on the Northern Frontier of New Spain," *American Indian Quarterly*, Vol. 11, No. 1 (Winter 1987), 2.

[38] Kevin Greene, "Technological Innovation and Economic Progress in the Ancient World: M.I. Finley Reconsidered," *Economic History Review*, New Series, Vol. 53, No. 1 (February 2000), 30.

[39] Henri Pirenne, *Mohammed and Charlemagne* (London: George Allen & Unwin, 1954).

[40] Matthew P. Fitzpatrick, "Provincializing Rome: The Indian Ocean Trade Network and Roman Imperialism," *Journal of World History*, Vol. 22, No. 1 (March 2011), 27–54.

[41] Goldsworthy, *How Rome Fell*, 106–107. It also appears that even before their westward push, the leaders of German tribal forces were often armed with Roman swords. See Peter Brown, *The Rise of Western Christendom* (Malden, MA: Blackwell Publishing, 2003, original 1996), 47.

[42] Christopher I. Beckwith, *Empires of the Silk Road* (Princeton, NJ: Princeton University Press, 2009), 264. For a geographic description of the "Silk Road," see René Grousset, *The Empires of the Steppes: A History of Central Asia* (New Brunswick, NJ: Rutgers University Press, 1970), 40–41. For the diffusion of technology under Mongol rule, see

therefore, was often characterized by commercial interactions that favored the spread of technology.

Three further factors made it exceedingly challenging to halt trade of military technology. First, it was difficult to enforce an arms embargo because from Roman times to the European expansion in North America, trade with many barbarian groups was conducted mostly by private individuals, driven by profits and less by long-term security concerns.[43] This was particularly the case when state monopoly of weapon manufacturing was relaxed or decentralized, as, for instance, it occurred toward the end of the Western Roman Empire. Furthermore, placed in distant frontier outposts, soldiers were in many cases the main sources of contraband, including weapons, forcing the exasperated imperial authorities to reiterate their prohibitions of uncontrolled trade.[44] But such official prohibitions may have resulted in dramatic increases in the price of weapons, creating even greater incentives for individual merchants or soldiers to trade with barbarians.[45]

Second, weapons were a source of political influence, and empires used them to befriend and support tribes considered as potential bulwarks against other, more bellicose groups. By introducing select barbarian groups to more powerful or better manufactured weapons, the empire altered the balance of power in its favor on the other side of its frontier. It gained a friendly tribe, but at the cost of spreading its military know-how. Often arms were accompanied by training, including service in imperial armies. The danger was, of course, that, once diffused, the technology and training could be used directly or indirectly against imperial forces. In the seventeenth century, for instance, the Spaniards in the southwestern North American continent armed Pueblo tribes that they considered to be friendly, but those tribes often resold the newly acquired weapons to neighboring groups or rebelled, and Spanish weapons ended up being used against Spanish soldiers. Centuries earlier, the stunning defeat of Varus's legions in the 9AD battle of Teutoburg was, at least in part, due to the knowledge of Roman tactics that the

---

T. Allsen, "The Circulation of Military Technology in the Mongolian Empire," in Nicola Di Cosmo, ed., *Warfare in Inner Asian History* (Leiden 2002), 265–293.

[43] On the mechanics of trade between Rome and Germanic tribes, see Olwen Brogan, "Trade Between the Roman Empire and the Free Germans," *Journal of Roman Studies*, Vol. 26, Part 2 (1936), 195–222. For trade with New England Indians, see Malone, 53.

[44] See, for instance, the case of Ming-Mongol contraband, Morris Rossabi, "The Ming and Inner Asia," in D. Twitchett and J. K. Fairbank, eds., *The Cambridge History of China*, Vol. 8, Part 2, chapter 4, 240 and 254–255.

[45] Hugh Elton, *Warfare in Roman Europe, AD 350–425* (Oxford: Oxford University Press, 1996), 57–58.

Germanic leader, Arminius, acquired as an auxiliary soldier in the Roman army.[46]

The third factor that made it difficult to limit the spread of military technology was the existence of great power competition. Peer rivals often vied for the support of barbarian tribes, calculating that they would create greater security woes to the adversary's interest than to them. Of course, there are episodes when traditional great power rivals occasionally collaborated against barbarians, as Rome and Parthia did in the Caucasus. But such cooperation was temporary and did not exclude concurrent attempts by the competing powers to woo barbarian groups to their own side. If the goal was merely to deflect a barbarian attack, bribes of gold or other valuables often sufficed to push groups in other directions. But great powers often pursued more offensive objectives and sought to incite and arm barbarian groups to destabilize and threaten frontiers of their great power competitors. The Spaniards, for instance, armed Northern California tribes to counter Russian expansion.[47] In brief, the more pronounced the competition between great powers, the greater the likelihood of arms transfers to barbarian groups. Proxy wars between peer competitors led to the diffusion of military technology.

While battlefield spoils and trade – the first two factors that aided the spread of military technology – were essential sources of lethality for the barbarians, they are not sufficient to explain the tactical advantages that in many cases these groups exhibited. Barbarians, in fact, were not mere recipients of superior equipment but were capable of great technological innovations, both of the hardware and of the ways of using it. States and empires had no monopoly over innovation. The composite bow developed, produced, and adopted by the steppe tribes since ancient times was, for instance, an incredibly powerful weapon, difficult to manufacture and to use.[48] Similarly, the long sword, produced by Slavic and Germanic metallurgists in later Roman times, was a deadly weapon, capable of keeping its sharp edge for prolonged periods, and it replaced the shorter Roman *gladius* after the collapse of the Western Roman Empire in the fifth century AD. The long sword favored a battle formation more relaxed and less disciplined than the one adopted by the well-trained Roman

---

[46] Peter S. Wells, *The Battle That Stopped Rome* (New York, NY: W.W. Norton & Co., 2004), 110–111.
[47] Schilz and Worcester, 8.
[48] For a description of the bow, see Edward Luttwak, *The Grand Strategy of the Byzantine Empire* (Cambridge, MA: Harvard University Press, 2009), 22–28; Heather, *The Fall of the Roman Empire*, 154–158.

legions, and consequently its adoption was probably due to lower military training standards.[49] But this barbarian sword and the way of fighting that came with it also gave a clear advantage in forested lands where a tight formation was impossible or in raids conducted by bands that coalesced quickly for the plundering and had limited experience fighting together. The types of weapons adopted or developed fit the geological environment in which these groups fought and the tactics they used.[50]

The use of the horse was another example of a successful indigenous tactical adaptation by barbarian groups. The barbarians, such as the Huns in late Roman times or the various steppes tribes in Central Asia or the Plains Indians in the eighteenth to nineteenth centuries, excelled at horsemanship, making them into fearsome fighters capable of engaging the enemy from a safe distance and at high speeds.[51] High mobility and great speed allowed barbarians to conduct quick raids and avoid set battles, giving them clear advantages over the heavier and larger armies, burdened by long logistical trains.

The difference between states and barbarians was in the end not as much in the technical quality of weapons but in how they were used. Even though a state such as the Roman Empire or Ming China or the British Empire could manufacture the most advanced weaponry, barbarian groups were often capable of adopting the latest technologies with greater efficiency. Robert Gilpin noted that "the imitators, who have lower standards of living and less wasteful habits, can use the imported technology more efficiently. Moreover, they can adopt the most advanced and most thoroughly proven techniques, whereas prior research and development costs and vested interests deter the more advanced economy from substituting the very latest techniques for obsolescent techniques. Thus, with lower costs, untapped resources, and equivalent technology, backward societies frequently can outcompete the more affluent advanced society economically and militarily."[52] William McNeill similarly observes that "Steppe populations ... had a cheaper and more mobile

---

[49] Lynn White, Jr., "The Act of Invention: Causes, Contexts, Continuities and Consequences," *Technology and Culture*, Vol. 3, No. 4 (Autumn 1962), 493.
[50] Michel Kazanski, "Barbarian Military Equipment and its Evolution in the Late Roman and Great Migration Periods (3rd-5th C. AD)," in Alexander Sarantis and Neil Christie, eds., *War and Warfare in Late Antiquity*, 2 vol. (Leiden: Brill, 2013), 493–521.
[51] Heather, *The Fall of the Roman Empire*, 155; Elton, 59; Allan R. Millett and Peter Maslowski, *For the Common Defense* (New York, NY: The Free Press, 1994), 254; Pekka Hämäläinen, *The Comanche Empire* (New Haven, CT: Yale University Press, 2008), 19.
[52] Robert Gilpin, *War and Change in War Politics* (New York, NY: Cambridge University Press, 1983), 178–179.

armed force at their command than civilized people could easily put into the field."[53]

Such a pattern was visible on a tactical level too. The various tribes facing Rome, for instance, often developed tactics that took into consideration their material inferiority and that Roman forces could not match. In fact, tactical innovation was more pronounced among the barbarian forces than Roman legions.[54] Similarly, in the mid-eighteenth century Comanche tribes outmatched Spanish forces by employing European weapons in hit-and-run tactics, a combination that the Spaniards could not defeat. As a historian of that period writes, "weapons technology, from stone-pointed spear to nuclear bomb, has never remained exclusively in the hands of its inventor. Sooner or later it is acquired by an enemy who will use it with less restraint and greater barbarity; and violence inevitably escalates."[55] In fact, in some cases, barbarian groups adopted a more advanced technology quicker and more effectively than their more developed enemy. For instance, seventeenth-century New England Indians quickly adopted flintlocks over matchlocks in contrast to British colonists, because the new firearm ignition system performed considerably better in guerilla-type ambushes in forests.[56]

The relative ease with which these barbarian groups acquired and adopted nonindigenous weapons is a symptom of the simplicity of their use. The simpler the weapon, the faster and easier its diffusion. In fact, weapons that required expert knowledge and complex machinery presented often insurmountable difficulties to groups that happened to acquire them but without the necessary knowhow. In 814, for example, Bulgar tribes captured some "Greek fire" but were unable to employ it on the battlefield because of their lack of knowledge of how to operate the machinery and how to handle the liquid.[57] Similarly, naval power falls into the category of capital- and skill-intensive technologies, and as such it was more difficult to acquire by barbarians. Navies always consumed large amounts of natural resources (timber, then iron, coal, and oil) and in premodern times also required large numbers of trained and disciplined crews.[58] The Mongols failed to project power across the sea to Japan in the late thirteenth century, in part because of stormy weather but

---

[53] McNeill, *The Pursuit of Power*, 16.   [54] DeVries, 8.
[55] Robert S. Weddle, *After the Massacre: The Violent Legacy of the San Sabá Mission* (Lubbock, TX: Texas Tech University Press, 2007), 2.
[56] Malone, 45.
[57] Alex Roland, "Secrecy, Technology, and War: Greek Fire and the Defense of Byzantium, 678–1204," *Technology and Culture*, Vol. 33, No. 4 (October 1992), 663.
[58] Jonathan Grant, "Rethinking the Ottoman 'Decline': Military Technology Diffusion in the Ottoman Empire, Fifteenth to Eighteenth Centuries," *Journal of World History*, Vol. 10, No. 1 (Spring 1999), 179–201.

in part because they were fairly new to maritime warfare. In Late Antiquity, the great "migrations" of barbarian tribes in Europe occurred by land, and even the Vandals crossed the Mediterranean to North Africa in effect by walking around it through Spain. Piracy was certainly a problem in premodern times, but it tended to be very localized.

There were periods throughout premodern history when to be a warrior one needed to be wealthy, making lethality a possession of the few. For instance, in the Middle Ages few could afford to buy the equipment necessary to be a powerful warrior. As Stanislav Andreski observes, "[e]ven the possession of a horse was beyond the means of an ordinary peasant." Because "the heavily armed cavalry could disperse any number of footmen, the only alternative to defeat was the institution of a small stratum of professional warriors whom the rest of the population would support."[59] The professionalization of the military class was driven by the cost of weapons and by the need to train constantly. In the Middle Ages the invention of the stirrup, a simple but "catalytic" invention that altered the mode of warfare, contributed to this development: "[m]ounted shock combat was not a business for part-time warriors," and "one had to be a skilled professional, the product of a long technical training," creating an aristocratic class of warriors.[60] But even in these cases, professional armed forces could not control populations without heavy costs because military technology by virtue of its relative simplicity could not be monopolized. It was easy to manufacture weapons. In Roman times, for instance, "[e]verywhere, even in remote villages, there will have been skilled smiths with materials at their disposal which were needed for the production of the tools used in fields, houses and workshops; both craftsmen and materials could rapidly be turned over to making weapons and armour."[61] It was impossible to disarm a conquered population for a prolonged period of time, resulting in a recurrent threat of rebellions.

Therefore, more so on land than on the sea, which demanded advanced skills and resources, it was not necessary to have large concentrations of capital or complex bureaucratic organizations to develop or utilize lethal weapons. To use Charles Tilly's argument, capital and coercion were separated in ancient times, and a political entity could have one or the other and still be a serious strategic actor in international relations.

---

[59] Stanislav Andreski, *Military Organization and Society* (Berkeley: University of California Press, 1968), 34.
[60] Lynn White, *Medieval Technology and Social Change* (London: Oxford University Press, 1962), 31. For a criticism of White's "stirrup thesis," see P. Saqyer and R. Hilton, "Technical Determinism, the Stirrup, and the Plough," *Past and Present*, no. 24 (1963), 90–100.
[61] P. A. Brunt, *Roman Imperial Themes* (New York, NY: Oxford University Press, 1990), 263.

Commercial city states (e.g. Venice) were not better off than groups that were purely coercive in nature (e.g. mercenaries or the early Ottomans). The ability to coerce was not necessarily linked to the possession of capital.

The main consequence was that the proliferation of violence allowed the proliferation of actors, including nomadic tribes and mercenary groups. And, although some groups such as the *ghazis* who established the foundations of the Ottoman Empire settled and developed state institutions and administrative capabilities, they did not need to do so to remain a strategic actor.[62] The "military revolution" of the fifteenth to sixteenth centuries, grounded mostly in the development of artillery and firearms, altered this situation. It demanded large, well-trained, standing armies equipped with increasingly more costly weapons, that in turn required the centralization of state authority and power, indispensable to garner the financial and technological resources upon which modern military strength was becoming increasingly based.[63] From then on, the strategic impact of a political actor was increasingly dependent on the "systematic organization and extraction of taxes from all resources" as much as a on the "possession of fire-arms."[64] This also meant that a professional, and thus expensive, military elite became increasingly more important to the survival of a polity. As Andreski puts it, "Swords or even rifles can be manufactured clandestinely but not tanks or bombers .... [The] predominance of the armed forces over the populace grows as the armament becomes more elaborate."[65] To be lethal and a strategic actor, one had to manage vast amounts of resources with which one could develop the military force necessary to compete.[66] Capital and coercion converged.

b. Control over men, not things: Because technological superiority was more difficult to achieve and did not give a decisive advantage in

---

[62] Paul Wittek, *The Rise of the Ottoman Empire* (London: The Royal Asiatic Society, 1938); Karen Barkey, *Empire of Difference* (New York, NY: Cambridge University Press, 2008).

[63] See Parker, *The Military Revolution*. Also Carlo Cipolla, *Guns, Sails, and Empires: Technological Innovation and the Early Phases of European Expansion, 1400–1700* (New York, NY: Pantheon Books, 1966); William H. McNeill, *The Pursuit of Power* (Chicago: University of Chicago Press, 1982), especially chapters 3–5, 63–184; Brian M. Downing, *The Military Revolution and Political Change* (Princeton, NJ: Princeton University Press, 1992). For an overview of historical literature on military technology and warfare, see John France, "Recent Writing on Medieval Warfare: From the Fall of Rome to *c.* 1300," *Journal of Military History*, Vol. 65, No. 2 (April 2001), 441–473.

[64] Andrew C. Hess, "The Ottoman Conquest of Egypt (1517) and the Beginning of the Sixteenth-Century World War," *International Journal of Middle East Studies*, Vol. 4, No. 1 (January 1973), 58.

[65] Andreski, 35.

[66] For an analysis of how "financial intensity" and "organizational capital" impact the diffusion of military technology, see Michael Horowitz, *The Diffusion of Military Power* (Princeton, NJ: Princeton University Press, 2010).

ancient history, to be powerful meant to control people, not things. Control over people meant the ability to supply manpower to armies, and thus be a respectable actor in international relations as well as in domestic politics. Whoever was capable of coalescing around him a large group of people could wage war either for his own or, as a mercenary, for somebody else's interests. Julius Caesar, for instance, observes that in Gaul the "possession of such a following [of warriors] is the only criterion of position and power" that the local population recognized.[67] An individual who had a large number of people indebted to him could exercise political influence as well as gain wealth through tributes and other payments. The political power of Roman emperors, for instance, was grounded to a large degree on their vast *clientela*, a network of people who sought legal, political, and sometimes financial support from the more powerful and prestigious family. And this power accumulated over generations, as one emperor (e.g. Octavian Augustus) inherited the *clientes* of his predecessor (e.g. Julius Caesar).[68] The flip side of this logic of power was that to expand a polity meant to extend control over more people, not territory. Foreign *clientelae* were one way through which imperial power expanded and maintained control over distant populations, whose elites sought Roman support for their own local political advancement.[69] As a historian notes, "like the Greeks before them, Romans first ruled people; then they dealt with land. Land without people was of no concern, and the proven way to rule people was through patron-client relationship."[70]

---

[67] Julius Caesar, *The Conquest of Gaul* (New York: Penguin, 1982), 141 (VI, 15). Also, Adrian Goldsworthy, "War," in P. Sabin et al., eds., *The Cambridge History of Greek and Roman Warfare* (New York: Cambridge University Press, 2007), Vol. 2, chapter 3, 81. The Roman political environment was also similar, placing a premium on the ability to employ an army. See Ronald Syme, *The Roman Revolution* (Oxford: Oxford University Press, 1960), 12.

[68] Everitt, 44. On developing a network of friends through *beneficia* and having a *clientela*, see Ramsay MacMullen, "Personal Power in the Roman Empire," *American Journal of Philology*, Vol. 107, No. 4 (Winter 1986), 512–524; Numa Denis Fustel de Coulanges, *The Ancient City* (Baltimore, MD: The Johns Hopkins University Press, 1980), 247–260; Finley, 40–41; P. A. Brunt, *The Fall of the Roman Republic* (Oxford: Clarendon Press, 1988), 383–442; Matthias Gelzer, *Caesar: Politician and Statesman* (Cambridge, MA: Harvard University Press, 1968), 3–4; Azar Gat, *War in Human Civilization* (New York, NY: Oxford University Press, 2006), 216–217.

[69] Ernst Badian, *Foreign Clientelae (264–70 B.C.)* (Oxford: Clarendon Press, 1958).

[70] Thomas S. Burns, *Rome and the Barbarians, 100 BC–AD 400* (Baltimore, MD: The Johns Hopkins University, 2003), 173. See also Greg Woolf, "Roman Peace," in John Rich and Graham Shipley, eds., *War and Society in the Roman World* (London: Routledge, 1993), 179; Susan Mattern, "Imperial Power in the Roman Republic," in D. E. Tabachnick and T. Koivukoski, eds., *Enduring Empire* (Toronto: University of Toronto Press, 2009), 132–133; Roger Batty, *Rome and the Nomads* (New York, NY: Oxford University Press, 2007), 451–452.

A version of a patron–client patronage continued in the Middle Ages. The sinews of power were the ties that linked different leaders through personal bonds of obligations and rights, establishing a web of allegiances and a hierarchy of power.[71] In a way that is reminiscent of the Roman concept of power, feudalism, as Hendrick Spruyt observes, was "rule over people rather than land."[72] A symbol of the importance of having the people's allegiance was the fact that often kings referred to themselves as leaders of a group (for example, king of the Goths, or the French) rather than of a specific territory. It was also difficult to exercise control over a territory for reasons mentioned earlier: Arming a population was relatively easy and rebellions were recurrent. A political leader had to first and foremost control the people by developing and nurturing their personal allegiance. Power was personal, stemming from the charisma that emanated from the leaders and that the populations respected and revered.[73]

As a result, for instance, many kings were constantly on the move, in part because their territories were widely dispersed, often geographically incongruous, requiring constant travel and delegation of authority. In some societies, such as Castile in the late medieval period, even fixed positions such as fortresses did not serve as administrative centers because "wealth which supported them was constantly on the move." The ties linking people did not arise from a circumscribed territory but from personal loyalty, and this was something that was not linked to a specific land. In fact, a "gentleman was not primarily a man who held land by a particular kind of tenure. He was a man who owned a horse and was prepared to ride it into battle in his lord's support."[74]

But in part, as Benno Teschke observes, "the peripatetic nature of the royal households is indicative of the structural difficulty of maintaining effective state authority over the territory."[75] If kings ruled people rather

---

[71] See Marc Bloch, *Feudal Society* (Chicago, IL: The University of Chicago Press, 1964), Vol. 1, 123–175; Duby, *The Chivalrous Society*; Robert S. Hoyt, *Feudal Institutions: Cause or Consequence of Decentralization?* (New York, NY: Holt, Rinehart and Winston, 1961).

[72] Hendrick Spruyt, *The Sovereign State and Its Competitors* (Princeton, NJ: Princeton University Press, 1994), 40. See also Gianfranco Poggi, *The Development of the Modern State* (Stanford, CA: Stanford University Press, 1978), 19–27; Palmira Brummett, *Ottoman Seapower and Levantine Diplomacy in the Age of Discovery* (Albany, NY: State University of New York Press, 1994), 13; Benno Teschke, "Geopolitical Relations in the European Middle Ages: History and Theory," *International Organization*, Vol. 52, No. 2 (Spring 1998), 345; Benno Teschke, *The Myth of 1648: Class, Geopolitics, and the Making of Modern International Relations* (London, New York, NY: Verso, 2003); Duby, *The Early Growth of the European Economy*, 162.

[73] Thomas N. Bisson, *The Crisis of the Twelfth Century* (Princeton, NJ: Princeton University Press, 2009), 2.

[74] J. H. Parry, *The Spanish Seaborne Empire* (Berkeley: University of California Press, 1990), 32.

[75] Teschke, "Geopolitical Relations," 345.

than land, they had to be visible to and in touch with their subjects as much as travel logistics of those centuries allowed. Of course, in an age of limited and slow communications, it was impossible for a ruler to be in charge of his entire domain. That is why medieval polities were a mosaic of influence and control. Historian Georges Duby observes that this "subdivision between smaller and smaller territorial units of the right to command and punish, to ensure peace and justice, constituted an adjustment to the concrete possibilities of exercising effective authority in a rural and barbaric world where it was difficult to communicate over any distance. Political organization was being adapted to the ordering of material life."[76]

Because manpower mattered more than territorial control, some of the key protagonists of ancient history were stateless, non-territorial groups, such as nomadic tribes or migrating groups. Modern states occupy, control, and administer territory; tribes, mercenaries, or brigands rule over men. Unlike in modern times, these groups were in some cases more than a match for established states and their armies, which in several famous instances (e.g. the 9AD Teutoburg massacre, the 378 battle of Adrianople, the 1449 battle of Tu-Mu) suffered devastating defeats at the hand of an apparently inferior enemy.[77] Only in premodern times, could a group of mercenaries, such as the "Ten Thousand" Greeks under Xenophon's command, defeat the army of a large empire (Persia), hack their way through enemy territory (modern Iraq and Turkey), and return to their home with booty and glory.[78] The effectiveness of such warrior groups derived from their leaders' ability to gather a growing number of fighters whose loyalty was to their chiefs and the group, rather than to a territory. The leadership of the chief, in fact, provided these warriors with the possibility of wealth and security, and their loyalty was directly correlated to the chief's skill at directing the group toward rich areas. As Azar Gat writes, "[c]ommand over men in successful wars was the major avenue to kingship, because it could enrich the successful war leader and expand his retinue and clientele above those of his peers and contenders, the other tribal powerful; because it could win him prestige and empower him with popular support and legitimacy within the tribe, again with the same result; or, indeed, because it could attract to him a host of warriors from far afield, thus creating around him an independent power base outside his original tribe."[79] The size of the assaulting group increased with the success of the initial raids, quick and short assaults on specific targets that guaranteed the highest payoff with limited

---

[76] Duby, *The Early Growth of the European Economy*, 162.   [77] See also Bloch, Vol. 1, 54.
[78] Xenophon, *The Persian Expedition* (New York, NY: Penguin, 1972).
[79] Azar Gat, *War in Human Civilization* (New York, NY: Oxford University Press, 2006), 241.

risks.[80] In fact, such groups often avoided large battles because they were too dangerous: a defeat would have discouraged other men, from runaway slaves to new tribes, from joining the warrior group. Military success, or at least absence of military defeats, was a powerful form of social cohesion.[81] The *ghazis*, for instance, were "essentially fighters and conquerors … and were uninterested in organized government."[82] A metric of their success was not how much territory they controlled or how well they administered it but how many men they could field in their plundering raids.[83] The Comanche tribes, a nineteenth-century remnant of a premodern actor, are another great example of this focus on manpower. Power was measured not by how much material wealth one possessed, but by how many followers one had accumulated through gifts and demonstrations of martial prowess.[84]

An additional effect of the personal nature of power was that even strong imperial centers were enfeebled by the web of allegiances linking people of different regions. Premodern state structures were contingent on the firm allegiance of powerful individuals whose influence was proportional to the clients, or more broadly, the manpower they could assemble on their side. In Rome, it was not the Senate that was powerful, but the senators. Of course, these personal relationships could also serve the interests of the distant clients who used their patrons in the capital to lobby on their personal behalf. A Roman individual who gathered large numbers of foreign clients often became an ancient version of a lobbying firm. One of the most lively descriptions of how a distant, foreign, and in the end hostile leader could use his personal connections in Rome to gain and for a while maintain local power was told by the Roman historian Sallust in his "War of Jugurtha." In a memorable scene, while leaving the city of Rome, the Numidian Jugurtha sums it up: "A city for sale and doomed to speedy destruction if it finds a purchaser."[85] This does not

---

[80] Batty, 23.
[81] See Goldsworthy, *How Rome Fell*, 311. A similar increase in the size of the raiding force occurred during the Viking and Magyar attacks on Western Europe in the ninth and tenth centuries. Duby, *The Early Growth of the European Economy*, 114–115. On the Ottoman *ghazi*, see Steven Runciman, *The Fall of Constantinople, 1453* (New York, NY: Cambridge University Press, 1990), 26.
[82] Runciman, *The Fall of Constantinople*, 26.
[83] Indeed, the raids of such fighters most often "resulted in the swift decay of roads and bridges, wells and irrigation channels," all products of a well-administered state. Runciman, *The Fall of Constantinople*, 26.
[84] Brian DeLay, *War of a Thousand Deserts* (New Haven, CT: Yale University Press, 2008), 96–97.
[85] "Urbem venalem et mature perituram, si emptorem invenerit." Sallust, "The War with Jugurtha," *Loeb Classical* #116, trans. J. C. Rolfe (Cambridge, MA: Harvard University Press, 1931), 212 (XXXV, 10).

necessarily mean that empires or premodern states were incapable of harnessing their populations and elites to defend a capital or common interests.[86] But it certainly weakened them and reinforced the necessity to figure out how to maintain the allegiance of their populations.

With the rise of the modern state, the requirements for survival changed. A fixed population in a delimited territory gradually became the prerequisites of strategic actors. Firepower demanded a large administrative apparatus and a substantial economic base. Taxes and resources had to be extracted, administered, managed, and translated into military strength – a series of activities that small and mobile groups could not pursue with great effectiveness.

c. Ungoverned spaces: Finally, until the late seventeenth and early eighteenth centuries, the map of the world was characterized by vast empty spaces, unexplored and outside of the reach of cities, states, or empires. Such large swaths of land allowed different ways of societal organization to arise, prosper, and at times even challenge the more established powers. For instance, until roughly the sixteenth century, several nomadic groups, such as the Huns and the Mongols, erupted on the Eurasian scene from the Central Asian steppes.[87] Similarly, as Tacitus recounts in his *Germania*, Central Europe in Roman times was populated by tribal groups with limited administrative and economic skills, and certainly without the large bureaucratic apparatus of the Roman Empire.[88]

The existence of these spaces outside of state control was due to three related reasons: geology, logistics, and politics. First, some areas of the known world were, and continue to be, simply too difficult to reach because of their geography. Marshes, distant valleys, heavily forested regions, deserts or jungles, high mountain ranges, and even islands create physical spaces where state officials and administrators have a difficult time functioning. Greek tragedian Aeschylus in *Prometheus Unbound* calls the distant lands of the Scythians, the barbarians of his time, "untrodden solitude."[89] In many cases, settled populations and imperial forces simply

---

[86] "Clients, like friends, if faced with a conflict in their personal obligations, had to make a choice, and that choice might be determined by consideration either of the relative strength of those obligations taken by themselves, or of their own advantage, or of the public interest, or, of course, by mixed motives. We must not assume that their views of the public interest counted for nothing. It might actually affect their choice of patrons." Brunt, *The Fall of the Roman Republic*, 399.
[87] René Grousset, *The Empire of the Steppes* (New Brunswick, NJ: Rutgers University Press, 2010 [1970]), in particular xxi–xxx; Nicola Di Cosmo, *Ancient China and Its Enemies* (New York, NY: Cambridge University Press, 2002), 13–43.
[88] Tacitus, *The Agricola and the Germania* (New York, NY: Penguin, 1970).
[89] Aeschylus, *Prometheus Bound in Aeschylus*, translated by Herbert Weir Smyth (New York, NY: G. P. Putnam's Sons, 1922), #1, 215.

could not reach the areas in question. Even when they did, a consistent state presence in the form of military forces or administrators was unlikely to succeed. An evocative description of the difficulty of surviving in such areas comes from a poem written by a young West Point graduate sent to Fort Brown, Texas, in the 1870s. In it he depicts the territories that the soldiers were expected to control, territories that according to his imagination had been bequeathed by God to the devil, who made a "good hell" out of them. He continued:

> He began to put thorns on all the trees,
> And mix up the sand with millions of fleas:
> And scattered tarantulas along all the roads;
> Put thorns on the cactus and horns on the toads.
> He lengthened the horns of the Texas steers,
> And put additions on the rabbits' ears;
> He put a little devil in the broncho steed
> And poisoned the feet of the centipede.
> The rattlesnake bites you, the scorpion stings.
> The mosquito delights you with buzzing wings;
> The sandburns prevail and so do the ants,
> And those who sit down need half-soles on their pants.
> ...
> The heat in the summer is a hunder and ten,
> Too hot for the devil and too hot for men,
> The wild boar roams through the black chaparral,
> It's a hell of a place he has for a hell.
> The red pepper grows on the banks of the brook;
> The Mexicans use it in all that they cook.
> Just dine with a 'greaser,' and then you will shout
> 'I've hell on the inside as well as the out.'[90]

These ungoverned and ungovernable regions were both inside and outside of imperial or state territories, presenting slightly different challenges. Inside, bandits, outlaws, and fugitive slaves often congregated, "periodically breaking the peace" and more broadly sowing instability and insecurity on roads and small communities.[91] These were safe havens for disaffected populations that often rebelled. "In olden days many successful revolts started in the outlying regions which were beyond the reach of effective supervision by the despot."[92] The weaker the control of the state, the greater was the likelihood of brigandage or even private wars,

---

[90] In Robert G. Carter, *On the Border with Mackenzie* (Austin: Texas State Historical Association, 2007; originally published in *c.* 1935), 294–295.
[91] Josiah Osgood, *Claudius Caesar: Image and Power in the Early Roman Empire* (New York, NY: Cambridge University Press, 2011), 5–6.
[92] Andreski, 36.

waged by wealthy individuals who in the absence of imperial authority hired and wielded their own forces to protect their properties or to extract resources from weaker parties.[93] Outside imperial territories, the spaces were much larger, permitting a wider spectrum of social organization as well as larger numbers of non-state actors who regularly threatened the imperial frontier and the settled, civilized communities along it.

Xenophon describes one such group of barbarians who were ensconced in a region that was difficult to access. While struggling to go through Persia's northern territories, the Greek mercenaries, among whom traveled the Greek historian, encountered several local tribes that did not pay allegiance to the king, who in any case could at best send occasional forces to keep them in check. These people, the Carduchi, "lived in the mountains and were very warlike and not subject to the King." Persian authorities were certainly eager to put them under their control, but "a royal army of a hundred and twenty thousand had once invaded their country, and not a man of them had got back."[94] The likely difficulties and costs associated with an imposition of imperial control would have been greater than the potential benefits.

The second cause for these ungoverned spaces was related to geography, but it is analytically separate. The logistics of state expansion or, to be more precise, of conquest were difficult in many areas. In part these territories were geographically too distant from the main ancient empires, whose expansion was often limited by technological limitations of power projection.[95] The perennial problem of a "loss-of-strength gradient," namely the fact that distance degrades power, was even more acute in premodern times because of the primitive means of communications.[96] A key logistical challenge that resulted from this was the difficulty of supplying sufficient food to soldiers. From Roman times to the conquest of the North American Plains, armies often marched with cattle that provided them with meat, but had a hard time carrying sufficient quantities of grain. It was too costly to transport it by land because over long distances the animals carting the grain ended up eating more than they carried. Sea transport was cheaper, and by extension, power projection on the sea or along waterways was easier than by land. A. H. M. Jones observed that it "was cheaper to ship grain from one end of the Mediterranean to the other than to cart it 75 miles."[97] Most cities far

---

[93] Ramsay MacMullen, *Corruption and the Decline of Rome* (New Haven, CT: Yale University Press, 1988), 72–73.
[94] Xenophon, *The Persian Expedition*, III:5, 173.   [95] Woolf, 185.
[96] Kenneth Boulding, *Conflict and Defense: A General Theory* (New York, NY: Harper, 1962).
[97] Jones, 842.

from a port or a river had to rely almost exclusively on local agricultural production, and if the annual harvest failed, they were at great risk of a famine.[98] Similarly, armies had to rely on local crops along their marching routes. Often it appears that armies were eager to take over a hostile city simply to find grain that would supplement their diet, which was dangerously limited to meat. Tacitus recounts a Roman expedition in the east where the soldiers "suffering no losses in battle, [were] becoming exhausted by short supplies and hardships, compelled as they were to stave off hunger solely by the flesh of cattle." They were undoubtedly relieved to reach "lands under cultivation, [where they] reaped the crops."[99]

Furthermore, projection of power was hampered by the absence of infrastructure such as roads and bridges. Imperial expansion occurred along existing roads and paths, slowing down, if not outright ending, where travel networks were nonexistent or underdeveloped. Julius Caesar conquered Gaul, albeit with some difficulty, but he could not do the same in Germania. In the former, he had roads as well as food, built and supplied by the local inhabitants who were either coopted or forced to support his legions. In the latter, he could barely find empty villages, and was forced to build from scratch the logistical apparatus – a bridge across the Rhine and food and forage for his soldiers – needed to project power. Similarly, the early expansion of Muscovite Russia into the steppes was hampered by the logistical challenges presented by distance. For instance, while conquering Kazan, Russian soldiers often were hungry and diverted their marches to capture abandoned towns where they could find food stores or not yet harvested crops.[100] Naturally, this slowed down a conquering army, and forced it to devote more attention to feeding itself than achieving the actual military objective. What Rome, as well as many other states and empires, needed was a fairly elaborate infrastructure that could sustain their conquering forces. A wish list included: "(1) a comprehensive fort network; (2) strong points and signal towers linked by all-weather roads and bridges, with massive building to assist movement; and (3) a strong naval presence on the internal rivers with fortified points of entry, jetties, quays arsenals,

---

[98] Jones, 844. See also Colin Adams, "Transport," in Walter Scheidel, ed., *The Cambridge Companion to the Roman Economy* (Cambridge: Cambridge University Press, 2012), 218–240.

[99] Tacitus, *Annals*, 14:24, in *The Complete Works of Tacitus* (New York, NY: The Modern Library, 1942), 334. For a very detailed study of Roman military logistics, see Jonathan Roth, *The Logistics of the Roman Army at War* (Leiden: Brill, 1998).

[100] Smith, "Muscovite Logistics," 49–50.

and granaries."[101] Without building such a massive infrastructure, a state could not conquer and later on keep the conquered land. It is not surprising therefore that, as Paul Claval put it, an empire is "surrounded by barbarians; ... its expansion stops at the boundaries of the cultivated universe."[102] An outright military conquest was difficult because geographic distance stretched the logistical lines while local inhabitants' "hit and run" tactics sapped the military strength of the invading armies.

Finally, the third factor that left vast spaces outside of state or imperial control was political or cultural. It was difficult to understand the social structures of the groups that arose in those areas. This prevented empires from extending indirect control over these lands. Direct conquest was too costly for the reasons mentioned earlier; indirect control was difficult because one could not understand with great clarity whom to coopt. To use more modern terms, formulated by James C. Scott, a population needs to be "legible" in order to be governed or ruled by a state, even a premodern one. "Legibility" means the ability "to arrange the population in ways that simplified the classic state functions of taxation, conscription, and prevention of rebellion." Premodern states were particularly handicapped because they "lacked anything like a detailed 'map' of its terrain and its people."[103] And such knowledge was even weaker of territories outside of their frontiers where the various groups tended to be small, mobile, and very diverse in terms of language, customs, and social hierarchy. "The more static, standardized, and uniform a population or social space is, the more legible it is, and the more amenable it is to the techniques of state officials."[104] Roman historian Tacitus suggests a similar challenge with a Numidian tribe led by Tacfarinas (see also Chapter 6): a group that bordered the deserts of Africa and lacked the civilization of cities ("nullo etiam tum urbium cultu" – "even then innocent of city life"), a situation that made it difficult for the Romans to understand and control this tribe.[105]

The difficulty of understanding the "human terrain" in these ungoverned spaces generated also a lot of fear among the civilized populations. The Greeks, for instance, were bewildered by the "barbarians" living beyond their borders.[106] Xenophon's tale of the Persian expedition is,

---

[101] James Lacey, "Conquering Germania: A Province Too Far," in W. Murray and P. Mansoor, eds., *Hybrid Warfare* (New York, NY: Cambridge University Press, 2012), 36. The same applies to Muscovite Russia. See Smith, 51–52.
[102] Paul Claval, *Espace et Pouvoir* (Paris, PUF: 1978), 109.
[103] James C. Scott, *Seeing Like a State* (New Haven, CT: Yale University Press, 1998), 2.
[104] Scott, *Seeing Like a State*, 82.   [105] Tacitus, *Annals*, II, 52.
[106] See Herodotus, passim, and especially the description of the Scythians, 4.2–4.82 (pp. 281–316).

among others, a description of various tribes, living in the hinterlands of Persia and in general outside of Persian control, who instilled dread because they were unknown to the Greeks and were assumed to be culturally and politically different. These tribes were simply not organized polities, like the Greek cities or the Persian Empire, and the Greeks and Persians alike did not know how to deal with them. Indeed, the gravest threat to Xenophon's Greek mercenaries story was not Persia, but the unruly and unknown tribes in Asia Minor occupying unclaimed territories. As the Spartan Clearchus, the leader of Xenophon's "ten thousand," puts it, "every river would be a difficult obstacle, every collection of people would inspire us with fear, but most fearful of all would be uninhabited places in which one is perplexed every way."[107]

As a result, these spaces were outside of the interstate system and did not participate in the development of regular interactions. They also allowed the proliferation of strategic actors other than territorial polities. The presence of regions that were difficult to reach by state forces (e.g. mountains, marshes) made it much easier to escape state control, establishing areas where non-state forms of societal organization prospered. This view of ungoverned spaces differs slightly from the modern one. One modern perspective on these spaces is that they increase competition among great powers. Africa, as an ungoverned space, generated a "scramble" for it. Or Civil Wars, which undermine the governance of a state, tend to draw in other powers that line up to protect their own factions. As a political scientist put it, "spaces that belong to no one or for which no one feels responsible offer temptations to plunder, exploit, or misuse, without regard to the interests of others or to the longer-term consequences of activities."[108] Another contemporary view is that failed states, or more broadly, areas of weak governance, cause humanitarian disasters with the possibility of dramatic spillover effects. But neither view necessarily denies the possibility that ungoverned spaces can become areas where different societal organizations, including dangerous and hostile groups, arise. This, rather than the fear of humanitarian disasters or exacerbated great power competition, was the preeminent fear in premodern times. One can see it in the problem facing Julius Caesar at the outset of his Gallic campaign. When the Helvetii left their region, the risk was that other, perhaps more threatening, groups would take over their former territories. As Julius Caesar wrote, having defeated the newly

---

[107] Xenophon, 124.
[108] Malcolm Anderson, "The Political Science of Frontiers," in P. Ganster et al., eds., *Borders and Border Regions in Europe and North America* (San Diego, CA: San Diego State University Press, 1997), 30. See also Jakub Grygiel, "Vacuum Wars," *The American Interest*, July 2009.

Objectives

mobile Helvetii, he "ordered the Helvetii themselves to rebuild the towns and villages they had burnt [and abandoned]. His chief reason for doing this was that he did not want the country they had abandoned to remain uninhabited, lest the Germans across the Rhine might be induced by its fertility to migrate into Switzerland, and so become near neighbours of the Roman Province."[109]

The gradual filling of these spaces by modern states eliminated most of such non-state actors.[110] In part this was made possible by the military revolution, which led to a clash between the artillery of states and the archers of the steppes, resulting in the defeat of the latter – and this development will be examined in a later chapter.[111] The sheer industrial power of states allowed them to spread into until then unconquered regions. But in part this "filling of space" was due to the growing ideological power of the modern state, which does not become well entrenched until the second half of the twentieth century with the decolonization process, and arguably until 1991 when the last of the truly multinational empires, the USSR, collapses, leaving several new states in its wake. This is the peak of the appeal of the state as the only, and best, way to organize society. And, one may argue, it is also the nadir of the proliferation of actors other than states in international relations. Yet, even then, the expansion of the modern state was never fully achieved. As James Scott has described, even now, regions outside of effective governmental control continue to exist, allowing for the survival of communities organized in non-territorial ways.[112]

1.3 Objectives

The second category of differences between premodern and modern history lies in the objectives pursued by the various political actors.[113]

---

[109] Caesar, *The Conquest of Gaul*, I. 28, 41–42.
[110] Peter C. Perdue, *China Marches West* (Cambridge, MA: Belknap Press, 2005), 10–11.
[111] Grousset, xi.
[112] James Scott, *The Art of Not Being Governed* (New Haven, CT: Yale University Press, 2010).
[113] Markus Fischer offers perhaps the best critique of the argument that modern international relations were different from medieval ones. He writes that "feudal discourse was indeed distinct, prescribing unity, functional cooperation, sharing, and lawfulness." But in reality, medieval actors behaved like modern states. "[T]hey really strove for exclusive territorial control, protected themselves by military means, subjugated each other, balanced against power, formed alliances and spheres of influence, and resolved their conflicts by the use and threat of force." Fischer, 428. Yet, his criticism is directly mainly against the idea that mere "discourse" of communal values can alter the practice of conflict. My argument is slightly different in that the difference between modern and ancient history is not based on "discourse" or the presence of "communal norms," but

These objectives stem from the previous characteristics – the nature of military technology, the importance of manpower, and the existence of ungoverned spaces. And they differ from those pursued in modern times. Even if often motivated by ideological goals, modern interstate wars tend to be about territory because the best way, and perhaps the only way, to achieve those was through expansion of territorial control. As Stalin famously argued toward the end of World War II, "This war is not as in the past; whoever occupies a territory also imposes his own social system. Everyone imposes his own system as far as his army can reach. It cannot be otherwise."[114] In ancient history, on the other hand, conflict tended to be motivated less by territorial demands than by concerns of status and prestige, by religious disputes and differences, and by the pursuit of violence as a source of social cohesion.

First, because control over men was more important than control over land, *conflicts were often over the allegiance of people* rather than about a specific piece of real estate or a territorial adjustment. The purpose of wars was to enlarge one's own manpower. James Scott observes that "[p]recolonial wars were more often about rounding up captives and settling them near the central court than asserting a territorial claim."[115] This was because "in premodern systems only power can guarantee property and wealth. And power, before the technological revolution in warfare, was largely a matter of how many men a ruler could field; power, in other words, boiled down to manpower."[116] And one way to extend influence over more people was by augmenting the status and reputation one possessed. They were instrumental to gathering more people under

---

on different military technology and the ability to form social groups other than territorially exclusive states. The nature of international relations is still the same, resulting in constant conflict through a variety of means including military, but the character this confrontation takes, and the character of its main actors, changes. Markus Fischer, "Feudal Europe, 800–1300: Communal Discourse and Conflictual Practices," *International Organization*, Vol. 46, No. 2 (Spring 1992), 427–466. For a critique of Fischer's argument, see Rodney Bruce Hall and Friedrich V. Kratochwil, "Medieval Tales: Neorealist 'Science' and the Abuse of History," *International Organization*, Vol. 47, No. 3 (Summer, 1993), 479–491.

[114] Milovan Djilas, *Conversations with Stalin* (New York, NY:Harcourt, Brace & World, Inc., 1962), 114.

[115] Scott, *Seeing Like a State*, 185.

[116] Scott, *The Art of Not Being Governed*, 68. He adds that warfare is a contest "for control over cultivators rather than arable land" (71). Some scholars argue that centralization, and thus some early forms of state, arose in the moment one group of people conquered another in order to exploit them. Raiders that did not limit themselves to plunder but sought to extract wealth in the form of taxes or labor from conquered populations had to centralize and settle. Conquest of people, therefore, led to the establishment of a state. See Franz Oppenheimer, *The State* (New York, NY: Free Life Editions, 1975); Michael Mann, *The Sources of Social Power* (New York, NY: Cambridge University Press, 1986), Vol. I, 53–55.

Objectives

one's political control.[117] For instance, many of the medieval confrontations that shook Europe were about the hierarchy of authority, or, in other words, about who controlled whom.[118] The scene of an emperor laying prostrate in front of the Pope at Canossa in 1077, acknowledging however briefly the superiority of the head of the Church over the temporal leader, is a vivid example of this.[119] Similarly, the Byzantine emperor "felt himself to be responsible for Christians living beyond his frontiers," clearly considering his authority to exceed the territorial extent of his empire and seeking the recognition of his status as a leader of a population much larger than the one circumscribed by imperial borders.[120] By gaining a reputation of being a protector of a group of people, the emperor could extend his influence and power beyond the territorial boundaries of its imperial domain. The Comanches were another group where a following of men was a metric of political success and power, and therefore to be a successful leader one had to develop a position of preeminence, which could be done by disbursing material benefits and honors. Such a leader "understood the social arithmetic of wealth: when hoarded, it divided people; when given away, it drew them together" under his command.[121]

The objectives of one side often were satisfied by the humble bowing of the other, and limited or no territorial adjustment had to be made. Conflicts, in this case in Medieval times, "were not political disputes [but] ... were concerned with status, not process."[122] This does not mean that the settlement of conflicts was easier than in modern times when map drawing became a source of tensions and wars. On the contrary, as I will point out in Chapter 2, changes in borders are easier to negotiate than questions of personal hostility, prestige, or religious differences. Political interactions at the domestic but also international level tended to be more personal because they were unfiltered by ideological and institutional considerations, and were more difficult to negotiate away; they were often zero-sum games that ended only with the

---

[117] That is why barbarian bands were not like modern national armies, conscripted or volunteer but trained for relatively long periods of time and remaining at the ready even during moments of peace. Rather they were "more like the 'Free Companies' of the Hundred Years War – diverse bands, brought together by ambitious impresarios of violence." Peter Brown, *The Rise of Western Christendom* (Malden, MA: Blackwell Publishing, 2003, original 1996), 105.

[118] "Mediaeval history ... is a history of rights and wrongs. Modern history, as contrasted with mediaeval, is a history of *powers*, forces, dynasties and ideas ... Mediaeval wars are, as a rule, wars of rights." Cyril E. Hudson, "The Church and International Affairs," *International Affairs*, Vol. 23, No. 1 (January 1947) 3.

[119] Rabb, 3.

[120] Steven Runciman, *The Byzantine Theocracy* (New York, NY: Cambridge University Press, 2003), 19.

[121] Hämäläinen, *The Comanche Empire*, 270.   [122] Bisson, 5.

submission of one side.[123] As historian J. R. Hale points out, "religion ... poisoned – or exalted – domestic tensions, led to interventions 'for defending friends', and, if it did not constitute a cause of open war between nations, made the very name of war more alarming by broadening its associations from the territorial ambition of monarchs to threats to the personal convictions of individuals."[124] Administrative borders can be adjusted, personal convictions and allegiances of people have to be replaced, and sentiments of personal enmity can be satisfied only by the total demise of the rival. Often this cannot be done without a massive exercise of violence.

It has to be noted that not all pursuits of status were instrumental. Individuals and polities defended their prestige and honor as ultimate goals.[125] As Daniel Markey defines it, prestige, the "public recognition of eminence as an end in itself," appears irrational to modern eyes but played a significant role in premodern times.[126] In fact, in some cases, polities engaged in *hubris* understood as "aggressive behavior involving the desire to bring dishonour to the victim."[127] While a perceived offense to one's honor needs to be redressed, the pursuit of honor or prestige is never fully satisfied; it is perpetual. Furthermore, it does not always match material calculations of costs-benefits.[128] As Gat writes, "glory ... was pursued by rulers (and others, of course) as a means of strengthening their hold on power and everything that it entailed, but also as an independent and most powerful source of emotional gratification."[129] Prestige, in other words, may, but does not necessarily, lead to greater influence over people. An individual who has acquired prestige, such as for instance

---

[123] For a fascinating description of the Roman concept of *inimicitia* (enmity), its causes and its outcomes, see David F. Epstein, *Personal Enmity in Roman Politics, 218-43BC* (Kent: Croom Helm, 1987).

[124] J. R. Hale, *War and Society in Renaissance Europe, 1450–1620* (Baltimore, MD: The Johns Hopkins University Press, 1986), 29.

[125] Some argue, convincingly, that pursuit of honor is deeply embedded in human nature and as such is not limited to premodern history. See Donald Kagan, "Our Interests and Our Honor," *Commentary*, April 1997, 42–45; MacMullen, *Corruption and the Decline of Rome*, 75.

[126] Daniel Markey, "Prestige and the Origins of War: Returning to Realism's Roots," *Security Studies*, Vol. 8, No. 4 (Summer 1999), 126.

[127] James A. Andrews, "Cleon's Hidden Appeals (Thucydides 3.37–40)," *Classical Quarterly*, Vol. 50, No. 1 (2000), 49. See also Gregory Crane's analysis of the role of prestige and status in the conflict over Corcyra, in Gregory Crane, "Power, Prestige, and the Corcyrean Affair in Thucydides," *Classical Antiquity*, Vol. 11, No. 1 (April 1992), 1–27; and his *Thucydides and the Ancient Simplicity* (Berkeley, CA: University of California Press, 1998). For an explanation of the Peloponnesian war as a conflict over status and rank, see J. E. Lendon, *Song of Wrath* (New York, NY: Basic Books, 2010).

[128] Markey, 159–160.   [129] Gat, 426.

a war hero, does not automatically become a political figure with a following of people.[130] Prestige is a reward on its own.

The second set of objectives and motivations pursued with greater frequency and passion in premodern rather than modern history was *religious in nature*. Religion infused and shaped many objectives pursued by various political actors throughout premodern history. For instance, religious impulses spurred large and lengthy projections of power. The Crusades were one such example of a conflict, which was, at least in part, "genuinely religious," motivated by the desire to "fight for the cross" and to attain spiritual rewards.[131] An analogous case was the prolonged conflict on the frontier between the Ottoman and the Hapsburg empires, where religiously motivated bands, the *ghazis*, relentlessly assaulted their Christian neighbors well into the seventeenth century.[132]

More broadly, even before the rise of monotheistic faiths, religion has always provided a very powerful source of social cohesion and of political motivation, particularly in moments of great political upheaval, such as the collapse of the Roman Empire. As Christopher Dawson writes, "religion was the only power that remained unaffected by the collapse of civilization, by the loss of faith in social institutions and cultural tradition and by the loss of hope in life."[133] And before Christianity and other monotheistic faiths, religion also played a role in the political life of states, cities, and other groups. For instance, in ancient Greece, religious considerations often decided whether two polities would be at war or at peace, and alliances were undertaken according to religious alignments.[134] In many cases, religion challenged and replaced the authority and power of states and empires by giving rise to groups whose identity and aspirations were stronger than those provided by the political entity of which they were a part. For instance, in the fifth century AD, the Nestorians, a heretical sect of the Christian

---

[130] Robert E. McGinn, "Prestige and the Logic of Political Argument," *The Monist*, Vol. 56, No. 1 (January 1972), 100–115.

[131] Steven Runciman, *A History of the Crusades*, Vol. 1 (Harmondsworth: Penguin Books, 1965), 92. See also Thomas F. Madden, *A Concise History of the Crusades* (Lanham, MD: Rowman & Littlefield, 1005); Jonathan Riley-Smith, *The Crusades, Christianity, and Islam* (New York, NY: Columbia University Press, 2008).

[132] John F. Guilmartin, "Ideology and Conflict: The Wars of the Ottoman Empire, 1453–1606," *Journal of Interdisciplinary History*, Vol. 18, No. 4 (Spring 1988), 721–747; Gunther Rothenberg, *The Austrian Military Border in Croatia, 1522–1747* (Urbana: University of Illinois Press, 1960); Hale, *War and Society in Renaissance Europe, 1450–1620*, 29; Normal Housley, *Religious Warfare in Europe, 1400–1536* (Oxford: Oxford University Press, 2002).

[133] Christopher Dawson, *Religion and the Rise of Western Culture* (New York, NY: Doubleday, 1991), 25.

[134] As Fustel de Coulanges writes, "two cities were two religious associations which had not the same gods," 197.

Church, left imperial territories and moved "their headquarters to the dominions of the Persian King, out of the Emperor's reach. They no longer saw themselves as citizens of the Holy Empire."[135] The objective of these groups was not to support the polity in which they lived but to maintain at all costs their independence, their unity, and their religion.

Finally, the third category of objectives was *violence and war itself*. Violence was a source of social cohesion, and as such it constituted an objective that could never be fully achieved.[136] Social cohesion required constant shoring up through war. According to our modern mindset, the objective of a polity is something of finite value that can be calculated, whether it is security or more resources or the triumph of a specific form of domestic regime. Violence can help us to achieve such an objective only if the costs of resorting to it are less than the potential benefits; it is a tool to attain something else. War, as Clausewitz famously said, is a continuation of politics by other means. It still falls in the realm of politics, that is, of something that can be rationally examined, calculated, defined, and perhaps negotiated. So much that violence can be seen as part of the larger process of negotiating with the rival. Thomas Schelling writes that war is a method of bargaining, an act of diplomacy – "vicious diplomacy, but diplomacy."[137]

In ancient history, however, violence was often seen as an objective in itself, and not one tool among many others to achieve some other finite goal. Specifically, there were two broad reasons why actors engaged in violence. The first one was instrumental because groups that engaged in violence solidified their internal unity and increased their attractiveness to outsiders. Violence was a social glue. Many groups, such as some nomadic tribes or the *ghazi* of Asia Minor, were aggressive in nature because only by engaging in violence against their neighbors could they attract increasingly larger numbers of followers. The sheer act of violence generated support and resources (that is, more manpower) especially when it was directed against groups or states deemed to be culturally and religiously different and inferior.[138] This meant that it was difficult, if not impossible, to dissuade some groups from warring. To use early Ottoman history again as an example, the *ghazi* warriors would have received no glory, and no new recruits, by seeking peace with Christian Byzantium.[139] In this sense, violence was a tool to achieve another objective, a concept then that is similar to the more modern one; it was a continuation of politics through

---

[135] Runciman, *The Byzantine Theocracy*, 41.
[136] Gat, 426; J. R. Hale, 22; also Martin Van Creveld, *The Culture of War* (New York, NY: Presidio Press, 2008), passim.
[137] Thomas Schelling, *Arms and Influence* (New Haven, CT: Yale University Press, 1967), 2.
[138] See Wittek.   [139] Runciman, *The Fall of Constantinople*, 30.

other means. But the difference was that the objective, social cohesion and, above all, greater appeal to potential new recruits, could never be fully satisfied. The pursuit of violence thus could never end.

The second related reason why some actors relentlessly pursued violence was that, together with material benefits derived from plunder and spoils, this was a way of increasing their status and reputation among their peers. War was a source of social advancement inside many communities, in particular barbarian groups. Among the Comanches, for instance, leading plundering raids on settled American or Spanish communities offered younger individuals "opportunities for economic and social advancement that simply did not exist in times of peace."[140] But such a dynamic was at work also among ancient polities, such as the Roman Empire, where the most effective way to increase one's own political power was by waging war on the frontier, in Gaul, Britain, or Asia.[141] The result was, in the words of the great historian Walter Prescott Webb describing the Plains Indians, that these tribes "were not amenable to the gentle philosophy of Christ nor were they tamed by the mysteries and elaborate ceremonials of the church. The warwhoop was sweeter to them than evening vespers; the crescent bow was a better symbol of their desires than the holy cross ... War was the end and aim of the Indian's life."[142]

To sum up, premodern history is characterized by actors pursuing objectives – a rightful position in a hierarchy of authority, the advancement of a religion, or violence as a source of social cohesion – that appear novel or perplexing to our modern eyes. These goals, as well as these actors, did not vanish completely but lost importance over the past three or four centuries, and ceased to be considered as defining features of our modern era. Yet, perhaps, as a result of not paying much attention to these premodern features we are so much less equipped to understand the present. The nature of these actors and of the goals that they pursued, in fact, did not simply add a different color to the political arena of the ancient world. It made it in many fundamental ways different from the modern world.

---

[140] DeLay, 97.
[141] Plutarch observed that the decline of war leads ambitious individuals to seek other areas where they could excel and gain glory and status. He writes in his *Moralia*, "Nowadays, then, when the affairs of the cities no longer include leadership in wars, nor the overthrowing of tyrannies, nor acts of alliances, what opening for a conspicuous and brilliant public career could a young man find? There remain the public lawsuits and embassies to the emperor, which demand a man of ardent temperament and one who possesses both courage and intellect." Plutarch, *Moralia*, Vol. X (Cambridge, MA: Loeb Classical Library, 1936), 193.
[142] Walter Prescott Webb, *The Texas Rangers* (Austin: University of Texas, 1995, original 1935), 8–9 and 13.

2 Barbarians and the Character of the Competition

> *"The 'nomad' ... is a 'soldier born,' always ready to take the field with his ordinary resources, his horse, his equipment and his victuals; and he is also served by a strategic sense of direction, as a rule quite absent in settled peoples."*
> March Bloch, *Feudal Society*[1]

> *"... where armed masses stand before each other, there the parchment for the inscription of treaties will be the fields, and the pens will be swords and lances."*
> Henryk Sienkiewicz, *Ogniem i Mieczem*[2]

The features that defined the premodern strategic environment had two related consequences. First, unlike in the modern period, barbarians were important strategic actors that competed with settled polities. The premodern period witnessed a variety of barbarian groups that were more than a match for large and powerful empires. Second, barbarian–state interactions were markedly more unstable and violent than interstate relations because the traditional tools of statecraft – military force, deterrence, and diplomacy – were less effective in resolving the conflict of interests between these two sets of actors. The result was greater uncertainty and violence, even though war along the frontier separating polities from barbarians was more diffused and less defined than in conflicts pitting city states or empires against each other.

This chapter examines, first, the nature of barbarians, focusing on three main features: their relatively small size, their high mobility, and their decentralized organization. Second, it describes the resulting character of international competition in premodern times, in particular analyzing the diminished utility of military force, deterrence, and diplomacy in the interactions between barbarians and polities.

---

[1] Marc Bloch, *Feudal Society*, Vol. 1 (Chicago, IL: University of Chicago Press, 1964), Vol. 1, 54.
[2] Henryk Sienkiewicz, *Ogniem i mieczem* (Warsaw: PIW, 1974), Vol. 1, chapter 33, 444 (translated by the author).

2.1 The Barbarians

The term "barbarian" carries now a pejorative connotation, referring to a foreign group that is deemed inferior according to many metrics. But originally the term referred simply to foreigners who were unintelligible. The Greeks used the term *barbaros* to include all who were non-Greek, including groups that they respected and considered as culturally equal but that spoke a different language. The linguistic difference also assumed political connotations. Barbarians were those who did not participate in the political life of a city, the *polis*, and lived according to lower standards of social organization. They were incapable of ordering themselves according to reason and laws, the foundations of political life, and as a result, were naturally more inclined to obey rather than rule, to be slaves rather than masters. As Aristotle writes in his *Politics*, "the poets say 'it is fitting for Greeks to rule barbarians' – the assumption being that barbarian and slave are by nature the same thing."[3] The idea that barbarians were incapable of reason and speech, roaming the world as "wild beasts" and acting not on the basis of reason but exclusively on physical strength, remained a powerful concept that distinguished intelligible from unintelligible social order.[4] But it increasingly acquired a meaning that justified conquest and slavery. The Roman view, for instance, differed from the Greek one because it allowed the possibility of the rule of law being extended to tribes on the periphery of the civilized world. It is also true, however, that ascribing all types of undesirable and nonhuman characteristics to the targeted group of "savages" justified the often-vicious conquest of these tribes.[5]

These negative connotations ascribed to the term "barbarians" have, however, obscured the underlying original concept. It is simply an attempt to distinguish two different ways of life. One is the civilized way of organizing social life, quite literally, in cities. Civilization is the political life of settled communities that organize themselves in cities and states. In order to instill order in such a social group, laws need to be written and administered according to objective rational standards; hence, the connection between reason through speech and political order through laws. When speech becomes impossible because, for instance, the meaning of words is perverted, political order collapses. The barbarian way of life is

---

[3] Aristotle, *Politics* (Chicago, IL: University of Chicago Press, 1984), trans. by Carnes Lord, I:2, 36.
[4] Anthony Pagden, *The Fall of Natural Man* (New York, NY: Cambridge University Press, 1982), 15–26; W. R. Jones, "The Image of the Barbarian in Medieval Europe," *Comparative Studies in Society and History*, Vol. 13, No. 4 (October 1971), 376–407.
[5] David Weber, *Bárbaros: Spaniards and Their Savages in the Age of Enlightenment* (New Haven, CT: Yale University Press, 2005).

the lifestyle outside of cities, led by groups that are unsettled and need only kinship and blood ties to keep them united. They are uncivilized in the literal sense that they do not live in cities, where they can protect themselves through walls, engage in commerce through markets, and participate in political debates in the public square. The difference in lifestyle undoubtedly led to a real hatred between the two groups. Late Antiquity historian Peter Brown observes that "[n]omads were seen as human groups placed at the very bottom of the scale of civilized life. The desert and the sown were held to stand in a state of immemorial and unresolved antipathy, with the desert always threatening, whenever possible, to dominate and destroy the sown."[6] But the term "barbarian" used in this book is therefore merely descriptive, not normative.

Barbarians had three broad features that set them apart from settled communities and states in general. First, each barbarian group was relatively small but there tended to be multiple groups challenging the state at the same time. Second, they were highly mobile. Third, they were organized in highly decentralized fashion as an amalgam of different families and clans.

2.1.1 Small

First, each barbarian group, whether the Goths in Late Antiquity or the Comanches in the nineteenth century, tended to be weaker than the forces of the empire that it faced. Barbarians usually did not control vast resources and could rarely field large armies capable of fighting a frontal war with imperial forces. The size of many of these groups is often hotly debated because we lack definitive information on most of them. After all, history was written mostly by the assaulted empires, not the raiding barbarians, and the numbers proposed by, for instance, Roman historians or Western observers of the Mongols are exaggerated. Marco Polo, for instance, claimed that the Mongol armies were close to 650,000, a number that is widely believed to be wrong.[7] In part, ancient historians exaggerated the numbers to increase the honor of the imperial defenders, whose glory was directly correlated with the size of their enemies. But the numbers were also believed to be large simply because the barbarians were deemed to be such a menace to the lifestyle of the settled communities; they loomed larger in the minds of civilized populations than they were in reality.

---

[6] Peter Brown, *The Rise of Western Christendom* (Malden, MA: Blackwell Publishing, 2003, original 1996), 43.

[7] John Masson Smith, Jr., "Mongol Manpower and Persian Population," *Journal of the Economic and Social History of the Orient*, Vol. 18, No. 3 (October 1975), 271–299.

It is also difficult to figure out the effective manpower of barbarians because they could field a higher proportion of their population than settled communities. Many barbarian groups, in fact, had most of their male population under arms, rather than having a semiprofessional army like empires or states did. They engaged in a premodern version of mass conscription or *levée en masse*. And when they were on the move while migrating, they often traveled with their entire populations, further confusing anyone who attempted to estimate their numbers. Julius Caesar, for example, in his first engagement in Gaul had to face the Helvetii tribe that had left its territory after having burnt its villages and fields. The entire population of the Helvetii was on the move, and any assessment of their military manpower was bound to be problematic.

It is plausible to argue that the size of individual barbarian groups was relatively small by observing two of their features. First, most barbarian groups, even the larger ones such as the Huns or the Mongols, tended to engage in raids or, what we now call, guerilla warfare, rather than seeking massive frontal battles. They consciously adopted a war fighting style that built on their advantages (mobility and topographical knowledge, among others) but also that recognized their relative weakness. The barbarian groups could not afford the risk of a large battle because a loss would likely have been catastrophic for them.[8] In other words, they sought to minimize their casualties in part because they did not have large reservoirs of manpower like the states they targeted; they chose hit-and-run tactics out of recognition of their weakness.

The second reason why it is possible to surmise that their numbers were relatively low was their mobility, a characteristic that will be examined later. But here I want to point out that to be mobile a group had to have either efficient logistical support or be small enough to survive off the

---

[8] Two qualifications are necessary here. First, casualty avoidance was also necessary because many tribal leaders derived their position of power and prestige from the claim of military success, which in its minimalist definition meant not losing men. A military defeat with large casualties would have blemished the reputation of the leader, even if it were not to destroy the bulk of his manpower. Second, in some cases, barbarian tribes did engage in a mass battle, risking and at times incurring massive casualties. For instance, a "last stand" type of battle where the barbarian tribes were cornered or had no other option but submission. The classic description of such a battle is by Tacitus in his *Agricola*, where he writes about the battle of Mons Graupius, which ended the rebellion led by Calcagus. Moreover, the other case is when a tribe, such as the Huns and Avars in the fifth century AD, controlled other, smaller and inferior, tribes, and a battle defeat would have caused greater casualties among them rather than the ruling elite tribe. Such groupings were therefore more likely to take greater risks, by engaging in large battles or assaulting and besieging cities.

land. Barbarians usually lacked the former and therefore relied almost exclusively on the food and forage provided by the territories they crossed. Their numbers, therefore, were limited by what the fields located along their path could sustain. One way of estimating their size is to measure the number of people and in particular horses that a given region could feed. For instance, some calculated that the Huns in the fourth century AD could have numbered around 15,000 once they reached the Hungarian plains, simply because that region could support around 150,000 horses (and ten horses per warrior are assumed to have been needed).[9] This calculation, as well as the conclusion that the Huns could not sustain high mobility when they reached Roman territories, is controversial, and its conclusion that the Huns had been "unhorsed" by the mid-fifth century most likely wrong. But the method of assessing the numbers by the fertility of the crossed land remains valid, and above all, indicates the severe limitations on the number of barbarians.

Each group may have been relatively small, but the strategic challenge for the targeted empire or settled community was that often there were many such groups threatening it in multiple places (in addition to, as it will be discussed later on, the danger of a peer competitor on a different frontier). Multiple raids across different spots on a long frontier presented peculiar operational challenges to imperial forces, and in some cases resulted in a decentralization of security provision. Each group alone was small, but many groups appearing roughly at the same time distracted the enemy and could penetrate deep inside imperial territories. Hence, in the case of the Roman Empire of the fifth and sixth centuries, there is a broad consensus that each barbarian group, from the Goths to the Vandals, fielded at most 20–30,000 fighting men.[10] Often, much smaller groups crossed the Rhine and the Danube, and while some of them were either defeated or assimilated by Rome, barbarians gradually moved into imperial territories from Gaul to Noricum and Thrace, overwhelming the ability of the Roman authorities and forces to oppose them effectively. As a historian puts it, it was a "seepage of barbarian peoples" rather than a mass assault that undermined the security of imperial territories.[11]

---

[9] Rudi Paul Lindner, "Nomadism, Horses and Huns," *Past and Present*, No. 92 (August 1981), 3–19.

[10] Herwig Wolfram, *The Roman Empire and its Germanic Peoples* (Berkeley, CA: University of California Press, 1997), 7; Walter Goffart, *Barbarians and Romans* (Princeton, NJ: Princeton University Press, 1980), 5 and 231–234; Heather, *Fall of the Roman Empire*, 446.

[11] Averil Cameron, *The Mediterranean World in Late Antiquity, AD 395–600* (London: Routledge, 1993), 56.

2.1.2 Highly Mobile

The second related feature of barbarians was their high mobility. In many cases, they led a pastoral and nomadic lifestyle, and in some periods, such as the late fourth century, they were migrating in vast numbers. Their mobility and unsettled nature was the most visible feature that also made them fearsome to civilized, that is, settled, communities. The fact that barbarians were seen as living off constant movement, with few fixed possessions to defend and with all their energies focused on the offensive, made them feared by those who did not lead that lifestyle.

The high mobility of these groups was made possible by two factors. One was their organizational structure, examined in the next point. The other was their great skill at horsemanship. Mongols, Huns, or Comanches were all superior horsemen, who acquired riding skills early in life simply by leading their regular lifestyle in the steppes or plains. In fact, the ability to ride horses (and in North America the introduction of horses to the continent) was the crucial factor that gave these groups an enormous comparative advantage. Horses were revolutionary, akin to the effects that railroads had in the nineteenth century, conquering an otherwise impossible space.

The empty or ungoverned spaces which made their rise possible also influenced their skills and warfighting. As many have observed, these regions have features, such as large distances and harsh conditions, that developed a type of warrior, in fact, a natural warrior, that was highly unlikely to arise among sedentary, agricultural groups.[12] Hunting in particular appears to have been a source of tactical innovations and instruction. Late sixth-century Byzantine emperor, Maurice, for instance wrote that "[w]arfare is like hunting. Wild animals are taken by scouting, by nets, by lying in wait, by stalking, by circling around, and by other such stratagems rather than by sheer force."[13] The Mongols were particularly adept at translating their hunting skills into battle tactics. In mass hunts they learned and practiced a tactic called *nerge*. This involved encircling the enemy, and then tightening the circle around him, preventing any escape. Large numbers of hunters, or warriors, were not necessary. As a historian observes, "[j]ust as skilled hunters were able to hold their positions to herd or direct the route of animals, so skilled warriors could do the same while encircling the enemy. Because of their archery skills

---

[12] David Christian, "Inner Eurasia as a Unit of World History," *Journal of World History*, Vol. 5, No. 2 (Fall 1994), 173–211; Erik Hildinger, 1–3; Fairbank, *Chinese Ways of Warfare*, 13.

[13] *Maurice's Strategikon: Handbook of Byzantine Military Strategy*, trans. by George T. Dennis (Philadelphia, PA: University of Pennsylvania, 1984), 65.

and great mobility, the Mongols did not require superior numbers of troops to encircle an enemy."[14] Similar tactics were adopted by other barbarian groups, including those who faced the late Roman Empire as well as the Spanish and American settlers in the North American Plains.

Mobility meant that the barbarian projections of power were small but quick and deep in unexpected places along the frontier. The barbarian way of warfare was to raid, rather than to conquer. A raid has a target, a timeframe, and an effect that are different from wars of conquest.[15] The target of a raid is very specific and narrowly defined: An undefended and not walled city, a particular region, and a small and isolated military or commercial outpost are all targets that could offer quick spoils at low risk. A raid is also of short duration because it is conducted with small numbers and with limited or no logistical support: a lighting strike and not a protracted campaign. Barbarians had little desire, as well as no capacity, to hold territory for long periods of times. And individual barbarian raids did not have the capacity to bring down an empire, even when directed at key centers of political or economic life. The 410 AD sack of Rome by Alaric's Goths was, for example, a direct attack against the by-then former administrative capital, and it was considered a shocking sign of the catastrophic collapse of the Roman power. In the late fourth century AD Saint Jerome dramatically wrote that the "city which had taken the whole world was itself taken."[16] But Alaric's assault was conducted out of a desire for gold and glory more than by a conscious decision to take over the Roman Empire. In brief, a raid was a short and in-depth penetration by small groups seeking booty in poorly defended targets, rather than full-scale and long-term territorial conquests.

Nonetheless, raids were terrifying. Saint Jerome wrote of the great fear the Huns generated among Roman populations. In a letter he wrote that "everywhere their [the Huns'] approach was unexpected, they outstripped rumour in speed, and, when they came, they spared neither religion nor rank nor age, even for wailing infants they had no pity."[17]

[14] Timothy May, "The Training of an Inner Asian Nomad Army in the Pre-Modern Period," *Journal of Military History*, Vol. 70, No. 3 (Jul., 2006), 620 (617–635). See also Morris Rossabi, "The Ming and Inner Asia," *Cambridge History of China*, Vol. 8, Part 2, 225–226.

[15] A partial list of characteristics of a raid: short duration, known route, safe return estimated, no families involved, no unnecessary vehicles, limited numbers, suitable transport (horses for short distances, or boats), and specific targets. Roger Batty, *Rome and the Nomads* (New York, NY: Oxford University Press, 2007), 23.

[16] Jerome, *Select Letters* (Cambridge, MA: Harvard University Press, Loeb Classical Library, 1933), Letter CXXVII, p. 463. See also Stefan Rebenich, "Christian Asceticism and Barbarian Incursion: The Making of a Christian Catastrophe," *Journal of Late Antiquity*, Vol. 2, No. 1 (Spring 2009), 49–59.

[17] Jerome, *Select Letters*, Letter LXXVII, 329–331.

The rapidity and the unexpected place of a barbarian raid left in its wake fears of further attacks in areas until then spared. The surprise of a raid, that is, generated expectations of other attacks, even if they may have been highly unlikely. Raids created a gap between the reality and the perceptions of the barbarians' capabilities.

Mobility, however, had also its operational costs. The most evident was the flip side of raids: albeit they were low-risk and induced terror among the targeted settled communities, plundering raids seldom translated into more permanent victories for barbarians. Raiding was, after all, the preferred tactic of barbarians because they recognized their inability to control and administer territories that were settled. Not surprisingly, nomads, for instance, rarely built long-lasting settlements, cities, or other centers of economic, political, and cultural life, and did not administer a piece of real estate. There are, of course, instances of nomadic groups, such as the Mongols or the Osmanli tribe, engaging in wars of conquest and extending their rule over large swaths of land.[18] Nonetheless, most often these represent either spectacular but brief moments of nomadic territorial empires that contracted as soon as their leader died (e.g. Tamerlane), or territorial conquest altered the structure of these tribes in fundamental ways, effectively ending their mobility and nomadic lifestyle (e.g. the Ottoman Empire, and some argue, the Huns).

The second negative consequence of mobility was the barbarians' inability to take cities or any other walled and defended settlement. In fact, throughout premodern history most barbarians avoided targeting cities because they did not have the logistics and the engineering necessary to conduct siege warfare. A siege of a city was in fact logistically more difficult for the besieging army than the besieged population. To besiege a city, it was necessary to stop the military advance while supplying the army with sufficient food and forage to wait out the besieged population. To win a siege, the attacking group had to prepare itself for months and even years of sitting or had to hope that discord inside the targeted city would lead to betrayal and the opening of the gates. For instance, in the famous case of Melos besieged by the Athenians, as Thucydides recounts, "some treachery occurred inside" the city that led to the surrender of the Melians. Moreover, siege warfare demanded technical knowhow necessary to build machinery to break down walls, tunnels to penetrate the city, and later artillery. The famous saying of Fritigern, a Gothic leader who led an assault on the Roman Empire in the fourth century AD, that he made "peace with walls," indicated clearly that simple defensive

---

[18] See, for instance, Thomas Barfield, *The Perilous Frontier: Nomadic Empires and China* (Blackwell Publishers, 1992).

56   Barbarians and the Character of the Competition

measures prevented barbarian tribes from attacking cities.[19] The Huns, and other later barbarian groups invading the Roman Empire, became more skilled at taking over cities but, again, these feats were not common and were achieved at the cost of losing mobility and time. Alaric sacked Rome in 410 AD but the city gates had most likely been opened to him by some traitor. In any case, he could not conquer other cities in Italy. Similarly, the Vandals failed to enter Palermo in Sicily.[20] A similar difficulty in poliorcetics faced the Mongols. Only Genghis Khan realized that his army needed engineers and specialized manpower, recruited mostly from China, in order to take over cities in Northern China and later in the Middle East.[21]

2.1.3 Decentralized Organizational Structure

Third, the organizational structure of barbarians is perhaps the most difficult feature to describe and analyze because of the often minimal knowledge that we have of these groups. History was written after all by historians of civilized empires and not by barbarians on the move. Yet, the glimpse that we can catch in the historical literature of how barbarians are organized points to a decentralized structure based on tribal affiliation.[22] In more modern terms, barbarian groups are networks of tribes, rather than hierarchically structured polities with clearly delimited administrative spheres. Barbarians organized as confederations composed of smaller units, whose allegiance was, first, to the clan or family and, second, to the larger band. It was a network of small clans, rather than a large

---

[19] See Ammianus Marcellinus, *The Later Roman Empire* (New York, NY: Penguin Classics, 2004), Book 31:6, p. 422; E. A. Thompson, "Early Germanic Warfare," *Past and Present*, No. 14 (November 1958), 2–29.
[20] See Kelly DeVries, *Medieval Military Technology* (Lewinston, NY: Broadview Press, 1992), 185. Constantinople, and with it the Eastern Roman Empire, may have been saved from barbarian destruction in part by the presence of large fortifications circumwalling the city, which was also located on a peninsula, enhancing its defensive advantage. The Western Empire was less fortunate: "more exposed to barbarian onslaughts which in persistence and sheer weight of numbers far exceeded anything which the empire had previously had to face," it collapsed. AHM Jones, *The Later Roman Empire*, Vol. 2, 1068.
[21] Kate Raphael, "Mongol Siege Warfare on the Banks of the Euphrates and the Question of Gunpowder (126–1312)," *Journal of the Royal Asiatic Society*, Series 3, Vol. 19, No. 3 (2009), 355–370.
[22] The decentralized nature of barbarian groups translated also into a way of fighting that was very different from that of settled polities. A Spartan general, Brasidas, noted that Illyrian groups fight in "no regular order" and hence "are not ashamed of deserting their positions when hard pressed; flight and attack are equally honorable with them, and afford no test of courage; their independent mode of fighting never leaving anyone who wants to run away without a fair excuse for doing so." Thucydides, *The Landmark Thucydides* (New York, NY: Free Press, 1996), 292, 4.126.5.

hierarchical organization. At times a charismatic leader imparted strategic consistency to these various tribes, but more often there was minimal political unity among these groups.

The main reason for such a decentralized organizational structure was the mobility, and thus the nonterritorial nature, of barbarians. Not being tied to a fixed place, the unity of these groups stemmed from common descent and kinship. Nomads for instance, are defined as a "social unit," an entity that is held together not by an administrative institution or written law or a centralized authority but by family ties and the authority of the elders.[23] The benefit of such units was that they could maintain remarkable stability while moving between regions or migrating because the main source of social cohesion (family, clan, descent) moved with the group. Because they maintain unity while on the move, nomadic groups are also capable of projecting power at great distances. This nomadic "social unit" is also small because its boundaries are determined by family connections that, by their very nature, extend to a limited number of individuals. Finally, blood ties create a strong unit that is very capable of courageous and bold acts, making it a remarkable fighting force.[24] Defining analogous groups as "trust networks," Charles Tilly writes that

> they often prove capable of feats that only occur extraordinarily in collaborative institutions and authoritative organizations; carrying on complex activities over great expanses of time and space without continuous monitoring, entrusting individuals with extensive resources likewise in the absence of continuous monitoring, eliciting dramatic sacrifices from individual members, and surviving large inequalities of rights, privileges, obligations, and power among nominally full-fledged participants.[25]

A decentralized nature of a group may mean, therefore, that there is only partial operational or strategic control exercised by a central authority or leader. This may create challenges for the group, encouraging centrifugal tendencies of smaller units interested, for example, in a more aggressive plundering behavior. A splintering of the group may be the extreme outcome, but most often it simply meant that without an authoritative leader there was little strategic cohesion. There were some groups, or some moments in the life of a group, that were characterized by the presence of a charismatic and often ruthless leader who directed his

---

[23] Anatoly M. Khazanov, *Nomads and the Outside World*, 2nd edition (Madison, WI: The University of Wisconsin Press, 1994; first published by Cambridge University Press in 1984), 150.
[24] See Harry H. Turney-High, *Primitive War* (Columbia, SC: University of South Carolina Press, 1949), 236–237.
[25] Tilly, *Trust and Rule*, 44–45.

tribe against a particularly lucrative target and in the process united other groups establishing a large confederation of tribes.[26] Yet, it tended to be an ephemeral concentration of power because such a large grouping followed the leader only as long as he is successful.[27] When he died, or when he stopped delivering victories and plunder, the various clans cease to pay allegiance to him and disperse.[28] A case in point is that of Attila and the Huns. After he was defeated at the battle of Chalons (or Catalaunian Plains) in 451 AD, he was forced to attack Italy largely to obtain the maximum amount of plunder he could in order to keep his mobile empire united. A few years later, after a night of drinking debauchery, he died, a "disgraceful end to a king renowned in war."[29] Immediately after his death, the Huns broke apart as a unified group because the various tribal leaders and Attila's sons fought among themselves, claiming their right to lead. The "minds of young men," wrote Jordanes, "are wont to be inflamed by ambition for power – and in their rash eagerness to rule they all alike destroyed his empire."[30] As a student of nomads succinctly puts it, a "successful chief led a growing tribe; the tribesmen elected (or reelected) him by voting – with their feet."[31] A large nomadic group could therefore expand or contract, unify and divide, very rapidly, depending on the warrior prowess of its chief.[32]

Small, mobile, and decentralized, barbarians could rarely survive on their means alone. Their political unity was strengthened by the benefits – the plunder and spoils, or if feasible, commercial exchanges – they derived from their interactions with the neighboring settled communities. Barbarians were not autarkic.[33] Throughout history, they needed goods produced by settled states (ranging from agricultural goods to manufactured products), and often thrived on the trading lanes in Central Asia

[26] On the relationship between war and the organization of society in primitive groups, such as the nomads, see also Turney-High, chapter 12, 227–253.
[27] Erik Hildinger, *Warriors of the Steppe* (Cambridge, MA: Da Capo Press, 1997), 10.
[28] Barfield, *The Nomadic Alternative*, 149.
[29] Jordanes, *The Gothic History of Jordanes*, trans. by Charles C. Mierow (Princeton, NJ: Princeton University Press, 1915), 123.
[30] Jordanes, 125 (#259). J. B. Bury argues that the "catastrophe of the Hun power was indeed inevitable, for the social fabric of the Huns and all their social instincts were opposed to the concentration and organization which could alone maintain the permanence of their empire." J. B. Bury, *The Invasions of Europe by the Barbarians*, 155. See also Christopher Kelly, *The End of Empire: Attila the Hun & The Fall of Rome* (New York, NY: W. W. Norton & Company, 2009).
[31] Rudi Paul Lindner, "What Was a Nomadic Tribe?" *Comparative Studies in Society and History*, Vol. 24, No. 4 (October 1982), 700. See also Rudi Paul Lindner, "Nomadism, Horses and Huns," *Past and Present*, No. 92 (August 1981), 3–19.
[32] Ammianus Marcellinus writes that the Alans "choose as their leaders men who have proved their worth by long experience in war." Book 31, 414 (Penguin edition).
[33] Khazanov, 3.

linking Europe and Asia.[34] This relationship between barbarian and sedentary groups could be peaceful, especially when trade between them was possible or when the nomadic tribes could serve as a conduit to other markets.[35] But when trade was not feasible or the group needed more resources than trade could provide, the relationship turned violent.[36] Barbarians had neither the interest nor the ability to practice agriculture on a scale sufficient to feed them, and resorted to raiding forays.[37] Violence between nomadic tribes and settled communities or states was more often than not the norm. As a historian of Byzantium observes, there "unquestionably was at least intermittent interdependence and mutualism [in state-barbarian relations]. But the empire did not commit hard to obtain, expensive, crack troops to posts there [on the frontier] merely to observe pastoral activities."[38]

2.2 The Challenges

Barbarians presented a particular set of security problems that were much greater than their relative strength (or rather, weakness) could suggest. Numerically small and technologically inferior, they created intractable problems for settled communities and empires, distracting them from rivalries with peer competitors and causing persistent instability along their frontiers and often deep inside their territories. As French historian Marc Bloch writes about the tenth-century invasions of Europe,

> Neither the Saracens nor the Northmen were better armed than their adversaries ... If the invaders possessed a military superiority, it was much less technical than social in its origins. Like the Mongols later, the Hungarians were fitted for warfare by their way of life itself. 'When the two sides are equal in numbers and in strength, the one more accustomed to the nomadic life gains the victory.' This observation is from the Arab historian Ibn-Khaldun. In the ancient world it had an almost universal validity – at least till such time as the sedentary peoples could call to their aid the resources of an improved political organization and of a really scientific military machine.[39]

---

[34] Nicola di Cosmo, "Ancient Inner Asian Nomads," *Journal of Asian Studies*, Vol. 53, No. 4 (November 1994), 1092–1093. See also Nicola Di Cosmo, *Ancient China and Its Enemies: The Rise of Nomadic Power in East Asian History* (New York, NY: Cambridge University Press. 2002), ix and 369.
[35] Barfield, *The Nomadic Alternative*, 149–150; William McNeill, *The Pursuit of Power* (Chicago, IL: University of Chicago Press, 1982), 56.
[36] Khazanov, 202–212.
[37] Andrew Bell-Fialkoff, ed., *The Role of Migration in the History of the Eurasian Steppe* (New York: St. Martin's Press, 2000), 184.
[38] Walter E. Kaegi, *Byzantium and the Early Islamic Conquests* (New York, NY: Cambridge University Press, 1992), 54.
[39] Bloch, Vol. 1, 54.

60 Barbarians and the Character of the Competition

The challenge of barbarians was threefold, stemming from their, as Block puts it, "social" features. First, it was difficult to use force against them; they rarely could be defeated because they avoided large-scale battles. Second, it was also hard to deter them, in part because of the inability to retaliate against them but also in part because they thrived on conflict and violence. And finally, third, it was difficult to reach a negotiated settlement of the conflict of interests that arose with barbarians because the process as well as the outcome of diplomacy were problematic. The three key tools of statecraft – use of force, deterrence, and diplomacy – were not as effective when dealing with barbarians, and forced states to adapt and pursue different strategies.

2.2.1 Use of Force

The first challenge was that barbarians were difficult to defeat militarily. Imperial armies could inflict upon them massive defeats but only when they could engage them on a battlefield. Even in the case of a direct clash, often imperial forces had a hard time achieving a clear victory. Julius Caesar observed that fighting with barbarians in Britain was "peculiar" because "our troops were too heavily weighted by their armour to deal with such an enemy: they could not pursue them when they retreated and dared not get separated from their standards."[40] But barbarians, cognizant of their relative weakness, usually avoided engaging enemy forces on a fixed battlefield unless they did so on their own terms through a surprise ambush. In fact, most of the great military engagements between imperial forces and barbarians were initiated by the latter, who often surprised the empire by choosing the place and time of the battle. The battle of Teutoburg in 9 AD that resulted in the massacre of three Roman legions led by Varus, the 378 AD battle of Hadrianople, in which Roman emperor Valens was killed, or the battle of Tu-mu in 1449, where a Ming army was annihilated by a small detachment of Oirat Mongols, are key examples of a direct military clash between barbarians and imperial forces ending in the defeat of the latter. In all of these cases, it was the barbarians who chose to fight by ambushing an unprepared foe or engaging a tired and confused one in geographic settings that did not allow the full employment of the military advantages that imperial armies possessed.

When a barbarian group decided to make a stand for reasons of honor or because of mistaken assumptions about its own strength, it was soundly defeated. Tacitus describes one such episode, the 83 AD battle of Mons Graupius in modern day Scotland, where Roman legions and

---
[40] Julius Caesar, *The Conquest of Gaul*, VI:16, 112.

The Challenges

their auxiliary forces inflicted a devastating defeat on the local rebels. After the battle, "everywhere was dismal silence, lonely hills, houses smoking to heaven." And the barbarian enemy vanished: Roman "scouts met no one ... and the enemy were nowhere uniting."[41] Such decisive victories by imperial forces were, however, rare.

More typical of barbarian–state relations was a prolonged period of frontier skirmishes, forest ambushes, barbarian raids on isolated imperial outposts, and imperial counterraids on the few barbarian encampments. Each military engagement with the barbarians was usually relatively small. The Romans fought bigger battles with the Carthaginians, Parthians, or even among themselves in the Civil Wars than with the various barbarian groups that crossed their northern borders. Julius Caesar was at greater risk, and took bigger casualties, facing Pompey than fighting against Vercingetorix's Gallic rebels or Ambiorix's Eburones. The clash between states and their armies, especially industrialized ones, kills more people than skirmishes with technologically primitive tribes. As an American Civil War veteran observed while roaming the Plains in search of Comanches, the "fighting was a mere bagateele [sic] as compared to even any skirmish the writer ever saw in front of our battle lines during the Civil War."[42] But, as it will be pointed out later, the clashes were individually small but constant.

From the perspective of the states, to use force was an exercise in managing expectations and containing frustration. The experience of war, and the theories derived from it, tend to be based on a clash between states, and thus the doctrines, training, and war fighting are tailored to a particular type of confrontation. But with barbarians, all those experiences and theories were less applicable. Julius Caesar observed in Gaul that the "battlefront was not formed according to rules of military theory" and the legions had to adapt quickly to the topography and the different ways of fighting.[43] The sixth-century Byzantine manual on strategy attributed to Emperor Maurice similarly suggested that a theory of war could not be developed because of the very different nature of the enemies that the empire faced: "all nations do not fight in a single formation or in the same manner, and one cannot deal with them all in the same way."[44] The experience of the US Army in the American West was an equally powerful demonstration that the knowledge acquired in fighting another state was less applicable to wars with the tribal groups on the prairies. A US Army Colonel commented that the tactics of the Indians "are such

---

[41] Tacitus, *Agricola*, Loeb edition, #38, 97.
[42] Robert G. Carter, *On the Border with Mackenzie* (Austin, TX: Texas State Historical Association, 2007; originally published in *c.* 1935), 53.
[43] Julius Caesar, Book II:22, 67.   [44] *Maurice's Strategikon*, book XI, Introduction, 113.

as to render the old system [of state warfare] almost wholly impotent ... [W]ith such an enemy the strategic science of civilized nations loses much of its importance."[45] Another officer commented in the 1870s that the warfare in the West

> differed so greatly from what we old Civil War veterans had seen, and so little was known of it that it proved to be an absolutely new kind of warfare, and the experience we had to gain, and that quickly – as we had no time in which to study or any books from which to gain it – was to everybody in that command of a kind we have never seen or encountered. Amidst all of this solitude of the vast plains, with its impressive – almost painful silence, and so remote then from all civilization and ordinary routes of travel, it required more patience and really more human endurance than civilized warfare calls for.[46]

The effectiveness of most projections of power by imperial forces was dubious, or at least difficult to be evaluated. The fact that state armies could not locate and defeat the barbarian enemy is a recurrent fact in premodern history. The end of the Western Roman Empire (see also Chapter 4) is a cautionary tale of a power that, however weakened and corrupted by inferior leadership and economic decline, could not find an appropriate military approach to defeat the invading tribes. Surely, part of the problem was Rome's inability to field consistently capable armies due to a decrease in state revenues and a general decline of leadership, recruitment, and training. But the nature of the military confrontation was also part of the problem: Roman soldiers could not engage an enemy that could not be found, that trickled into the empire, and that moved with great speed in search of plunder and food.

The same challenge faced the US Army in the West. As a soldier fighting in the 1870s observed:

> When the Indians scattered, what should be done? Should they be pursued singly or in pairs? That required the almost impossible task of hunting for individual trails ... [They would divide] to meet again, by some prearranged plan, at some point 40 miles beyond, at some lone peak, tree, butte or passway, all the country about which the Indians knew so well, and of which his newly arrived white brother was in doleful ignorance. The trail had been lost, and the command ... usually rode slowly back to the ranch; buried the dead, and from thence to the post a disappointed and baffled column of brave, hard worked, tired out men.[47]

During one of the early trips along the Santa Fe Trail, the high mobility of the Indians frustrated US soldiers. As a US Army officer recounted, it

[45] Randolph B. Marcy, *The Prairie Traveler: A Hand-book for Overland Expeditions* (New York, NY: Harper & Brothers, 1861), 200–201; see also William H. Leckie, *The Military Conquest of the Southern Plains* (Norman, OK: University of Oklahoma Press, 1963), 8–9.
[46] Carter, 535–536.   [47] Carter, 293.

The Challenges

"was a humiliating condition to be surrounded by these rascally Indians, who, by means of their horses, could tantalize us with the hopes of battle, and elude our efforts; who could annoy us ... and who could insult us with impunity."[48]

The most common military approach in response to barbarian raiding was to lead a punitive counterraid. Julius Caesar did that in retaliation to German tribes' forays into Gaul, but his expedition across the Rhine, albeit a feat of logistics, was inconclusive. The targeted tribes vanished before the arrival of Roman legions, escaping "their country with all their belongings and hidden themselves in forests and uninhabited districts."[49] There was not much left for Caesar to do but to burn whatever villages he could find, and after eighteen days he crossed the Rhine again, dismantled the bridge built by his engineers, and returned to Gaul. This was far from a glorious campaign, but it achieved the "show of force" effect it sought (and more precisely, it displayed the great logistical and engineering capabilities of the Romans). A war fought in the forest would have been too dangerous for the legions that would have been deprived of the tactical advantages they had in an open battle.[50]

Almost two millennia later, at the tail end of the premodern period, the Spanish faced an analogous problem on their Texas frontier. When one of the Spanish northernmost missions, Santa Cruz de San Saba, was plundered by a group of Comanches in 1758, the Spanish authorities ordered a punitive raid.[51] It took them almost a year to fund and organize it, while in the meantime the Comanches again raided the area. The Spanish expedition, supported by a small number of friendly Indians, managed early on to win a small skirmish. But in the end, it turned into a rout. Deep in hostile territory, the Spanish soldiers met a surprisingly well-organized opposition from the Comanches who had fortified a small village. Having lost about fifty men (about 10 percent of their total number) and in fear of being cut off from their return route, the Spanish retreated, never recovering the desire to push further north into the Plains.[52]

---

[48] Quoted in Ray Allen Billington, *The Far Western Frontier* (New York, NY: Harper & Row, 1956), 38. A similar description was offered by Col.
[49] Julius Caesar, *The Conquest of Gaul* (New York, NY: Penguin, 1982), 96.
[50] J. F. C. Fuller, *Julius Caesar* (New Brunswick, NJ: Rutgers University Press, 1965; DaCapo Reprint), 121.
[51] John Francis Bannon, *The Spanish Borderlands Frontier: 1513–1821* (New York, NY: Holt, Rinehart and Winston, 1970), 137–139; Henry Easton Allen, "The Parrilla Expedition to the Red River in 1759," *The Southwestern Historical Quarterly*, Vol. 43, No. 1 (July 1939), 53–71; William Edward Dunn, "The Apache Mission on the San Sabá River: Its Founding and Failure," *The Southwestern Historical Quarterly*, Vol. 17, No. 4 (April 1914), 379–414.
[52] Robert S. Weddle, *After the Massacre: The Violent Legacy of the San Sabá Mission* (Lubbock, TX: Texas Tech University Press, 2007), xvi.

Punitive raids were therefore risky undertakings. At worst, they were an expenditure of resources and manpower that resulted in a setback, more by sheer overextension than battlefield defeat. At best, counterraids were pursued for reputational purposes, to show the ability to project power, rather than for any hope of achieving a decisive military victory. But in either case they were a symptom of a clear recognition that it was difficult, if at all possible, to vanquish the barbarian enemy. As Owen Lattimore put it in the context of Chinese–Mongol relations, the "mobility of the Mongols, and the lack of 'nerve-centers' in Mongolia, in the way of cities that could be seized, paralyzing the economic and political life, made it unsatisfactory to send out expeditions to occupy and hold the country."[53]

It was unclear, in fact, what the center of gravity of the barbarian enemy was. In the modern European theater composed of states, an army could translate a military victory into a political one because the ultimate target was the government of the hostile state. The purpose of a military engagement was to alter the calculation of the enemy's government, and to do so, it was unnecessary (at least until the twentieth century) to target the population. And even when the population was targeted, the goal was to break its will to fight and to pressure its government to surrender or alter its behavior in the desired direction. But when facing an enemy that had no government, or at least that had no recognizable hierarchy, the only option was to attack everything one could find as suitable target: empty villages, fields, and entire populations. Alexis de Tocqueville, observing political developments in North Africa, wrote that in Europe "we [the French] wage war on governments and not on populations."[54] But in Algeria the European style of warfare was impossible to employ and one had to target the entire population in order to change the security conditions. Such a drastic undertaking, however, diminishes the legitimacy of using force. Targeting civilian populations today is considered a war crime, and rightly so. In premodern times, this was less of an issue and it was relatively common to exterminate entire populations of a hostile city. But even then it was not an action that was pursued lightly and it carried serious material and reputational costs. Killing hundreds of disarmed people meant losing potential revenue from selling them as slaves. Moreover, it damaged the reputation of the polity that engaged in that act, as in the case of the Athenians massacring the Melians. At a minimum, the leader that chose to target a hostile population writ

[53] Owen Lattimore, "On the Wickedness of Being Nomads," in *Studies in Frontier History – Collected Papers 1928–1958* (London: Oxford University Press, 1962), 415.
[54] Alexis de Tocqueville, *Writings on Empire and Slavery*, ed. by Jennifer Pitts (Baltimore, MD: Johns Hopkins University Press, 2001), 70.

The Challenges

large had to justify doing so in the eyes of his domestic audience as an act necessary to maintain control over a territory or as revenge for some equally brutal action suffered by his own forces. In brief, attacking entire populations, as opposed to specific, narrowly defined military or economic targets, made conflicts with barbarians more difficult.

2.2.2 Deterrence

The decreased effectiveness of force meant also that deterrence was less likely to stabilize the relationship between states and barbarians. The conceptualization of deterrence is relatively new, and much of the language we use to explain it is a product of the post-World War II era. But the concept is ancient and perennial, as Thomas Schelling indicated by using examples dating back to Thucydides and Julius Caesar. The existence of deterrence is, of course, not constant and there are plenty of examples of its failure.[55] The clearest examples of failure are when weaker states attack stronger ones, and this occurs when the weaker are more motivated, when they misperceive their relative strength, and when they see a vulnerability of the strong state that they can exploit.[56] More pertinent to the subject of this book, the effectiveness of deterrence fluctuates in history, varying with changes in the nature of the competing strategic actors. The relationship between barbarians and states, in particular, has been characterized by weak deterrence.

There are three broad reasons why deterrence did not hold between states and barbarians, and more precisely, why states had difficulties deterring barbarians. First, barbarians presented few targets against which one could retaliate. Second, for a variety of reasons it was difficult to communicate the threats to the barbarians, breaking a key mechanism

---

[55] Richard Ned Lebow, *Between Peace and War: The Nature of International Crisis* (Baltimore, MD: The Johns Hopkins University Press, 1981); Richard Ned Lebow, "Thucydides and Deterrence," *Security Studies*, Vol. 16, No. 2 (April–June 2007), 163–188. For a critique of the argument that deterrence failed, see John Orme, "Deterrence Failures: A Second Look," *International Security*, Vol. 11, No. 4 (Spring 1987), 96–124.

[56] In a cogent paper, Barry Wolf examined the question why weak states attack the stronger, a clear case of deterrence failure. He lists three reasons. First, the weaker state was highly motivated, either because of a deep belief in a particular idea or value or a strong psychopathological leader. Second, the weaker state misperceived the strategic reality, thinking the rival to be weaker and expecting no retaliation, or believing that its own allies would rally after the attack. Third, the weaker state sees a vulnerability of the stronger state that justifies an attack. Barry Wolf, "When the Weak Attack the Strong: Failures of Deterrence" (Santa Monica: Rand, 1991), N-3261-A, at www.rand.org/content/dam/rand/pubs/notes/2005/N3261.pdf.

of deterrence. The cultural differences between states and barbarians made the calculation of threats and costs challenging. Finally, third, it was difficult to deter groups for whom the pursuit of violence was a way of life and a source of cohesion.

The first reason for a weak relationship of deterrence between states and barbarians is the most self-evident and most examined, and is tightly related to the ineffectiveness of using force against barbarians. The basic logic of deterrence is predicated on the credible ability to punish a potential aggressor.[57] One can deter a rival by promising to retaliate and inflict unacceptable costs after an attack had occurred. In many cases, it was sufficient to threaten the destruction of military assets in order to alter the calculus of the rival state. The risk of losing a large portion of one's own military strength understandably led to more cautious behavior. An offensive that results in a considerable loss of military strength is at best a Pyrrhic victory for a state, and at worst it makes that state in turn vulnerable to being attacked. Deterrence can also be achieved by threatening the sources of the enemy's economic wellbeing, such as cultivated fields and, in the modern age, industrial centers. A state than cannot feed its own population is in danger of losing its legitimacy and ultimately may collapse or surrender. Consequently, as a nineteenth-century French officer in Algeria observed, "In Europe, once [you are] master of two or three large centers of industry and production, the entire country is yours." When a state can control the political fate of a rival through the destruction of a few targets, it can also deter him with greater ease. But, the officer continued, "in Africa, how can you impose your will on a population whose only link with the land is the pegs of their tents?"[58] The answer tended to be to retaliate against the population writ large, a more cruel but not totally ineffective way of deterring the enemy (but such an answer carried moral and domestic costs, and thus diminished credibility, mentioned earlier). In brief, one can deter by threatening to destroy a variety of targets, pursuing "countervalue" or counterforce" retaliation.

The challenge presented by most premodern barbarians was that they offered neither "countervalue" nor "counterforce" targets. They were not settled, did not control a well-demarcated territory, did not live in cities, and did not till fields. As a result, such highly mobile groups did not

---

[57] The literature on deterrence is vast. For a sample, see Schelling, *Arms and Influence*; Patrick M. Morgan, *Deterrence Now* (New York, NY: Cambridge University Press, 2003); Keith B. Payne, *The Fallacies of Cold War Deterrence and a New Direction* (Lexington, KY: University Press of Kentucky, 2001).
[58] Quote in Thomas Rid, "Razzia: A Turning Point in Modern Strategy," *Terrorism and Political Violence*, Vol. 21, No. 4 (2009), 622.

present a clear "countervalue" target that could be threatened and, if deterrence failed, destroyed. In the late Roman period, it was simply impossible to threaten a countervalue retaliation because most of the invading barbarian groups were migrating *en masse*, abandoning their territories and thereby effectively depriving imperial forces of a target. With nothing to defend but themselves, they were an impressive offensive machine. But even when barbarian groups left behind a portion of their population, like the Comanches did while on a plundering raid, it was difficult for states to threaten credible retaliation. Often the nonraiding barbarian party left behind was too far away, creating enormous logistical difficulties for state forces. And if reachable, it was also prepared to put up a serious fight because barbarian tribes considered all of their members as warriors. Walter Prescott Webb argues that the fact that the Plains Indians "were nomadic, had no settled village life, and therefore could not be destroyed in their own homes" made them fundamentally different, and more threatening, than the Indians in the East.[59] The ability to threaten destruction makes relations with a hostile group more manageable; vice versa, the inability to do so removes a key stabilizing factor in a strategic interaction.

Moreover, as discussed earlier, a counterforce approach to deterrence was impossible when the enemy did not present fixed military assets, such as staging area, fortifications, weapons depots, "soft targets" of logistical units, and large formed units. By engaging in hit-and-run tactics, barbarian groups deprived their opponents of the ability to target them and thus to threaten credible retaliation. It is not surprising, therefore, that as Azar Gat puts it, relations between mobile, nomadic bands and settled groups were extremely violent, "accounting for some of the most horrendous pages in history ... [because] not only did the exponents of the two alien ways of life look down on each other, with the nomads lacking sympathy for the property and toil upon which sedentary life depended, but the nomads also had little fear from retaliation, a major constraining factor between two sedentary or pastoral societies."[60]

The second reason why deterrence between states and barbarians was problematic is related to the difficulty of communication, a challenge also examined in the next section on diplomacy. A deterrent threat has a chance of succeeding when it is communicated clearly to the enemy, and the enemy understands it and believes it to be realistic. A threat that is held secret or that is not otherwise communicated to the enemy is not a threat but merely an aspiration.

[59] Walter Prescott Webb, *The Great Plains* (Lincoln, NE: University of Nebraska Press, 1981; original 1931, 1959), 59.
[60] Azar Gat, *War in Human Civilization* (New York, NY: Oxford University Press, 2006), 379.

Barbarian–state relations were characterized by two sets of communication challenges that affected deterrence. First, the two strategic actors were culturally so different as to make communication fraught with problems. It was not a matter simply of linguistic diversity, a problem that was readily remedied by the presence of, for instance, merchants who traveled back and forth between the two. Rather it was a problem that stemmed from the inability to comprehend each other due to the fundamentally different lifestyles led by the barbarian and state communities. In the absence of common cultural values, deterrence is more difficult because taboos as well as the expected forms of punishments for breaking them are not shared. As Lawrence Freedman writes, deterrence is more likely to succeed when the two strategic actors "are working within a sufficiently shared normative framework ... [that has the effect of establishing] social pressures and a sense of fair and effective punishment."[61] Unable to understand the barbarian enemy, imperial strategists were also less capable of understanding how their rivals perceived the costs and benefits of specific actions and punishments. The animosity that also characterized these relationships from both sides was a symptom of the underlying cultural gap, but it also reinforced the difficulty of deterrence: not only did they not understand each other, but they thought poorly of each other and were eager to fight, rather than seeking ways to coexist.

On top of the often unbridgeable cultural differences, the relations between individual barbarian groups and states lacked temporal permanence, diminishing the effectiveness of any communication that may have existed. Deterrence is more likely to hold when there is a history of interactions from which the two parties can learn, establishing expectations about their behavior and building their reputations and credibility.[62] These are relational concepts that depend on the existence of the other actor: a state or a group would have no reputation were it to exist in perfect solitude.[63] Moreover, a reputation does not arise immediately, merely because of the possession of military strength. It requires time and

---

[61] Lawrence Freedman, *Deterrence* (New York, NY: Polity Press, 2004), 5.
[62] Credibility is defined as "the perception by the threatened party of the degree of probability that the power-wielder will actually carry out the threat if its terms are not complied with or will keep a promise if its conditions are met." Glenn H. Snyder, "Deterrence and Power," *Journal of Conflict Resolution*, Vol. 4, No. 2 (June 1960), 164.
[63] Jonathan Mercer, *Reputation and International Politics* (Ithaca, NY: Cornell University Press, 1996), 26–27. The relational nature of reputation distinguishes it from honor, an intrinsic concept the existence of which does not depend on the perceptions of others. One acquires or keeps his honor by doing the right thing regardless of the personal costs incurred, and the honorable act may not be valued by others. Honor is not evaluated by the spectators, but by the actor himself; reputation, on the other hand, is in the eyes of the others.

a pattern of behavior upon which credible threats of retaliation can be built. Credibility is also a perishable good that requires a recurrent demonstration of its worthiness, something that can be done only when the two actors compete for a certain period of time.[64] In many cases of state–barbarian interactions, the permanence of the state was matched by the transience of the barbarian group. While the barbarian threat in general remained, the individual groups appeared and vanished often in quick succession, and with them the memory and the lessons of the strategic interaction went away. The reputation that a state built with one group did not automatically transfer to another, which had to develop its own knowledge of the state rival through direct experience and observation.

The third factor that diminished the efficacy of deterrence stemmed from the organizing principle of barbarian groups. It was difficult to deter groups for whom violence was a way of life and a source of power and glory. For such entities, war was preferable because being deterred would have supplied little fame and plunder and would have thus weakened their social bonds.[65] The cult of violence that characterized many groups, especially nomadic tribes, many of which had a powerful aristocratic class devoted to war, left no space for being deterred.[66] A Germanic leader, Arminius, who defeated three Roman legions at the battle of Teutoburg, became the tribal chief because "he advocated war": for the barbarians, "the readier a man is to take a risk so much the more is he the man to trust."[67] The Comanches, for instance, engaged in war not simply for material reasons, which arguably could have shaped a cost-benefit calculation leading to deterrence. Rather, the "inner workings of the Comanche society required violent external action."[68] To be deterred meant to be dissuaded from offensive actions, thereby fraying the ties linking the various members of the tribe and undermining the authority of

---

[64] Kenneth Boulding writes that "[d]eterrence is successful as long as it deters, but deterrence itself seems to be unstable. The reason for this ... is that the credibility of threats depreciates with time if threats are not carried out. Hence threats occasionally need to be carried out in order to re-establish their credibility." Kenneth E. Boulding, "Towards a Pure Theory of Threat Systems," *The American Economic Review*, Vol. 53, No. 2, Papers and Proceedings of the Seventy-Fifth Annual Meeting of the American Economic Association (May, 1963), 429.

[65] This is true for many actors that are often reluctant to end a conflict because of fear of internal strife. Fred Iklé, *Every War Must End* (New York, NY: Columbia University Press, 2005), 87, and chapter 4, 59–83.

[66] In fact, in tribal societies there is little or no distinction between the people and the army. Rather, "they do not have armies [but] they themselves are armies ... What we have is warriors." See Van Creveld, *Transformation of War*, 56. On the idea of a warrior class devoted to violence, see also Michael Howard, *War in European History* (New York, NY: Oxford University Press, 1993), especially 1–20.

[67] Tacitus, *Annales*, I:57.   [68] Hämäläinen, 39.

the group leader. Sedentary communities, and wealthy empires in particular, were a lucrative target that generated envy among poorer nomads and incited adventurous leaders who sought glory and wealth. The strength and wealth of an empire, therefore, were an attraction more than a deterrent for nomadic tribes.

Moreover, the objective of barbarian groups was not merely plunder, or the occupation of a specific territory, but the actual act of the attack, which unified them. In fact, many barbarian tribes that assaulted the Roman Empire in the fifth and sixth centuries became gradually more united rather than the opposite. Together they were more effective in facing imperial forces but also their success attracted others to their side: unity stemmed from being on the attack, not from being deterred.[69] In a sixth-century Byzantine military manual, the writer observed that barbarian groups similar to the Huns do not, "as do the others, give up the struggle when worsted in the first battle. But until their strength gives out, they try all sorts of ways to assail their enemies."[70] For leaders of warrior societies, historian Michael Howard writes, "prolonged peace was often ... a disaster."[71]

There was an additional challenge peculiar to the ability of states to deter by denial, namely to dissuade barbarians from attacking by preventing them from achieving their objectives.[72] Sedentary communities tried to harden the potential targets of nomadic and barbarian raids, hoping to dissuade these tribes from attacking. In particular, this meant fortifying cities. The inability of barbarians to conduct protracted sieges, as described earlier, was a serious handicap that only a few groups managed to overcome in history. And walls were effective at protecting cities from the raiding groups. Yet, they have a very limited deterring effect on the strategic level and did not stop nomadic raids. Even large fixed defensive positions built by Roman or Chinese empires, for instance, could not thwart an enemy whose main strength was his high mobility and therefore unpredictability. Although built to "separate the barbarians from the Romans,"[73] Hadrian's Wall had probably only a "symbolic value as

---

[69] Ward-Perkins, 51.   [70] *Maurice's Strategikon*, book XI, 118.
[71] Michael Howard, *Lessons of History* (New Haven, CT: Yale University Press, 1991), 167. This was also true to a certain degree of more settled societies in which martial glory was a source of power. Ammianus Marcellinus recounts that Emperor Valens was jealous of the successes of his nephew, "whose exploits irked him" and wanted to gain equal glory "by some glorious deeds of his own." As a result, he did not wait for reinforcements and went to fight the Goths with only his forces: the result was the massive defeat at Hadrianople in 378 AD. Ammianus Marcellinus, Book 31, 432 (Penguin edition).
[72] For a classic text on the distinction between deterrence by punishment and deterrence by denial, see Glenn H. Snyder, *Deterrence and Defense: Toward a Theory of National Security* (Princeton, NJ: Princeton University Press, 1961).
[73] *Historia Augusta*, trans. by David Magie, Vol. 1 (Cambridge: Loeb Classical Library, 1921), L139, 34–35.

a line of trespass."[74] Similarly, the Ming Chinese hoped, especially after their disastrous defeat in 1449 at Tu-Mu, that the monumental wall built in the north would suffice to keep the Mongols out.[75] But highly mobile nomadic groups could cross the frontiers at the weakest spots, outmaneuvering imperial forces.[76] Furthermore, the relative safety of walled cities was accompanied by the inability of imperial forces to defend less-fortified settlements and agricultural areas as well as to guarantee the security of roads linking various parts of the empire. The success of deterrence by denial in walled urban areas was matched by a failure of defending much of the imperial territory, hurting the ability of the state to provide food and maintain commerce. The success of walling cities against barbarian attacks was predicated on the hope that the raid would be brief and that the damage inflicted on the surrounding areas would not be devastating and prolonged.

The immediate consequence of weak deterrence in state–nomadic relations meant that the frontier separating sedentary from nomadic communities was highly unstable.[77] Through much of premodern history, steppes nomads could raid civilized territories "almost with impunity, unless rulers were able to replicate barbarian levels of mobility and morale within their own establishments," a task that was hard to put into practice.[78] Absence of deterrence, rather than momentary failures of

[74] Everett Wheeler, "Methodological Limits and the Mirage of Roman Strategy," Part I, *Journal of Military History*, Vol. 57, No. 1 (January 1993), 29.
[75] On the Great Wall, see Owen Lattimore, "Origins of the Great Wall of China: A Frontier Concept in Theory and Practice," *The Geographical Review*, Vol. 27, No. 4 (October 1937), 529–549.
[76] Bell-Fialkoff, 187; Khazanov, 222. In fact, there is evidence that Roman troops manning Hadrian's Wall, at least originally, were meant to be a "mobile frontier army, not fortress troops" – clearly indicating awareness that the wall could not hold the line against a highly mobile enemy. "The Wall is not a Maginot Line defended by fortress troops, nor is it a corral; it is a device to divide the Romans from the barbarians, and as an after-thought a base for a field army." David J. Breeze and Brian Dobson, "Hadrian's Wall: Some Problems," *Britannia*, Vol. 3 (1972), 190 and 192.
[77] For instance, in the case of Rome, some argue that Roman–Persian relations were inherently more stable than Roman–barbarian ones. Several factors, most of them absent in state–barbarian relations, made the difference: "(1) show of force, (2) small land actions, (3) alliances with a third power, (4) the building of fortifications, (5) establishment of military colonies, (6) instigation of civil unrest within the deterred power, (7) the use of subsidy payments, (8) utilization of women as a reward, (9) an outward observance of titles and tokens of respect toward each other, and (10) the exchange of missionaries, (11) merchants and traders, and (12) other cultural contacts with each other." Vern L. Bullough, "The Roman Empire vs. Persia, 363–502: a study of successful deterrence," *Journal of Conflict Resolution*, Vol. 7, No. 1 (March 1963), 55.
[78] McNeill, 16. An analogous debate is occurring in US military circles on whether, and how, to increase the mobility of US armed forces to respond to multiple, diffused, and low-intensity threats presented by highly mobile groups. See, for instance, Nina Bernstein, "Strategists fight a war about the war," *New York Times*, 6 April 2003;

deterrence, resulted in relations characterized by a low-intensity but persistent level of violence, in contrast to a more predictable, even though prone to highly destructive outbursts of fighting, rapport among states or empires. In fact, states seem to engage in violence with each other less often, and for shorter periods, than non-state, tribal societies.[79] In contrast to Bernard Brodie's statement that in the modern (and especially nuclear) age the chief purpose of armies was to avert and not to fight wars, premodern imperial armies had a limited deterrent effect on barbarians.[80] Their purpose was to fight, not to avert, wars with barbarians.

It is important to note that it was difficult to deter barbarians not because they were irrational – a view that was easy to espouse as they were considered culturally inferior and incapable of reasoning beyond their impulses. On the contrary, barbarians calculated perfectly that the threat of retaliation by the polity they targeted was minimal, while the denial was only partial and limited.

2.2.3 Diplomacy

Finally, a crucial tool of statecraft, diplomacy, was also less effective. Defined as the negotiated settlement of a conflict of interest, diplomacy is an alternative to the actual use of force. It may be preferable to war if the latter is considered too costly in relation to the potential objectives and to the likelihood of attaining them through force. Diplomacy, however, is not separated from the threat of force; in fact, negotiations often occur under the shadow of violence, spurring the negotiating parties to seek an accommodating settlement. The difficulties of force and deterrence mentioned earlier also affected the ability of the competing strategic actors to reach a diplomatic settlement.

The challenges facing diplomacy in premodern times went, however, beyond the inability of states to threaten barbarians in a credible fashion, thus forcing them to the negotiating table. Diplomacy was more difficult both as a process and as an outcome.[81]

The process of diplomacy was less developed than in modern times and it faced systemic difficulties that were difficult, if not impossible, to

---

Eliot Cohen, "Change and Transformation in Military Affairs," *Journal of Strategic Studies*, Vol. 27, No. 3 (September 2004), 395–407; Michael Evans, "From Kadesh to Kandahar," *Naval War College Review*, Vol. 56, No. 3 (Summer 2003).

[79] Lawrence Keeley, *War before Civilization* (New York, NY: Oxford University Press, 1997), 33. Keeley also argues that war between primitive societies killed a much larger percentage of their populations than wars among states. Keeley, 93–94, and on frontiers, 130–132.

[80] Bernard Brodie, *The Absolute Weapon* (New York, NY: Harcourt Brace, 1946), 76.

[81] Gat, 379.

The Challenges

overcome.[82] First, political communication among polities, as well as between states and barbarians, was slow and irregular. Many scholars consider the Renaissance as the beginning of modern diplomacy, in part because of the development of a professional diplomatic corps at the service of sovereign polities.[83] At this time, the idea of resident embassies was introduced, and it allowed the establishment of continuous relations among polities, even though this did not imply automatically more peaceful interactions. In premodern times, diplomacy was conducted by envoys and heralds, often considered to be sacred and inviolable to facilitate the flow of information even in moments of heightened tensions and war.[84] We know that Roman emperors, for instance, communicated with foreign leaders and that provincial governors and commanders exchanged information and instructions with Rome, but we have very few surviving documents, suggesting perhaps that such communications were not decisive.[85]

Moreover, the practice of sending envoys to exchange information and to negotiate made interactions extremely slow because of the status of premodern communications (which really did not change dramatically until the nineteenth century).[86] It could take years for an embassy to travel back and forth and complete its mission. Even important messengers that were given full logistical support and priority could travel perhaps no more than 100 miles per day, making a trip from, for

---

[82] I do not argue, however, that diplomacy has been characterized by a steady progress from a primitive status of ancient times to the more sophisticated one of the nineteenth century and an even loftier one of the twenty-first. Diplomacy is an outcome of underlying political and strategic conditions, such as the nature of the competing polities, and not an institution that can be manipulated and improved by illuminated political managers. It waxes and wanes with the changing political conditions; it depends on them, rather than shaping them.

[83] Garrett Mattingly, *Renaissance Diplomacy* (Boston, MA: Houghton Mifflin Company, 1955; republished by New York: Dover Publications, 1988); Christopher Dawson, *The Dividing of Christendom* (New York, NY: Sheed & Ward, 1965).

[84] See Amos S. Hershey, "The History of International Relations During Antiquity and the Middle Ages," *American Journal of International Law*, Vol. 5, No. 4 (October 1911), 901–933. For an example of the inviolability of envoys, see Caesar, 54 (I. 47).

[85] See Fergus Millar, "Emperors, Frontiers, and Foreign Relations, 31 BC to AD 378," *Britannia*, Vol. 13 (1982), 1–23; Fergus Millar, "Government and Diplomacy in the Roman Empire during the First Three Centuries," *International History Review*, Vol. 10, No. 3 (August 1988), 345–377. Diplomacy also seems to be less necessary when there is one hegemonic or imperial power, and in fact, the number of envoys and the extent of political communications increased as the number of political actors increased. The gradual weakening of Roman hold over the Mediterranean region raised the need for communications, even though it did not necessarily lead to more successful diplomacy. See Andrew Gillett, *Envoys and Political Communication in the Late Antique West, 411–533* (New York, NY: Cambridge University Press, 2003).

[86] Christern Jönsson and Martin Hall, "Communication: An Essential Aspect of Diplomacy," *International Studies Perspectives*, 4 (2003), 206–207.

instance, Antioch to Rome, in about a month.[87] The waging of war was of course also fairly slow (armies moved at an average of fifteen miles per day), and thus diplomacy could take its leisurely time.[88] The slowness of diplomacy was, however, less appropriate when one of the strategic actors had the capacity to move swiftly, attacking and withdrawing before even the first news of the assault reached the imperial authorities. Barbarians often raided imperial territories, surprising the defenders, raiding their lands, and disappearing in the ungoverned and unreachable spaces. Not only did the speed of such attacks make a centralized response difficult but also diplomatic interactions that may have been attempted to forestall or mitigate such a raid required a swiftness that was simply impossible.

A partial solution to the sluggishness of diplomatic communication was to give authority to foreign citizens so that they could represent the interest of a particular polity. In Ancient Greece, this was the role of the *proxenos*, who was given the official task to protect and represent the interest of another city.[89] But this worked relatively well when the two states were not in "serious conflict ... [because when they were] the loyalties of the proxenos are bound to be torn between the interests of his own city and those of the one he represents."[90] And in any case, there is little evidence that these local representatives made much difference in the interactions among cities. Moreover, it was impossible to institute similar systems of representation with actors, such as the barbarians, who were culturally very different and who were often unknown.

This leads to the second difficulty of the diplomatic process, namely the lack of permanence of the actors in conflict. Diplomacy, like deterrence, is more effective when there are recurrent interactions among the actors, and for this, permanence is necessary. Diplomacy increases as states acquire greater spatial and temporal permanence. Not only is it difficult to establish communications with newly arrived actors, but the brevity of many such interactions did not allow development of routines necessary to maintain a certain level of contact and limited the ability to develop a modicum of knowledge of each other's nature, interests, and

---

[87] Fergus Millar, "Emperors, Frontiers, and Foreign Relations, 31 BC to AD 378," *Britannia*, Vol. 13 (1982), 10.
[88] Harry Sidebottom, "International Relations" (chapter 1), in P. Sabin, H. Van Wees, and M. Whitby, eds., *The Cambridge History of Greek and Roman Warfare* (New York, NY: Cambridge University Press, 2007), 9.
[89] On *proxenia*, see Lynette Mitchell, *Greeks Bearing Gifts: The Public Use of Private Relationships in Greek World, 435–323 BC* (New York, NY: Cambridge University Press, 2002), 28–37.
[90] Adam Watson, *Diplomacy*, 88.

capabilities.[91] The shorter the lifespan of a barbarian group (or, to be more precise, of the contact with the barbarian group), the more difficult it was to engage in diplomacy. The rapid rise and disappearance of many barbarian groups, often tied to the fortunes of individual leaders, simply did not allow the physical stability necessary to develop diplomatic exchanges. The process of diplomacy presupposes a modicum of knowledge among the parties involved, and this was missing in many premodern interactions exactly because of the impermanence of the barbarian groups. Absence of information led to greater uncertainty and instability in these relations because it often deprived the two parties of knowledge of the social structures, the customs, and the objectives pursued by the other side.[92] The limited information concerning internal political developments as well as foreign policy decisions of external actors combined with the inability to convey one's own decisions or resolve meant that violent confrontations were almost inevitable.[93] Geographic and temporary permanence is certainly not sufficient to maintain diplomatic interactions and to negotiate peacefully a conflict of interests: The many interstate wars are a testament to that. But without such permanence, the necessary but insufficient condition, diplomacy has little chance to be successful.[94]

The impermanence of the barbarian rival, and in particular his quick projections of power, have also an impact on the ability of the state to engage in effective diplomacy. From the perspective of the state, in fact, the constant raiding by barbarian groups may have hindered the ability to foster a diplomatic approach toward them because it made the targeted society unstable, hindering its political development. Rapid and

---

[91] A similar dynamic affected the establishment (or lack thereof) of legal rules and social norms. Without "territorial propinquity and temporal stability" it is more difficult to give the sense of permanence and continuity that is necessary to develop and implement such rules. Michael Mann, *The Sources of Social Power* (New York, NY: Cambridge University Press, 1986), Vol. I, 420. Mann also observes that "[w]here states' territoriality increased, interstate relations were politically regulated." Mann, 431.

[92] A. D. Lee, *Information and Frontiers* (New York, NY: Cambridge University Press, 1993).

[93] Eckstein, *Mediterranean Anarchy*, 59. See also Martin Wight, *Systems of States* (Leicester: Leicester University Press, 1977), 50.

[94] Gordon Craig and Felix Gilbert write that the duties of diplomats, in particular in the golden age of diplomacy between the sixteenth and eighteenth centuries, were "facilitated by the fact that the European states of this period were autarchical entities and that the factors that determined their international behavior and their intercourse with their neighbors – such things as political ambition, economic power, and military resources – were, or seemed to be, easily calculable." In brief, they "possessed a conceptual framework within which they could move with confidence." Such a framework is missing in most premodern history. Gordon Craig and Felix Gilbert, eds., *The Diplomats: 1919–1939* (New York, NY: Atheneum, 1965, reprint of Princeton University Press edition), Vol. 1, 4.

persistent raiding induces panic and fear, rather than the relative tranquility necessary to promote the patience required for negotiations.[95] If a state engaged in diplomacy directly with a barbarian group, it tended to be as an attempt, often temporarily successful, to appease them and to redirect their military assault away from their own territory, rather than a process to settle a conflict through negotiations. As Harold Nicholson observes, diplomacy with tribal groups was often limited to attempts (a) to divide them by favoring one over the other, (b) to bribe them, and (c) to assimilate or convert them. None of these involved settling differences through negotiations.[96] Appeasement was attractive to states because it carried the promise of no military engagement, a costly and risky endeavor, especially if a defeat was engraved in the memory of imperial administrators, as well as the hope that the postponement of a direct confrontation would have bought sufficient time to let the group move on farther away or disintegrate because of internal discord. Fifth-century Byzantium, for instance, could not forget the 378 AD disaster at Hadrianople, and when the Huns started to push into imperial territories, it was eager to buy them off. The protection of the Balkan territories, key sources of revenues and manpower, drove much of Byzantine foreign policy and the Huns threatened to plunder them.[97] Hence, through the

[95] Marc Bloch observed that raids on Europe stopped around the tenth century AD, affecting only its Eastern frontier (today's Central and Eastern Europe). While this did not lead to peace as various European potentates fought each other for power and glory with great ferocity, it did mean that there was no external assault on the region. "This meant the possibility of a much more regular cultural and social evolution, uninterrupted by any attack from without or any influx of foreign settlers ... It is surely not unreasonable to think that this extraordinary immunity, of which we have shared the privilege with scarcely any people but the Japanese, was one of the fundamental factors of European civilization, in the deepest sense, in the exact sense of the word." Bloch, 56.
[96] Harold Nicholson, *Diplomacy* (Washington, DC: Institute for the Study of Diplomacy, Georgetown University, 1988; reprint of 3rd edition), 10.
[97] See Alexander Sarantis, "War and Diplomacy in Pannonia and the Northwest Balkans during the Reign of Justinian: The Gepid Threat and Imperial Responses," *Dumbarton Oaks Papers*, Vol. 63 (2009), 15–40. But it needs to be added that a war against barbarians also did not supply the emperor with much glory, and Roman emperors tended to prefer the Asian theater of action. As historian John Haldon observes, "Warfare was thus not necessarily conducted with a purely material advantage in mind, since ideological superiority played an important role in Byzantine notions of their identity and role in the order of things' nor was it conducted with any longer-term strategic objective in mind. Any damage to the enemy was a good thing, but some ways of hitting the enemy also carried an ideological value: Heraclius' destruction of the Zoroastrian temples, the sack by Nikephros I of the Bulgar khan's capital at Pliska, Theophilos' attack on Melitene and Sozopetra in 837, [etc.] ... In turn, some theatres were ideologically more important than others. Fighting the barbarians in the Balkans and north of the Danube was regarded as much less prestigious and glorious than combating the religious foe, the Muslims, in the east: as the eleventh-century intellectual and courtier Michael Psellos remarks: 'There seemed nothing grand [in fighting] the barbarians in the West ... but were he [the emperor Romanos III] to turn to those living

diplomacy of subsidies and gifts of gold, Byzantium succeeded in deflecting the Hunnic assault to the detriment of the Western rump of the Roman Empire.[98] And it was doubly successful because of the collapse of the Huns after Attila's death: The impermanent nature of the particular group allowed for appeasement to buy sufficient time. Barbarian impermanence makes diplomacy as a settlement of a conflict difficult, but it puts a premium on deflecting or postponing the direct confrontation.

Of course, counting on the eventual disappearance of the barbarian group was not the only justification for pursuing appeasement by bribing. Other, less strategic, reasons were often at play. For instance, Emperor Commodus (r. 180–192 AD), son of Marcus Aurelius, abandoned the fight with the barbarians along the Danube. His military advisers, wise and experienced, urged him to continue the war in person, because "to leave this war unfinished is both disgraceful and dangerous. That course would increase the barbarians' boldness; they will not believe that we long to return to our home, but will rather accuse us of a cowardly retreat." There was no compelling reason to return home before winning that war; in fact, it was dangerous and dishonorable to do so. But other courtiers, "who gauge their pleasure by their bellies and something a little lower," appealed to Commodus' nostalgia for the pleasures of Rome and repeatedly tempted him to leave the frontier and return to the capital. "'Master,' they said again and again, 'when will you stop drinking this icy liquid mud? In the meantime, others will be enjoying warm streams and cool streams, mists and fine air too, all of which only Italy possesses in abundance.' By merely suggesting such delights to the youth, they whetted his appetite for a taste of pleasures." The sycophantic courtesans won; the wise advisors lost. Commodus returned, leaving the frontier in the hands of leaders he deemed capable and trustworthy. The approach taken by them was to buy the barbarians off. "The barbarians are by nature fond of money; contemptuous of danger, they obtain the necessities of life either by pillaging and plundering or by selling peace at a huge price. Commodus was aware of this practice; since he had plenty of money, he bargained for release from care and gave them everything they demanded." Of course, the abdication of leadership on the frontier has its security consequences. The Roman army, and presumably the allied forces with it, was not eager to remain on the frontier. "All the soldiers wanted to leave with him [Commodus], so that they might stop wasting their time in the war and enjoy the pleasures at Rome." Wars cannot be

in the East, he thought that he could perform nobly'" John Haldon, *Warfare, State and Society in the Byzantine World, 565–1204* (London: UCL Press, 1999), 42.

[98] Gabriela Simonova, "Byzantine Diplomacy and the Huns," *Macedonian Historical Review*, Vol. 2, No. 2 (2011), 67–85.

led from well-appointed tables in Rome. We do not know much about how that war ended. But Commodus' disengagement from the frontier, contrary to the strategy pursued by his predecessor and father, left a vast region unstable that a few years later ended up demanding even larger numbers of Roman manpower. Commodus merely postponed a problem, aggravating it in the process.[99]

Finally, the last reason why the process of diplomacy was more difficult was the incompatibility of the objectives pursued. Even when the various parties exchanged envoys, a diplomatic outcome was more difficult to attain because the goals pursued by them were nonnegotiable. Talking with each other is, in other words, not the same as resolving divergent interests and claims through political means.[100] As mentioned earlier, many of the ancient clashes were not about territory, but about issues of allegiance or glory or plunder, all of which are much more difficult to resolve through a negotiated compromise. These are indivisible questions that lend themselves only to an either-or solution, unlike territorial claims that are relatively easy to adjust and settle by shifting borders and moving populations. Hence, a Congress of Vienna that through hard bargaining dealt with conflicting aspirations of the European great powers was possible in the early nineteenth century and was followed by many analogous agreements, but was a rarity in ancient times.[101] This is not to say that there were no treaties or other types of agreements in ancient history. The Persian war that wrecked Greece in the fifth century BC ended with a treaty (the Peace of Callias around 450 BC); the Peace of Nicias (412 BC) negotiated between Athens and Sparta paused their conflict; Rome built a web of treaties with its Latin neighbors; and the conflict between the Western and Byzantine empires was mitigated by the Pax Nicephori (803). The list could go on. Nonetheless, often these agreements came after a conflict, merely confirming the results of the war rather than representing a compromise reached at the negotiating table. It was post-victory diplomacy pursued by actors, such as Rome, that believed that peace was possible only after the total defeat of the enemy.[102] Moreover, such agreements represented only a portion of ancient international politics, those dealing with relations among similar actors such as cities, empires, kings, or emperors. The growing importance of territorial control that characterizes the advent of the modern era made

---

[99] Herodian, *Roman History*, I:6, 1–9.   [100] Eckstein, *Mediterranean Anarchy*, 58.
[101] See also Strayer, 27.
[102] Goldsworthy, *Cambridge History of Greek and Roman Warfare*, 112–113.

the process of political compromise more feasible in international relations.[103] There was simply something, for instance territorial adjustments, that could be the subject of negotiations.

The existence of such nonnegotiable objectives also points to the difficulty of reaching and implementing an outcome. The process of diplomacy was itself problematic as described earlier, but even when it occurred, a positive outcome of diplomacy was highly unlikely. Besides the nature of the objectives pursued, the nature of the actors engaged in diplomacy made its outcome tenuous. Some of the strategic actors were too decentralized and did not have the administrative framework necessary to conduct diplomatic negotiations and then to implement the agreements.[104] This was a general problem in premodern times as states rarely had clear boundaries, and thus foreign and domestic policies overlapped. The Roman Empire, for example, considered many internal revolts as foreign wars, and lacked a cadre of experts, diplomats, or strategists that characterize a modern ministry of foreign affairs or defense.[105] Similarly, in the Middle Ages, the multiple layers of sovereignty made the conduct of diplomacy complicated as there was no clear actor who could negotiate and implement an agreement. As Joseph Strayer observes, "[i]n a Europe without states and without boundaries the concept of 'foreign affairs' had no meaning, and so no machinery for dealing with foreign affairs was needed."[106] This impacted the process, but also the implementation of any agreement the leaders may have reached. The "foreign affairs machinery" is needed to allow the political authorities to impose upon their own population the settlement reached with the external actors.

The negotiations pursued by the leaders are rarely sufficient by themselves to establish and maintain a compromise between the parties in conflict. As the president of the United States needs to seek the approval of the Senate for international treaties, so premodern actors had to obtain

---

[103] Territory can also become an indivisible issue, especially when it assumes quasi-religious connotations. See Monica Duffy Toft, *The Geography of Ethnic Violence* (Princeton, NJ: Princeton University Press, 2005; Stacie Goddard, "Uncommon Ground: Indivisible Territory and the Politics of Legitimacy," *International Organization*, Vol. 60, Issue 1 (January 2006), 35–68; Ron Hassner, "To Have and to Hold: Conflicts over Sacred Space and the Problem of Indivisibility," *Security Studies*, Vol. 12, No. 4 (Summer 2003), 1–33; Ron Hassner, "Fighting Insurgency on Sacred Ground," *Washington Quarterly*, Vol. 29, No. 2 (Spring 2006), 149–166.

[104] Martin Van Creveld, *The Transformation of War* (New York, NY: The Free Press, 1991), 56.

[105] Susan Mattern, *Rome and the Enemy* (Berkeley, CA: University of California Press, 2002), 1–23.

[106] Joseph Strayer, *On the Medieval Origins of the Modern State* (Princeton, NJ: Princeton University Press, 2005), 27.

the acceptance of their subordinates and populations. But the less hierarchical and more decentralized nature of premodern entities, and of barbarians in particular, made that process of wide approval all the more difficult. The Byzantines, rightly considered as masters of diplomacy, faced serious difficulties when they attempted to negotiate with their northern barbarian neighbors. The "stateless nature of Slav society" was particularly problematic because diplomacy "only work[s] if there is an acknowledged leader with whom one can establish binding agreements. No one in Slav society had that kind of lasting authority."[107] The challenge of negotiating with a stateless group was even greater in moments characterized by peace or at least no active military conflict because then there was less need for a centralized decision-making structure; only in war, when the demands for discipline and a unitary command are greater, do decentralized groups adopt greater capacities for coordination and subordination. As Andreski points out, war "is on the whole an emergency in which the co-ordination of actions of great numbers is more than ever imperative."[108] Of course, when relations have already degenerated to the point of war, negotiations become attempts to postpone or divert the attack rather than to resolve the conflict of interest. Paradoxically, when barbarians assumed the greatest capacity to engage in the process of diplomacy, they were also less likely to be willing to do so; they were on a warpath, not in search of a compromise. It is not surprising then that from an imperial perspective, the barbarians' unwillingness to engage in diplomacy was puzzling and had to be ascribed to their nature, which was torn by unbridled passions. As Roman historian Ammianus Marcellinus colorfully put it, "you cannot make a truce with them, because ... like unreasoning beasts they are entirely at the mercy of the maddest impulses."[109]

To be fair, relations between states and barbarians were not always conflictual. Sedentary and nomadic communities could coexist in a fragile peace, based on a certain symbiosis that was a mix of deterrence and diplomacy. In large measure this was driven by commercial interests: Sedentary communities needed the horses that many nomadic groups bred, while nomads were eager to acquire manufactured or agricultural goods that settled civilization produced. Chinese Ming officials, for instance, thought that the barbarians beyond their northern frontiers were always interested in tea. As one put it, "All the barbarians need tea to survive. If they cannot get tea, they become ill and die."[110] Chinese

---

[107] Whittow, 49.   [108] Andreski, 92.
[109] Ammianus Marcellinus, Book 31, 412 (Penguin).
[110] Peter C. Perdue, *China Marches West* (Cambridge, MA: Belknap Press, 2005), 69.

administrators therefore regularly sent large-scale shipments of tea to the frontier and exchanged them for the horses that the nomadic tribes bred.[111] A similar policy was pursued by Muscovite Russia with some of the steppe tribes: Moscow bought thousands of horses with a certain regularity, driven by its military needs on the northwestern frontier. The preferred, but not always attainable, outcome was a tense stalemate, summed up by a saying of the Nogais steppe groups: "we won't break the chicken's leg, don't you break the colt's leg" – where the chickens were the animals of sedentary lifestyle and horses those of the steppes.[112] In any case, these exchanges were less commercial in nature than forms of subsidies paid by the empire to the barbarians (tea for China, grain or gold in the case of Rome) in the hope that this would have satisfied the immediate economic needs of these groups and decrease their incentives to plunder.[113]

But these were rare moments of stability, quickly undermined by the fundamentally opposed interests. States did not constantly need the supply of horses from the barbarians, and that need usually coincided with military campaigns on a different front (as in the case of Muscovite Russia). Once that campaign or war had ended, the demand for horses abated and states refocused on the barbarian threat. From the perspective of barbarians, the decision not to engage in plundering raids depended on a variety of reasons, from the internal leadership dynamics of the tribe to the availability of manpower sufficient for the attack. An interruption in trade could lead to a barbarian attack, perhaps because tea was deemed so vital for survival. But by and large, as common sense would dictate, if the barbarians calculated that it was easier to acquire the needed goods through a raid rather than through trade, then they chose the violent way. And the challenge was that more often than not it was indeed easier and cheaper to raid than to trade: A raid brought gold, grain, tea, and glory with little expenditure of horses, whereas trade brought only material goods, it generated no glory, and it cost horses.

2.3 The Consequences

The consequences of less effective diplomacy, deterrence, and use of force were predictable: more violence. The premodern strategic landscape was characterized by a violence that was more frequent and

---

[111] See Rossabi, "The Ming and Inner Asia," 221–271.
[112] Edward Louis Keenan, Jr., "Muscovy and Kazan: Some Introductory Remarks on the Patterns of Steppe Diplomacy," *Slavic Review*, Vol. 26, No. 4 (December 1967), 552.
[113] Olwen Brogan, "Trade between the Roman Empire and the Free Germans," *Journal of Roman Studies*, Vol. 26, Part 2 (1936), 195–222.

pervasive, even though less destructive, than in modern times. The frequency was due to the ineffectiveness of diplomacy and deterrence, whereas the pervasiveness was made possible by the proliferation and relative cheapness of military technology, which meant that the costs of a violent act tended to be less than the potential benefits. In brief, the result was that violence was much more likely to erupt in ancient than modern times.[114] As historian M. I. Finley writes, "There is nothing in modern experience quite like this. War was a normal part of life; not all periods compared in intensity with the Persian and Peloponnesian wars or with the Hannibalic War, but hardly a year went by without requiring a formal decision to fight, followed by a muster and the necessary preparations, and finally combat at some level."[115]

The interactions between many actors tended to degenerate easily into violence, mitigated only by the capability of the two parties to fight and usually ending in either the complete annihilation or the withdrawal of one side. If a political settlement was not attainable, then violence was the only way to solve the conflict between the various parties. Similarly, if a group or leader sought glory rather than territory or wealth, then war was more likely to be the tool of choice because compromises supply little fame. Also, wars over rank and prestige are more difficult to assess because there are few hard, tangible metrics of victory. As a historian put it, "victory had to be judged not by a statistical exercise, but in the gut."[116] In such circumstances, escalation is more likely to occur, up to wars of extermination.

Violence on the frontiers between settled populations and barbarians tended to be vicious and allowed no quarter. In the contest for the American Plains, for instance, there was no concept of surrender. As the great historian of the Plains puts it, the "Plains Indians were by nature more ferocious, implacable, and cruel than the other tribes ... The Indians rarely, if ever, surrendered themselves, and they had no concept of the white man's generosity to a vanquished foe. If one cannot surrender, then one must flee or fight, and in the end must die rather than fall alive into the hands of the enemy."[117] It is not surprising therefore that most white soldiers, if under attack, would leave a bullet for themselves.

---

[114] Eckstein, *Mediterranean Anarchy*, 42–43, 93; Arthur Eckstein, "Bellicosity and Anarchy: Soldiers, Warriors, and Combat in Antiquity," *International History Review*, Vol. 27, No. 3 (September 2005), 497; Daniel Deudney, "'A Republic for Expansion': The Roman Constitution and Empire and Balance-of-Power Theory," in S. Kaufman, R. Little, and W. Wohlforth, eds., *The Balance of Power in World History* (New York, NY: Palgrave Macmillan, 2007), 166–167.

[115] M.I. Finley, *Politics in the Ancient World* (New York, NY: Cambridge University Press, 1983), 67.

[116] Lendon, 132.   [117] Walter Prescott Webb, *The Great Plains*, 59.

The Consequences

Moreover, violence was more pervasive because of the proliferation and relative cheapness of military technology, which meant that the costs of a violent act tended to be less than the potential benefits. An industrious individual, with great charisma and leadership skills, could gather around him a band of men, eager for wealth and glory, arm them, and thereby create another powerful actor that thrived on violence. In fact, as some have argued, during prolonged periods of premodern history, there is little, if any, distinction between international and domestic war because, "within states and between states, lords stood principally in nonpacified relations to each other."[118] Moreover, premodern war often differed from its modern incarnation in that it did not have clear boundaries and frontlines and well-defined timeframes. As a historian put it, there was little warfare but much violence.[119] John Guilmartin observes that "far more common in the broad sweep of history are prolonged conflicts where the transition from peace to war is blurred, where guerilla and positional operations are more important to the outcome than field or naval campaigns of limited duration, and where objectives tend to be total. This type of conflict – the term war is frequently inadequate – tends to end only with the elimination or cultural absorption of the losers."[120] War was often fought without any possibility of a political compromise and without any norms moderating its conduct.[121]

At best, there was a dualism of sorts in international politics with, on the one hand, relations among states or similarly organized polities, and on the other, interactions between states and non-state actors. Political scientists Buzan and Little rightly argue that "[p]rehistory reveals the enormous difference made by whether the units in the system are mobile or territorially fixed."[122] This dualism was quite evident throughout the history of the Roman Empire, which through war and diplomacy achieved a degree of stability with the Parthian Empire, a similarly hierarchic and

---

[118] Teschke, 348.
[119] Gat, quoting a historian of Ireland, 183. See also Lawrence Keeley, *War before Civilization* (New York, NY: Oxford University Press, 1997), 33.
[120] Guilmartin, 722. Thomas Schelling observes that "Ancient wars were often quite 'total' for the loser, the men being put to death, the women sold as slaves, the boys castrated, the cattle slaughtered, and the buildings leveled, for the sake of revenge, justice, personal gain, or merely custom ... Pure violence, like fire, can be harnessed to a purpose; that does not mean that behind every holocaust is a shrewd intention successfully fulfilled." Schelling, *Arms and Influence*, 9.
[121] Fustel de Coulanges, 198–199. See also Thomas Schelling, *Arms and Influence*, 2; Jack Levy, Thomas Walker, and Martin Edwards, "Continuity and Change in the Evolution of Warfare," in *War in a Changing World*, ed. Zeev Maoz and Azar Gat (Ann Arbor, MI: University of Michigan Press, 2001), 27.
[122] Barry Buzan and Richard Little, *International Systems in World History* (New York, NY: Oxford University Press, 2000), 160.

84   Barbarians and the Character of the Competition

territorially defined polity, but until its very end struggled to pacify the Rhine-Danube frontiers with the Germanic tribes, a loose network of highly mobile and decentralized groups.[123] In the latter relationship, the length of war was not under Roman control because the military superiority of imperial forces was insufficient to deter and to inflict decisive and quick defeats on unsettled groups.[124] A similar challenge faced the Spanish Empire in part of the Americas. As historian J. H. Parry writes, "Significantly, the only lasting military defeats suffered by Spaniards were inflicted by wild people living a scattered life in wild country. The Araucanians of southern Chile, the Chichimecas of northern Mexico, the Caribs of the lesser Antilles, having no great temples or capital cities, were less vulnerable, more mobile, more dangerous."[125] War was more difficult to prevent and to mitigate.

Another example of the dual security threat often facing territorial polities was thirteenth-century Livonia. Its eastern frontier with Russian principalities was relatively stable, and any attack from the east could be met with an organized force because of advance warning. Established tools of statecraft – diplomacy, deterrence, and armed confrontation – could be employed here. In the south, the situation was different because the threat was coming from bellicose pagan tribes that frequently attacked Livonian villages, surprising their targets and returning to their lands as quickly as they had arrived. Conquering these tribes proved to be too difficult and retaliatory counterattacks were costly and ineffective. The Livonian knights, therefore, had to organize some sort of frontier defense. This was based on a string of castles and fortified settlements that, however, were not built to hold the line but to allow for patrolling the region and supporting an area defense – and most often for the organization of a counterraid. The result was that plundering raids of nearby pagan tribal forces were almost never caught inside Livonian territory, but outside it, after they had devastated an area. Heavy with booty and with a train of slaves, the tribal party was slower and could be attacked by a force that was organized inside the castles and other frontier

---

[123] See also C. R. Whittaker, *Frontiers of the Roman Empire* (Baltimore, MD: The Johns Hopkins University Press, 1994), especially 49–53; Vern L. Bullough, "Rome vs. Persia: A Study of Successful Deterrence," *Journal of Conflict Resolution*, Vol. 7, No. 1 (1963), 55–68. Tacitus even claimed that the Germans were more dangerous than Parthia. Tacitus, *The Agricola and the Germania* (New York, NY: Penguin 1970), 132 (Germania, 37). Chester Starr, *The Roman Empire* (New York, NY: Oxford University Press 1982), 174. See also Richard Frye, "The Sassanians," in *Cambridge Ancient History*, Vol. XII, 473–474.

[124] Michael Whitby, "War," in *Cambridge History of Greek and Roman Warfare*, Vol. 2, chapter 9, 320–321.

[125] J. H. Parry, *The Spanish Seaborne Empire* (Berkeley, CA: University of California Press, 1990), 97.

fortifications. This did not of course give much hope to the targeted populations inside Livonia that they would be protected from the next raid. Frontier defense was not preventing the attacks and at best could only retaliate after the fact.[126]

The big question of whether these premodern characteristics are making a comeback is examined next.

---

[126] William Urban, "The Organization of Defense of the Livonian Frontier in the Thirteenth Century," *Speculum*, Vol. 48, No. 3 (July 1973), 525–532.

3 The Return of Premodern History?

The preceding description of premodern history and of the barbarians is sweeping and, therefore, undoubtedly imperfect and superficial. Nonetheless, the broad point is not to establish the existence of a historical period extending through several centuries, if not millennia, with uniform features in its security landscape. To make such a claim would be not just incorrect but outright silly. There are good reasons – based on changes in the nature of domestic political regimes or of philosophical thought, and also differences in political interactions among strategic actors – why historians distinguish the years of Republican Rome from Late Antiquity, and Late Antiquity from the Middle Ages, and so on. The purpose of the previous chapters is only to convey the idea that some of the complexity of international politics was lost in modern times, and not that the centuries of the premodern era were uniform in how political entities competed with each other.

Modern, post-Westphalian international relations are no less difficult, tragic, and destructive, but are perhaps more one-dimensional than the preceding centuries. Premodern times are characterized by a geopolitical pluralism of multiple actors of disparate nature competing with each other according to a variety of rules, a pluralism only occasionally encountered after the seventeenth century. And this proliferation of actors, pursuing a spectrum of objectives more variegated than those in the modern age, was made possible because of certain underlying conditions such as the proliferation of tools of violence and the presence of ungoverned spaces.

Some of these conditions are seeing a resurgence in a format consonant with the existing geopolitical and technological circumstances. These conditions, namely the proliferation of strategic actors due to the wide availability of weapons and the presence of ungoverned spaces, had disappeared gradually over the past two or three centuries, or at a minimum have been suppressed by the rise and expansion of modern states. But to assert that such a disappearance is eternal, a symptom of a progressive nature of history moving toward greater predictability and rule-based interactions, is dangerous because it closes the mind to the possibility of a more complex and perhaps even more chaotic international system.[1] It is also unmoored from the historical reality of constant, albeit gradual, change that characterizes the modern age, and the international relations associated with it. While it is plausible that we may enter into a period with no parallels in history, perhaps due to the presence of nuclear weapons or to the existence of economic ties of interdependence, it is equally plausible to see a return of features that went into remission. Moreover, it is also inescapable that we seek historical analogies, past stories that promise and often deliver glimpses of knowledge useful for the present. Historians and political scientists alike often focus on the misuses of historical analogies.[2] But dangerous as they may be, we need them because we think by analogies. As John Lukacs aptly put it, "[w]e are all historians by nature, while we are scientists only by choice."[3]

The question examined in this chapter is whether premodern history has relevance for the current, and perhaps future, strategic environment. There is a proliferation of military technology, including of weapons of mass destruction, and there is a rise of ungoverned spaces across vast swaths of land. Lethality is no longer tied to a well-administered, resource-rich state. In fact, many states have a difficult time maintaining control over their own territories, in part at least because the modern monopoly over violence is weakening. In a nutshell, the question is this: Are premodern conditions reappearing? And if so, would their reappearance signal a return to an international situation more akin to premodern times?

The answer provided in this chapter is a tentative yes. It is at least plausible to suggest that the features described in the previous chapters are making a comeback of sorts and, in combination with other factors such as the diffusion of power to non-Western regions and the gradual degradation of international norms of behavior, are breaking the modern mold of international relations. The proliferation of violence and the rise of ungoverned spaces are making statelessness feasible and

---

[1] Randall Schweller, *Maxwell's Demon and the Golden Apple* (Baltimore, MD: The Johns Hopkins University Press, 2014).

[2] On thinking by historical analogies, see Ernest May, *"Lessons" of the Past: The Use and Misuse of History in American Foreign Policy* (New York, NY: Oxford University Press, 1975); Robert Jervis, *Perception and Misperception in International Affairs* (Princeton, NJ: Princeton University Press, 1976); Michael Howard, *The Lessons of History* (New Haven, CT: Yale University press, 1991); Margaret McMillan, *Dangerous Games: The Uses and Abuses of History* (New York, NY: Modern Library, 2010). History, and analogies, are also a source of practical knowledge as they can serve to develop "error avoidance." See William Inboden, "Statecraft, Decision-Making, and the Varieties of Historical Experience: A Taxonomy," *Journal of Strategic Studies*, Vol. 37, No. 2 (2014), 9–10.

[3] John Lukacs, *At the End of An Age* (New Haven, CT: Yale University Press, 2002), 50.

perhaps even desirable. This is allowing the rise of new strategic actors, motivated by new objectives that do not fit neatly into the modern international setting and, because of their loose organization and small size, more difficult to detect and monitor. The end result is that, like in premodern history, diplomacy and deterrence may not be as effective as they had been over the past two or three centuries. And the world will be characterized by more pervasive, geographically diffuse, even if low-intensity violence.

In what follows, I delineate two related trends that may make current and future international relations more akin to premodern history. These two trends – namely, the rise of new actors and the prominence of new objectives – are not marking the end of the modern state, and are certainly not altering the anarchic structure of international politics.[4] There is a fundamental continuity in international relations, from ancient to modern times (namely, international anarchy) as well as since the seventeenth century (the modern state). But these trends, if they continue to develop, have the potential to alter international relations and make them more similar to premodern history. The underlying theme is that the exercise of monopoly of violence, the defining trait of the modern state, may be increasingly more difficult to attain. As a consequence of these developments, deterrence and diplomacy, the two main tools to mitigate the violence of strategic interactions, are likely to be less effective. And the resulting security landscape will be characterized by more violence, geographically spread out and affecting local communities rather than entire states, and with the potential of inflicting increasingly larger casualties and destruction.

3.1 The Rise of New Actors

Over the past few decades the world has witnessed a marked expansion in the spectrum of political actors in international relations. These actors effectively compete with the traditional modern state as sources of political expression and of wealth, and sometimes of security. Some new actors are "above" the nation state, forming large conglomerates of states, such as the United Nations or the European Union, the latter compared

---

[4] The literature on the decline of the modern nation state is vast. See, for example, Martin Van Creveld, *The Rise and Decline of the State* (New York, NY: Cambridge University Press, 1999); Susan Strange, "The Defective State," *Daedalus*, Vol. 124, No. 2 (Spring 1995), 55–74; Susan Strange, *The Retreat of the State* (New York, NY: Cambridge University Press, 1996); Richard Rosencrance, *The Rise of the Virtual State* (New York, NY: Basic Books, 1999); Jean-Marie Guehenno, *The End of the Nation-State* (Minneapolis, MN: University of Minnesota Press, 1995).

by some to the old Holy Roman Empire.[5] The effect, or at least the desired effect, of these international institutions is to pool sovereignty into a larger, regional or global, entity, thereby weakening the ability of individual states to act alone. Other actors are small states or even cities (e.g. Singapore or Hong Kong), akin to the commercial cities that flourished in the Middle Ages. The promise of such polities is that their economic potential is not related to territorial size and endowment of natural resources, two features that defined the strength of the modern state.[6] Rather their skill in integrating into a global web of trade as hubs or service providers would determine their ability to be relevant strategic actors on the global scene. A very different set of strategic actors that attracted renewed attention in the 1990s are tribes and clans, such as those that tore Somalia apart. And finally, the terrorist attacks of 9/11 brought to the fore the most elusive and yet the most problematic new actor, the transnational networks of terrorists. All of these actors are not the typical modern nation state that was the preeminent and often only actor on the international scene of the past two or three centuries.

More importantly, they are all part of a larger trend that is creating competition for the modern state. The state may still claim to be the supreme authority over a demarcated territory, but arguably it is losing some of its attributes of power because of globalization, broadly defined.[7] Perhaps this decreased autonomy of the state is most visible in the economic sphere, where traditional policy tools, such as monetary policy, are rendered less influential.[8] But a more worrisome and dangerous development is in the security realm, as the state is increasingly less capable of maintaining its modern monopoly over violence.

Some of these actors are not necessarily disruptive of the existing modern international order as they benefit from the presence of international institutions and rule-based interactions, reinforcing them in the process. In fact, the bigger challenge to the geopolitical *status quo* is likely to arise from revisionist powers such as China and Russia, rather than from international institutions, commercial hubs, or multinational corporations. But the biggest question mark, and potentially the most difficult problem, may arise from violent non-state groups. They present a

---

[5] Harold James, *The Roman Predicament* (Princeton, NJ: Princeton University Press, 2006), 118–140.
[6] Jeffrey Herbst, "Let Them Fail: State Failure in Theory and Practice," in Robert Rotberg, ed., *When States Fail* (Princeton, NJ: Princeton University Press, 2004), 305.
[7] Strange, *The Retreat of the State*.
[8] See, for instance, Ben Bernanke, "Globalization and Monetary Policy," Remarks at the Fourth Economic Summit, Stanford Institute for Economic Policy Research, Stanford, CA, March 2, 2007, online at www.federalreserve.gov/boarddocs/speeches/2007/20070302/.

serious challenge because they are becoming increasingly more capable of greater lethality and can sustain themselves outside of the political and economic order established by states. They thrive, in fact, on criminal activities, which are enhanced by porous borders and global communications – the dark side of globalization. Their objectives and nature vary, but they are united by three related trends that are making them possible and desirable: a proliferation of tools of violence, the rise of ungoverned spaces, and the importance of controlling men rather than territory. These parallel the trends described in Chapter 1 that have characterized premodern history.

3.1.1 Proliferation of Violence

The first trend is the growing availability of lethal technologies, empowering small groups and even individuals, and tilting the balance in their favor. The increased lethality of military technology is part of a long historical trend, moving from "crossbow to H-bomb."[9] One side effect of this trend is that the relationship between lethality and manpower has changed. The ability to inflict casualties and destruction is no longer directly related to the ability to organize large numbers of people and manage vast stores of resources. For instance, the destruction of a city – or even an entire state – no longer requires the involvement of a large army or a mass invasion led by armor, air power, and infantry divisions. Economist Martin Shubik put it most clearly in a 1997 article where he argues that since the 1950s the historical necessity to have large and well-organized groups or states in order to be lethal has been weakening. The modern age in particular was characterized by the growth of a centralized state driven by rapid technological developments. "The shifts, as units such as the battleship grew larger, called for more centralized organization and formalized routine for running many hundreds of individuals, who were strangers, in the same ship. Better logistics enabled army size to grow and called for the creation of a general staff to aid the commanding general. But, not all innovations call for bigger size and more organization. An increase in lethality or mobility of a small unit, be it a ship, tank, or a commando group, can send the size requirements down, not up."[10] As a result, "the size of the group needed to become an organized agency of mass destruction is fast shrinking to a handful of individual, less in number

---

[9] Bernard Brodie and Fawn Brodie, *From Crossbow to H-bomb* (Bloomington, IN: Indiana University Press, 1973).
[10] Martin Shubik, "Terrorism, Technology, and Socioeconomics of Death," *Comparative Strategy*, Vol. 16, No. 4 (October–December 1997), 406.

than most terrorist organizations."[11] You can be poor, small, and lacking a vast administrative apparatus, and yet be very lethal. Fewer men and resources are needed to inflict increasingly larger damage. As became clear in September 2001 in the United States, and in countries from Spain and France to India in the succeeding years, a few, relatively impoverished individuals can disrupt the political and economic lifestyle of a major state that by all metrics should be capable of deterring, defeating, or absorbing an attack without too great an effort.

Parallel to this effect of empowering small groups there is the impact that more lethal technologies have on states. Some argued decades ago that the state has been undermined by advances in air power and nuclear weapons.[12] The development of technologies capable of inflicting "megadeath," effectively terminating the life of the targeted state, has weakened the central claim of the modern state, namely, of being the main and perhaps only provider of security to its citizens.[13] It is true that the ability of states to deter a nuclear attack by developing their own nuclear weapons, a technical feat that so far has been firmly in the hands of modern states, has somewhat countered this trend. The state was indispensable, and thus accepted as the main source of security and legitimacy, because advances in modern military technologies required the infrastructure and resources provided only by states, and every offensive capability (e.g. artillery, air power, or nuclear weapons) has been countered by technologies provided by states – and only by states (e.g. fortresses, thicker armor, larger armies, and nuclear weapons as deterrent). There is no guarantee, however, that this cycle can be maintained, and it is conceivable that at a certain point states will be incapable of providing countermeasures against a technology or a strategic actor. If, for instance, the ability of states to provide nuclear deterrence weakens, such states will have a difficult time justifying their existence and generating allegiance of people.[14] In brief, the claim of the state to be the most effective and only security provider is under challenge.

---

[11] Shubik, 400.
[12] John H. Herz, "Rise and Demise of the Territorial State," *World Politics*, Vol. 9, No. 4 (July 1957), 489.
[13] The term "megadeath" is from Herman Kahn, *On Thermonuclear War* (Princeton, NJ: Princeton University Press, 1961). Kahn, however, thought that states had an important role in preventing such a war through deterrence, in winning it were deterrence to fail, and in guaranteeing the survival of society in the aftermath of the war.
[14] The "return address" problem of non-state actors is particularly problematic for deterrence. For a contrary view, see Caitlin Talmadge, "Deterring a Nuclear 9/11," *The Washington Quarterly*, Vol. 30, No. 2 (Spring 2007), 21–34; Michael Miller, "Nuclear Attribution as Deterrence," *The Nonproliferation Review*, Vol. 14, Issue 1 (March 2007), 33–60.

On top of being more lethal, military technology is also proliferating. The proliferation of the most destructive forms of weapons, such as nuclear, biological, and chemical capabilities, is of course the most worrisome. And the problems of nuclear proliferation – how to hinder it and, if that does not succeed, how to mitigate the consequences of a polynuclear world – attract most of the attention in policy and academic circles. But the problem of proliferation is wider, and the spectrum of the technologies that are widely spreading ranges from small arms to nuclear weapons. The diffusion of technology has four mutually reinforcing causes that are tilting the balance away from modern states and are empowering stateless actors.

First, most technologies can be used in multiple ways: Civilian airplanes can be turned into guided missiles, cars can be transformed into bombs, and computers and cell phones can be used to disrupt the economic and political life of a society. These tools are readily available, especially in developed countries, which can as a result be more vulnerable. The more technologically advanced the society, the easier it is to find technologies that can be used against it. As an article in *Wired Magazine* put it, insurgents in Iraq "cherry-pick the best US tech: disposable email addresses, anonymous Internet accounts, the latest radios ... And every American-financed move to reinforce Iraq's civilian infrastructure only makes it easier for the insurgents to operate. Every new Internet café is a center for insurgent operations. Every new cell tower means a hundred new nodes on the insurgent network."[15] With relatively limited resources and knowhow, a small group can find the most effective technologies to inflict serious costs on a state. The case of UAVs is also indicative. A few years ago their development and use was limited to a handful of states, with the United States being the most visible adopter in Iraq and Afghanistan. But some of the low-end, reconnaissance UAVs are now widely used by small states but also non-state groups, from Hamas to the all-volunteer "Donbass" battalion fighting against Russian forces in Ukraine.[16]

Second, military technological advances are undoubtedly increasing the power of states by giving them greater firepower, longer reach, more

---

[15] Noah Shachtman, "How Technology Almost Lost the War: In Iraq, the Critical Networks Are Social – Not Electronic," *Wired Magazine*, 15: 12, online at www.wired.com/politics/security/magazine/15-12/ff_futurewar.

[16] Some of these platforms can be built with off-the-shelves material and can be used by individuals with little training. See the site DIYDrones at http://diydrones.com/. Moreover, even a small UAV can be used as a precision-guided missile to strike at a civilian plane or a stationary target. See "Hamas unveils new UAV," *Jane's Defence Weekly*, July 15, 2014, at www.janes.com/article/40768/hamas-unveils-new-uav. For a video of the UAV of the Ukrainian "Donbass" battalion in action in July 2014, see http://youtu.be/uzu1eUxgN20.

precise and timely information, and in the case of the most developed powers, stealth.[17] Yet, history also indicates that for every technological advance there is a corresponding advance in the tools and skills to counteract its effect. For every new weapon, sooner or later there is an instrument or behavior that minimizes its power and usefulness. In many cases, it seems that it is cheaper to build and implement countermeasures to a new technology. A telling example was the widespread availability of relatively cheap and easy-to-use IEDs in Iraq, adopted by insurgents to inflict serious costs on US forces. Expensive vehicles, often heavily armored, could be seriously damaged by these homemade bombs.[18] The cheapness of these countermeasures has the effect of empowering individuals and groups that with few resources can make expensive, state-built platforms vulnerable and perhaps even useless in the field. An immediate impact of this development is that, as will be pointed out later on, it is more difficult to conquer and control territory through coercion because the effectiveness, availability, cheapness, and ease of use of these technologies creates incentives to resist foreign forces and imposes upon them costs that may be operationally as well as politically prohibitive.[19]

Third, there is a wide availability of weapons. In part, this is made possible by stocks of mothballed Cold War arsenals that can be purchased from states with relative ease. But in part, the flow of weapons is facilitated by the weakening of states, which in some regions are increasingly losing control over their territories. As a result, it becomes possible to acquire a vast array of munitions, including some, such as portable surface-to-air missiles or sophisticated antitank mines and missiles, that require the

---

[17] As the US military calls it, "full spectrum dominance" is based on "dominant maneuver," "precision engagement," "focused logistics," and "full dimensional protection," all of which require investment in new state-of-the-art technologies. The assumption behind this vision seems to be that (a) it is possible to achieve clear and unchallenged superiority (or even dominance) over potential enemies, and (b) this can be attained only by a state with massive resources, such as the United States. See US Department of Defense, *Joint Vision 2020* (2000), available online at www.dtic.mil/jointvision/jvpub2.htm.

[18] Rick Atkinson, "Left of Boom," September 30–October 3, 2007, *Washington Post*. Online at www.washingtonpost.com/wp-srv/world/specials/leftofboom/index.html.

[19] The spread of precision-guided weapons is particularly important because it gives great leverage to small groups. As Thomas Mahnken observes, "In a world where many states possess precision-strike systems, traditional conquest and occupation will become much more difficult. They may, in fact, become prohibitively expensive in some cases. Imagine, for example, if the Iraqi insurgents had been equipped with precision-guided mortars and rockets and had reliably been able to target points within Baghdad's Green Zone. Or imagine that the Taliban were similarly armed and were thus able to strike routinely the US and Afghan forward operating bases that dot the Afghan countryside. US casualties could have amounted to many times what they have been in either theater." Thomas G. Mahnken, "Weapons: The Growth & Spread of the Precision-Strike Regime," *Daedalus*, Vol. 140, No. 3, The Modern American Military (Summer 2011), 53.

backing of a state's industrial resources to design and produce.[20] Offensive technology is increasingly available on the open market for low prices and requires little knowledge of how to operate it.[21] This is particularly the case for small arms, which are widely available. One impact is that, as a RAND monograph observes, maritime piracy is on the rise because, among other reasons, "the global proliferation of small arms has provided pirates (as well as terrorists and other criminal elements) with an enhanced means to operate on a more destructive and sophisticated level."[22] Another widely available platform is the GPS (Global Positioning System). While the GPS signal is under US control, access to it is widespread, as anyone with a smartphone knows. This gives capabilities to third parties, from less-developed hostile states to individuals, that were not available a few decades ago. The enemy now can self-locate as well as target a stationary objective with great precision, giving him an enormous capability, especially in the initial stages of a conflict because the United States could limit access to the system in the case of a war. This also, incidentally, puts a premium on surprise attacks by these actors as once hostilities have been initiated the United States is likely to turn off free access to GPSsignals.[23]

Fourth, technology in general, and military technology in particular, is diffusing rapidly because it is becoming easy to use. The modern technological trend of the past few centuries has been to favor large states with skilled manpower. Lethality required wealth and resources, and therefore access to it was restricted to well-organized (and to a certain degree,

---

[20] A NATO program for states participating in a variety of agreements with the alliance, the "Trust Fund," has destroyed or cleared over the past decade an astounding quantity of weapons, among them 10,000 surface-to-air missiles and 1,470 man-portable air defense systems (MANPADS). See www.nato.int/cps/en/natohq/topics_52142.htm.

[21] See also Frank G. Hoffman, "Small Wars Revisited: The United States and Nontraditional Wars," *Journal of Strategic Studies*, Vol. 28, No. 6 (December 2005), 925–926.

[22] Peter Chalk, "The maritime dimension of international security: terrorism, piracy, and challenges for the United States," RAND Monograph 697 (2008), p. xii, available online at www.rand.org/pubs/monographs/2008/RAND_MG697.pdf. On modern piracy, see also Gal Luft and Anne Korin, "Terrorism Goes to Sea," *Foreign Affairs*, Vol. 83, No. 6 (November/December 2004), 61–71. Martin Murphy, "Contemporary Piracy and Maritime Terrorism," *Adelphi Paper*, No. 388 (International Institute for Strategic Studies, 2007); Martin Murphy, "Suppression of Piracy and Maritime Terrorism," *Naval War College Review*, Vol. 60, No. 3 (Summer 2007), 23–45.

[23] US rivals have been developing competing systems (Russia's GLONASS, China's BeiDou, EU's Galileo). For a dated but still interesting analysis of the GPS system and its effects on international security, see Scott Pace et al., *The Global Positioning System: Assessing National Policies* (Santa Monica, CA: RAND, 1995), especially chapter 3, at www.rand.org/pubs/monograph_reports/MR614.html; Irving Lachow, "The GPS Dilemma: Balancing Military Risks and Economic Benefits," *International Security*, Vol. 20, No. 1 (Summer, 1995), 126–148.

territorially large or at least resource-rich) states. The examples that are most often adduced are artillery (the "gunpowder revolution"), airpower, and nuclear weapons combined with missile technology.[24] In all of these cases, larger, wealthier, and better-administered states tended to have an advantage over actors that did not possess the resources and organization necessary to develop, acquire, and use increasingly more expensive and complex weapons. In part this had to do with the costs associated with the production of these platforms. But in part these "revolutions in military affairs" (RMA) favored complex training and technical skills that only well-organized states could generate in large enough numbers and with sufficient consistency. This includes the most recent technological revolution that put a premium on the capacity to integrate complex flows of information, surveillance, target identification, and acquisition to achieve a superior ability to "see and hit" enemy forces in real time. Such view of the RMA may benefit states, such as the United States, that have the intellectual knowhow and the material resources to plan, organize, train, and implement progressively more complicated technologies. In brief, this line of thinking posits that technological progress put a premium on societies and individuals capable of managing and employing increasingly more complex systems.

But it is also plausible to argue that the trend in technology is favoring the less sophisticated, the less wealthy, and the less organized. Technology and the ability to kill and inflict damage may be becoming cheaper and easier to use, with the effect of equalizing power among a variety of strategic actors. It has a democratizing effect. The technical knowledge is no longer confined to a few states, and is being replicated in states that have minimal resources (e.g. North Korea) and among groups with no deep reservoir of Ph.Ds. in engineering or computer science.[25] In a 1961 RAND study, Malcolm Hoag argued that the then security environment was beneficial to the United States because, among other factors, it demanded high wealth to be able to inflict casualties in war. As we move backward in history, that ratio of cost for casualties decreased,

---

[24] For good histories of these developments, see William McNeill, *The Pursuit of Power* (Chicago, IL: University of Chicago Press, 1982); Geoffrey Parker, *The Military Revolution* (New York, NY: Cambridge University Press, 1988); Macgregor Knox and Williamson Murray, eds., *The Dynamics of Military Revolution, 1300–2050* (New York, NY: Cambridge University Press, 2001). A recent book is Max Boot, *War Made New* (New York, NY: Gotham Books, 2006). Also, Andrew F. Krepinevich, "Cavalry to Computer: The Pattern of Military Revolutions," *The National Interest*, Vol. 37 (Fall 1994), 31–36; Eliot A. Cohen, "A Revolution in Warfare," *Foreign Affairs*, Vol. 75, No. 2 (March/April 1996), 43–44.

[25] On the diffusion of military technology, see Emily Goodman and Richard Andreas, "Systemic Effects of Military Innovation and Diffusion," *Security Studies*, Vol. 8, No. 4 (Summer 1999), 79–125.

and arguably in the future could decrease as well. It was, and it may be in the future, very cheap to kill. Moreover, some tools in history were so easy to use that anyone who had access to them became capable of threatening others, and thus of exercising coercion and engaging in strategic interactions. If a large number of actors acquire access to lethal weapons, the United States and any other great industrial modern state would lose some of their inherent advantages. As Hoag put it, an "era of cheap nuclear weapons and of spears are both disadvantageous to us."[26] Or to put it another way, there is a big difference between what is required to fly an F-22 or operate an aircraft carrier and what one needs to be able to build IEDs, use antitank missiles, fly small UAVs, or disrupt internet access.[27] The greater lethality and availability of the latter platforms empower the untrained, the less organized, the less educated, and less skilled. In fact, it can lead to a point when "super-empowered" individuals, even amateurs, can present serious threats to states.[28]

The result of this diffusion of technology is a proliferation of violence. Smaller and poorer – and stateless – groups can achieve more lethal results than a few decades ago. Globalization, understood here as the spread of technology and of knowhow, leads to the splintering of the world, and may generate the seeds of its own demise by undermining the authority and power of states. It is true that the technologies at the disposal of non-state groups – the modern day "barbarians" – are rarely of the same caliber in terms of lethality and complexity of those wielded by states. But they do not need to be because they are sufficient to inflict serious costs and damages on states, likely resulting in a change of their domestic and foreign policies.[29] Moreover, the objective of many of the modern non-state groups is not to replace a state, in part because they do not have the capabilities to lead a frontal assault on the state or, once destroyed, to rebuild and administer a state, and in part because they do not aspire to the responsibility of having a state. Their objective is to

---

[26] Malcolm W. Hoag, "On Local War Doctrine," RAND, P-2433 (August 1961), 18.
[27] The latter platforms are "demanding" technologies while the former are less so. The definition of "demanding technology" is, according to Tim Wu, that it "takes time to master, whose usage is highly occupying, and whose operation includes some real risk of failure." Tim Wu, "The Problem with Easy Technology," *New Yorker*, 21 February 2014.
[28] The "super-empowered" term is from Thomas Friedman, *The Lexus and the Olive Tree: Understanding Globalization* (New York, NY: Anchor Books, 1999), 14–15. On the role of amateurs and their growing power, see Jeff Howe, *Crowdsourcing* (New York, NY: Crown 2008), especially chapter 2.
[29] As some have observed, a further goal of these groups, as in the case of Al-Qaeda, is perhaps to spur the target state to react (or rather, overreact) to an attack in a way that would lead to its weakening. See James Fallows, "Declaring Victory," *The Atlantic Monthly*, September 2006.

weaken, disrupt, and delegitimize the state, thereby creating the space for the group to function and gain authority.[30]

3.1.2 Ungoverned Spaces

The ability of non-state actors to compete with states and be a disruptive force for the political order in various regions of the world is also tied to the existence of ungoverned spaces. These spaces are both an enabler of non-state groups and a result of the enhanced power of such groups. The gradually filling of the entire world with states – effectively closing the frontier that allowed barbarians to prosper – may be reversing for two reasons. First, despite appearing on maps as clearly delimited entities, many modern states are frail and incapable of exerting control over their territories in several regions of the world. Second, new communication technologies are allowing the rapid organizations of large groups outside of states' purview.

Since the early 1990s, many regions, vacated by the superpowers, became heavily destabilized, collapsing into a cycle of violence and turmoil.[31] In Sub-Saharan and East Africa, as well as in Southeastern Europe and Central Asia, states and their governments either disintegrated or lost their ability to impose order within their own territories.[32] Failed states or "ungoverned territories" are becoming the modern equivalent of the "barbarian" lands of Central Europe in Roman times or Central Asia until the eighteenth century or the North American Plains for the Spanish or early United States – places where empires had limited or no reach, and different forms of societal organization could arise and prosper. These areas, in fact, give rise to other ways of organizing social relations, often along tribal and clan lines (such as Somalia) or ethnic and religious affiliation (such as the former

---

[30] As David Kilcullen points out, in many cases, especially in Europe, the objective of terrorist groups is subversion, an early stage in the struggle between extremists and states. See David Kilcullen, "Subversion and Countersubversion in the Campaign against Terrorism in Europe," *Studies in Conflict & Terrorism*, Vol. 30 (2007) 647–666.

[31] Robert I. Rotberg, ""The New Nature of Nation-State Failure," *Washington Quarterly*, Vol. 25, No. 3 (Summer 2002), 85–96; Michael Desch, "War and Strong States, Peace and Weak States?" *International Organization*, Vol. 50, No. 2 (Spring 1996), 237–268. On the impact of external threats on the size of polities, see Alberto Alesina and Enrico Spolaore, "War, Peace, and the Size of Countries," *Journal of Public Economics*, Vol. 89 (2005), 1349–1350; Phil Williams, *From the New Middle Ages to a New Dark Age: The Decline of the State and US Strategy* (Carlisle, PA: Strategic Studies Institute, US Army War College, June 2008).

[32] Angel Rabasa et al., *Ungoverned Territories* (Santa Monica, CA: RAND, 2007); John Rapley, "The New Middle Ages," *Foreign Affairs*, Vol. 85, No. 3 (May/June 2006), 95–103.

Yugoslavia). These deeply rooted associations provide the public goods, from order and security to social services and education (as the Hezbollah in Lebanon), that the state has traditionally supplied in modern times. There is a logic to these regions, but it is not the logic of the state as a centralized hierarchical entity. It is the logic of decentralization based on allegiance to leaders rather than institutions, to ancient codes rather than laws, to ethnic and religious bonds rather than states.

These areas offer a space also to groups of terrorists, such as Al-Qaeda, that can organize out of the attentive sight of a state.[33] Over the past few years, the cases of Pakistan and Iraq, but also Somalia and to a degree Indonesia, have been used as examples of this connection between state failure and terrorism, especially of the Islamist kind.[34] The link between empty spaces or failed states and terrorists should not be exaggerated, however. Terrorists do not live in a vacuum, and can prosper in failed states only if they defeat or coexist with the local tribes and clans, as in the case of Waziristan in Pakistan. In fact, they are more likely to thrive in weak rather than failed or collapsed states. They need the cover of state sovereignty to protect them from foreign intervention and are better off in an environment that is relatively stable and not wrecked by uncontrollable violence and crime.

Technological changes are the second set of forces that have played a key role in creating spaces outside of state control. In fact, non-state groups, including terrorist ones, can organize quite effectively within well-functioning states, from Germany and Spain to Saudi Arabia, because states, especially liberal democracies, do not have full control over every aspect of social life. And arguably, these empty spaces have increased across the globe thanks to the widespread adoption of the internet as the preferred tool for communication. The internet is by its nature difficult to control by a state or any other organization, and it is

---

[33] See Princeton Lyman and J. Stephen Morrison, "The Terrorist Threat in Africa," *Foreign Affairs* Vol. 83, Issue 1 (January/February 2004), 75; R. W. Johnson, "Tracking Terror Through Africa," *The National Interest* (Spring 2004), 161–172; Robert Rotberg, "Failed States in a World of Terror," *Foreign Affairs*, July-August 2002, 127–140; Francis Fukuyama, *State-Building: Governance and World Order in the 21st Century* (Ithaca, NY: Cornell University Press, 2004), xi and 92–93; Ray Takeyh and Nicholas Gvosdev, "Do Terrorist Networks Need a Home?" *Washington Quarterly*, Vol. 25, No. 3 (Summer 2002), 97–108.

[34] Another effect of the presence of these ungoverned spaces is the rise in maritime piracy. See Martin Murphy, "Contemporary Piracy and Maritime Terrorism," *Adelphi Paper*, No. 388 (London: International Institute for Strategic Studies), especially 12–17; Peter Chalk, "The Maritime Dimension of International Security: Terrorism, Piracy, and Challenges for the United States," RAND Monograph 697 (2008), online at www.rand.org/pubs/monographs/2008/RAND_MG697.pdf.

analogous to the stateless regions of the world because it facilitates the formation of groups transcending borders.[35]

The great modern organizational ability is no longer restricted to the state. As in previous periods of dramatic improvements in communications (e.g. print, telegraph and railroad, and radio), new technologies lead to new ways of organizing people. It is becoming possible to organize and manage large groups without a state, using technologies (broadly speaking, the internet and its applications, but also widely available and relatively cheap tools like cell phones, digital cameras, and so on) instead of bureaucracies and institutions. New types of societies, often referred to as virtual networks, are arising outside of state control, across borders, and without the backing of governments. These networked groups are detached from a specific territory and thus do not need to administer it, setting them clearly apart from the state. They also lack a centralized, hierarchical structure typical of modern states.[36]

This trend is affecting the wealthy as well as the less-developed countries. While it is certainly true that there is a technological gap between the wealthy countries and the less-developed regions of the world, even in the poorest countries technologies are rapidly spreading. For instance, simple and common technologies, such as the cell phone and digital cameras, played an important role in popularizing the 2007 uprising in Burma, one of the most oppressive, isolated, and destitute countries in the world.[37] Similarly, in Egypt, "Facebook," a popular social network application, was an important space where tens of thousands (according to some estimates, close to 80,000) of individuals organized opposition to the government and mobilized for elections and demonstrations.[38] As

---

[35] Audrey Kurth Cronin, "Behind the Curve: Globalization and International Terrorism," *International Security*, Vol. 27, No. 3 (Winter 2002/03), 46–49; "A World Wide Web of Terror," *The Economist*, July 14, 2007, 28–30; Office of the Director of National Intelligence, National Intelligence Estimate, "The Terrorist Threat to the US Homeland," July 2007. Online at www.odni.gov/press_releases/20070717_release.pdf.

[36] On the rise of networks as effective forms of social organizations and their impact on war, see John Arquilla and David Ronfeldt, *The Advent of Netwar* (Santa Monica, CA: RAND, MR-789-OSD, 1996); John Arquilla and David Ronfeldt, eds., *Networks and Netwars: The Future of Terror, Crime, and Militancy* (Santa Monica, CA: RAND, MR-1382-OSD, 2001). On how new technologies will (or should) impact US warfighting, see Vice Admiral Arthur K. Cebrowski and John J. Garstka, "Network-Centric Warfare: Its Origin and Future," *Proceedings*, January 1998; Thomas Rid, "War 2.0," *Policy Review*, February/March 2007, online at www.hoover.org/publications/policyreview/5956806.html.

[37] Geoffrey A. Fowler, "'Citizen Journalists' Evade Blackout on Myanmar News," *Wall Street Journal*, September 28, 2007; Ben Arnoldy, "Downloading the Burma Uprising: Did It Help?" *Christian Science Monitor*, October 3, 2007.

[38] Maria Fam, "Egyptian Political Dissent Unites through Facebook," *Wall Street Journal*, May 5, 2008, A9.

became evident in many of these revolts, the internet, whether Facebook, Twitter, or any other platform, can serve as a tool to coalesce a large number of people quickly, but it is not an effective means of administering a polity. It aids in disrupting an existing political order, but not in building a new one.

Moreover, modern means of communications connect individuals and small groups that until now had limited contact or even knowledge of each other. A group in Grozny can communicate, and consequently, recruit, coordinate, spread the news, and fundraise, with an individual in a suburb of Paris or Peshawar or Moscow. As a result, the groups that arise from these interactions are deterritorialized, being based in what is essentially a virtual world.

Finally, these technologies are also exceptionally democratic. It is very easy to participate in a virtual group, and the main barriers are the availability of the technology and the ability to understand the language used. The *lingua franca* tends to be English, even on Islamist websites, in large measure because it allows them to reach a wider audience, spanning the entire globe. These technologies are also democratic in the sense that every participant can add his or her knowledge, skills, interests, and objectives without a central authority deciding the priorities or the hierarchy of values. The "open-source" nature of these technologies leads to a high level of decentralization of the group that does not possess a central repository of technical skills, ideological principles, or operational objectives.[39] As has been observed regarding the "Facebook" movement in Egypt, "young secular people can communicate, build relationships and express their opinions freely ... Every member in the 100,000-strong online community could be, at any given moment, a leader of a movement."[40]

Consequently, the growth and the direction of such groups are unpredictable because they do not follow a clear project but turn according to the inputs of all of its members. To use a metaphor adopted to distinguish two different methods of software development, these modern, networked, and stateless groups resemble a "bazaar" – a decentralized, rapid, and seemingly chaotic system – rather than a "cathedral" – a slow, methodical, and planned system.[41]

---

[39] On the "open-source" nature of terrorism and insurgency, see John Robb, "The Open-Source War," *New York Times*, October 15, 2005; John Robb, *Brave New War* (Hoboken, NJ: John Wiley & Sons, Inc., 2007).
[40] Sherif Mansour, "Egypt's Facebook Showdown," *Los Angeles Times*, June 2, 2008.
[41] See Eric S. Raymond, *The Cathedral and the Bazaar: Musings on Linux and Open Source by an Accidental Revolutionary* (San Francisco, CA: O'Reilly Media, 2001); Steven Weber, *The Success of Open Source* (Cambridge, MA: Harvard University Press, 2004).

The effect of these technologies is to facilitate the rise of political movements that are increasingly capable of playing a strategic role in international relations. Some have called this phenomenon "cyber mobilization" because it allows the rapid emergence of groups with a widespread reach and ability to inflict damage.[42] The state, with its large logistical infrastructure and management capacity, is not only being supplanted by these networked groups but also is unable to control them. This phenomenon, in fact, is occurring often in areas that are outside of state control, both geographically and virtually. It is difficult to extend centralized control over the internet, and even draconian attempts to filter or block it are only minimally effective. In brief, the railroad is being replaced by the internet as a different, more resilient, and decentralized mobilization tool.

Moreover, "cyber mobilization" is leading to the establishment of groups that can be more extremist than in the past. These technologies, in fact, link together individuals and groups that always existed across states and societies but lacked the capacity to meet and organize.[43] Without the ability to "cyber mobilize" they remained on the fringe of various societies; they were the small, oddball, and largely ineffective groups or the solitary individuals with large aspirations but limited or no power. An extremist individual in one state or one region was unable to participate in a larger group, unless he physically joined it. Hence, historically, the migration of people to join warrior groups (e.g. the *ghazi* that assaulted Byzantium from the thirteenth century on, or the Crusaders in Europe) was required to produce fearsome stateless actors. In the end, from the seventeenth century on, only a few large and efficient social organizations, such as the modern state, could garner the necessary power to compete in international relations, leaving the disconnected and individually small groups and individuals behind.

Now technologies are giving power to the motley groups and individuals that had been previously irrelevant as strategic actors on the international scene. Minority interests and passions can find expression, and individuals have greater choices as to what they can support and where they can belong. The logic behind this trend is analogous to what has been

---

[42] Audrey Kurth Cronin, "Cyber-Mobilization: The New *Levée en Masse*," *Parameters*, Summer 2006, 77–87; Timothy L. Thomas, "Cyber Mobilization: A Growing Counterinsurgency Campaign," *IOSphere*, Summer 2006. Online at www.army.mil/fm so/documents/cyber-mobilization.pdf.

[43] See also, Madeleine Gruen, "Online social networks expand a sense of community among members and supporters of extremists groups," online at http://counterterrorism blog.org/2008/06/online_social_networks_expand.php.

defined in business as the "long tail."[44] The many niche products, which previously had a small or no market, are now easy to find and can be matched with consumers. The market then may increasingly be composed of many small hits – the long tail – and a few great hits. By analogy, the international scene may be characterized by a few effective states but many small stateless actors (and they can also be on a spectrum ranging from a relatively large group to one or two individuals acting alone) – the long tail of international relations.

The strength and resilience of networked groups should not be exaggerated for three reasons. First, the sheer number of niche groups that arises in a network imparts a high level of instability, as they vie for more attention or as they seek to achieve their narrow objectives, which may be undermining the goals of others small groups. In other words, the "long tail" may be characterized by a chaotic, highly conflictual group of small non-state actors that are as opposed to existing states as they are to each other. Competition is more pronounced and life more difficult in the "long tail." Second, "cyber-mobilization" that creates networked groups is in a sense very ethereal. The resulting group lacks temporal stability as individuals and cells come and go. Without a territory that delimits the administrative scope of the organization and a set of institutions that imparts permanence, these groups can increase in strength as quickly as they can lose it. The ease with which they can incorporate new individuals is matched by the difficulty of retaining them. The open nature of the group also makes it vulnerable to being subverted by skillful propaganda or infiltration. Egyptian authorities, for instance, had most likely infiltrated the "Facebook" group of activists, many of whom were arrested and intimidated.[45] It is also very difficult for such groups to establish a political organization that can administer a polity: they arise as quickly as they can dissipate. They can therefore disrupt a polity but have a more difficult time rebuilding and administering it. The third reason why these stateless, niche groups are impermanent and vulnerable is that the technology they use can be used against them. It is impractical, and most likely impossible, to devise ways of preventing the spread of these technologies and of eliminating them. But these technologies, from the internet to the use of cell phones, are not invulnerable and have as many weak points as they have advantages. For instance, networks rely on a few, well-connected "nodes" or individuals,

---

[44] Chris Anderson, "The Long Tail," *Wired*, Vol. 12, No. 10 (October 2004). Online at http://web.archive.org/web/20041127085645/http://www.wired.com/wired/archive/12.10/tail.html.

[45] Ellen Knickmeyer, "Fledgling Rebellion on Facebook Is Struck Down by Force in Egypt," *Washington Post*, May 18, 2008, A1.

whose elimination can have a serious negative impact on the cohesiveness and effectiveness of the group.[46]

3.2 The Rise of New Objectives

The second feature of the current international environment that makes it similar to premodern times is that many strategic actors pursue nonterritorial objectives. They fight for the allegiance or respect of people, for glory and prestige, or for ideological and religious objectives that transcend material calculations.[47] Control over resources is, and will be, important and will continue to fuel conflicts, but it is clear that, because of the trends described earlier, many groups do not need large infrastructures and vast resources to inflict heavy damage on states, to force their enemies to change their behavior, and consequently to be considered strategic actors.[48]

Not only is there no need to seek a state, but also there are serious drawbacks associated with controlling a state. In fact, control over a state and its resources may be unappealing to many groups because it may force the groups to moderate their aspirations and reach. Often these objectives carry religious overtones, marking a revival of religion as a motivating factor in politics.[49] For instance, as some experts argue, many of today's terrorist organizations are motivated by religion, rather than by ideology, separatism, or nationalism as was the case in the previous decades.[50] And many domestic conflicts are similarly characterized

---

[46] Bruce W. Don et al., *Network Technologies for Networked Terrorists* (Santa Monica, CA: RAND, 2007), chapter 3, 49–64, and 66.

[47] See Richard Schultz and Andrea Dew, *Insurgents, Terrorists, and Militias* (New York, NY: Columbia University Press, 2006), 5–6.

[48] On resource-driven conflict, see Thomas F. Homer-Dixon, *Environment, Scarcity, and Violence* (Princeton, NJ: Princeton University Press, 2001); Michael Klare, *Resource Wars* (New York, NY: Henry Holt and Co., 2001); National Intelligence Council, *Global Trends 2025: A Transformed World*, online at www.dni.gov/nic/PDF_2025/2025_Global_Trends_Final_Report.pdf, especially 63–67.

[49] See Lilla; "The New Wars of Religion," *The Economist*, November 1, 2007; Thomas F. Farr, "Diplomacy in an Age of Faith," *Foreign Affairs*, March/April 2008, 110–124; Fabio Petito and Pavlos Hatzopoulos, eds., *Religion in International Relations: The Return from Exile* (New York, NY: Palgrave Macmillan, 2003); Scott M. Thomas, *The Global Resurgence of Religion and the Transformation of International Relations* (New York, NY: Palgrave Macmillan, 2005); Jonathan Fox, "Religion as an Overlooked Element of International Relations," *International Studies Review*, Vol. 3, Issue 3 (2001), 53–73. For a critical perspective, see Alan Wolfe, "And the winner is ... ", *The Atlantic Monthly*, March 2008.

[50] Jessica Stern, *Terror in the Name of God: Why Religious Militants Kill* (New York, NY: Harper Collins, 2003); Mark Juergensmeyer, *Terror in the Mind of God* (Berkeley, CA: University of California Press, 2001). A critic of this view is Pape, *Dying to Win*. For a debate on Pape's argument, see James D. Kiras, "Dying to Prove a Point: The

by religious divides, rather than ethnic or ideological differences.[51] The challenge for such groups is that managing a state requires some political compromise, which undermines the purity of the religious ideas.[52] Controlling a state, then, often leads to disillusionment, weakening the appeal and thus the power of the group. This is one of the reasons why, for instance, Islamist groups by and large remain stateless. As Oliver Roy points out, Islamic fundamentalists "distrust the state. Their quest for a strict implementation of *sharia* with no concession to man-made law pushes them to reject the modern state in favour of a kind of 'libertarian' view of the state: the state is a lesser evil but is not the tool for implementing Islam."[53] The disappointment with political Islam leads then to the search for a globalized "umma," a stateless community of believers. Moreover, this process of rejecting the state starts a cycle of radicalization: because a radical idea can never be fully implemented through the state, the group that believes in it will globalize its efforts (and become deterritorialized and stateless), and in turn it can become even more radical because it does not need to compromise its goals. Moreover, the possession of a state is not a good fit for those who pursue niche, narrow objectives. The technologies mentioned earlier allow the formation of groups that are held together by an often very narrow concern (ranging from worries about "carbon footprints" to human rights or anti-American sentiments, and more). Such groups have no interest in establishing a state not only because its members are most likely to be geographically very dispersed but also because there is no larger idea (whether ethnic or cultural similarity, or broader aspirations) uniting the various members.

The possession of a state is also risky, making the barbarian group more vulnerable. A state is a target that can be threatened, pressured, deterred, and, if necessary, destroyed. It functions because it has administrative entities with physical addresses; it maintains order over a territory

---

Methodology of *Dying to Win*," *Journal of Strategic Studies*, Vol. 30, Issue 2 (2007), 227–241; David Cook, "A critique of Robert Pape's *Dying to Win*, *Journal of Strategic Studies*, Vol. 30, No. 2 (2007), 243–254.

[51] Jonathan Fox, "The Rise of Religion and the Fall of the Civilization Paradigm as Explanations for Intra-State Conflict," *Cambridge Review of International Affairs*, Vol. 20, No. 3, September 2007, 361–382.

[52] The zeal that characterizes extremists is not a substitute for administrative skills. The everyday functioning of a state requires managers, not charismatic advocates for a millenarian cause that can perhaps move a mass of people in the pursuit of a distant and thrilling objective but cannot motivate people to work in a bureaucracy. An analogous situation arises in business settings when innovators need to implement their concepts by seeking financing, new markets, and production processes. Startups then often have to search for seasoned managers to administer their rise because innovators have great ideas but not always the experience or interest necessary to turn them into a working reality.

[53] Oliver Roy, *Globalized Islam* (New York, NY: Columbia University Press, 2004) 281.

Rise of New Objectives

through police and military forces; it draws resources from the local economy. All of these features present targets that either do not exist or are less well defined when the group maintains its barbarian, stateless characteristics. The advantages of being stateless increase when there is a state, or empire, that has clear military superiority.[54] The state becomes a burden because it has to be defended, a feat that is difficult to achieve in moments of great unbalance of power. It is not surprising therefore that many groups choose to keep a low, stateless footprint: they are "barbarians by design" in James Scott's phrase.[55]

To put it differently, for a great power the price of military supremacy is the rise of an enemy that tries to avoid presenting a target by maximizing his ability to seek cover, to conceal, and to disperse.[56] The best way to minimize military inequality is by not having state institutions and territory, which, combined with the responsibility to protect and organize a society as well as the industrial and economic infrastructure, come with a state. Unlike a state, a decentralized, dispersed, and stateless actor is better suited to act without the danger of retaliation. The rise of terrorist networks such as Al-Qaeda, therefore, can be seen as a response to the clear supremacy enjoyed by the United States in the last two decades of the twentieth century.

The desire to avoid the burden of the state is noticeable among even the most powerful and effective groups. For instance, albeit probably capable of taking over the weak central government of Lebanon, Hezbollah has preferred to maintain their "sub-state" role, thereby limiting their responsibility and hence their vulnerability to attacks. As their leader Hassan Nasrallah said in May 2008, "We don't want authority in Lebanon... We don't want to control Lebanon."[57] Having a state would most likely weaken the ability of Hezbollah to attack Israel, whose military forces could therefore find identifiable targets. As it is, Hezbollah can fade away when necessary, leaving Israel with the difficult decision to punish the state and people of Lebanon or try to find the concealed and dispersed Hezbollah fighters. In brief, it is difficult to bomb, and thus coerce and deter, stateless actors. Statelessness gives you impunity, and it allows you to survive the retaliatory actions of a powerful state.

[54] It has been often observed that asymmetric war and terrorism are tools of the poor. This is true on the tactical as well as the larger, strategic level. Statelessness is an asset of those who cannot, or do not want to, challenge directly a great power, or at least that are aware of the great power's reach and adapt their political nature to present the smallest target possible.
[55] Scott, *The Art of Not Being Governed*, 3.
[56] On the tactics of "cover, conceal, and disperse," see also Stephen Biddle, "The Past as Prologue: Assessing Theories of Future Warfare," *Security Studies*, Vol. 8, No. 1, 1–74.
[57] Robert F. Worth, "Hezbollah Leader Plays Down Group's Political Aims in Lebanon," *New York Times*, May 27, 2008.

Finally, another set of objectives that is coming back to the strategic landscape is religion. Until recently, religion as a key source of social cohesion, transcending state borders, has been understudied in security studies.[58] In part the modern reluctance to examine religion in international politics stems from the separation of "church and state," the secular conceit that the realm of politics can be neatly removed from religion, that the management of state administration does not intersect with the ultimate questions. According to this view, religion is a private matter and it ought not to have much impact on the public square. This modern view was reinforced by the Cold War, a clash between two ideologies that, albeit based on assumptions (that is, acts of faith) about human nature and society, denied the existence and the political relevance of the transcendental. It was an often violent confrontation between two different plans for organizing society, a seemingly nonreligious conflict that defined the geopolitical map of the second half of the twentieth century. The end of the Cold War, but also a broader sense that a modern perspective on politics that eliminates religion as a key variable did not account for important aspects of human behavior, brought religion back into the study of international politics. The academic swings of interest do not necessarily mean, therefore, that religion was not an objective or a motivation over the past decades, or two or three centuries, but merely that it was not studied with sufficient attention.

But it is also plausible to see a real resurgence of religion as a factor in international politics, and not just as a product of academic fashions. There are multiple reasons why this could be the case: the uprooting of large segments of populations through rapid urbanization or migration who then seek community in religious groups, the natural desire to seek answers to the ultimate questions, the dissatisfaction with the gap between promises and reality of modern ideologies, and so on. One overarching reason, however, is that the attractiveness of the modern state as an object of allegiance and a source of social cohesion may be on the wane. The modern territorial nation state maintains unity by drawing lines on maps and eliciting support from the population through a mix of national pride and claims of guaranteeing peace and wellbeing. In a sense, it is the outcome of a transactional relationship in which the state provides certain public goods (security, welfare, and order) in exchange for support. That transaction may be fraying because the provision of some of these public goods, including security, is not as consistent as

---

[58] Daniel Philpott, "The Challenge of September 11 to Secularism in International Relations," *World Politics*, Vol. 55, No. 1 (October 2002) 66–95; Eliot Cohen, "Religion and War," *SAISphere* (2009), 12–15.

promised. Also, the push to seek an alternative to nationalism, perhaps to be replaced by a wider regional or global identity (such as the European Union, or the idea of a "global community"), is contributing to weakening the claims nation states can make. But the outcome is not necessarily a new global source of cohesion, but rather a search for other forms of community, of which religious identity is one. The point here is that the search for religious affiliation is deeply ingrained in human nature and it increases as other sources of authority and allegiance weaken.

Religion provides a powerful alternative to the state, especially when the particular state rejects any religious affiliation or connection.[59] A flip side of this reality is that statelessness is possible when there is a powerful idea that holds that group together, and religion offers one of the most powerful sets of ideas. This in itself is not a threat and does not lead to violence, but it allows for strong social cohesion outside of the state. In this sense, this is a return to premodern times, when religious affiliation among individuals and groups crossed the weak political borders, creating challenges to the authority of the temporal leaders. Moreover, as I indicate later on, strategic actors, state and non-state alike, that are motivated by religious visions are likely to behave differently than secular modern states.

3.3 The Future Premodern Strategic Landscape

The aforementioned features of the security environment are not completely new. They existed in some form over the past decades and centuries, but were perhaps in remission, overwhelmed by the sheer material power and ideological attractiveness of the nation state. Some premodern features continued to persist at the periphery of the power of industrial states, as colonial wars pitted modern polities against a mosaic of groups that fought using asymmetric means. That periphery stretched along an arc of instability from the Eastern Mediterranean to East Asia, with pockets in Africa and the Americas, but it was seen as an increasingly less relevant area, with actors that were on their way out from the strategic landscape or that, especially in the post-World War II decades, sought to assume the features of modern states. The process of decolonization may

---

[59] Paradoxically, perhaps, the more "secular" the state asserts to be, the greater the appeal of religion is among the population. Soviet regimes throughout Europe, for instance, have never succeeded in eradicating the religious faith of their populations; on the contrary, they have created greater incentives to seek solace and freedom in churches. In different circumstances, the secular claims of today's European states have not led to the demise of religion, and may be contributing to the growing disaffection of many religious individuals and groups who see secularism as a threat to their faiths.

108   The Return of Premodern History?

have marked the decline of European empires but it gave further expression to the predominance of the modern state and all this meant for international relations, namely greater effectiveness of diplomacy and more stable deterrence.

This may change, and in fact, is already gradually altering. The future strategic environment may be characterized by the ineffectiveness of diplomacy, a weakening of deterrence, and consequently more violent international relations. In this, it will resemble premodern history. These three features – ineffective diplomacy, weak deterrence, and greater violence – are hypotheses based on a reading of premodern history and a sense that there are growing parallels between it and our times. They are also contested by many academics and policymakers, who, for instance, argue in favor of the continued effectiveness of diplomacy and deterrence. In fact, some go so far as to argue that a progressive trend in history is resulting in a decrease of the devastation and casualties from violence and in the gradual end of war due to the moral amelioration of man, the menace of nuclear annihilation, or the domestic and international institutions that mitigate conflict.[60] We can hope such a progressive view of history is correct, but it is more plausible to take a less optimistic view of the future. If there is some agreement that the current and future strategic environment will carry premodern characteristics, such as the presence of multiple non-state actors and the resurgence of nonnegotiable objectives (e.g. religion), then it is at least plausible to expect that there will be analogous consequences. In what follows I delineate three related trends concerning diplomacy, deterrence, and the nature of conflicts.

3.3.1   Diplomacy

Diplomacy, both as a process and as an outcome, is less likely to occur and succeed. First, diplomacy as a process refers to the act of negotiating among various actors. It is relatively easy to engage a state in a diplomatic interaction because there are more or less established venues and institutions facilitating it. An integral part of a state apparatus is a hierarchy that can take and implement decisions as well as a diplomatic corps consisting of representatives in foreign capitals. The diplomatic effectiveness of state

---

[60] For example, Steven Pinker, *The Better Angels of Our Nature: Why Violence Has Declined* (New York, NY: Penguin Books, 2011); Ian Morris, *War! What Is It Good For?: Conflict and the Progress of Civilization from Primates to Robots* (New York, NY: Farrar, Straus and Giroux, 2014). For older arguments arguing for a "democratic" or a "nuclear" peace, see the classics: Michael Doyle, "Kant, Liberal Legacies, and Foreign Affairs," part I and part II, *Philosophy and Public Affairs*, Vol. 12 (1983), 205–235 and Vol. 12 (1983), 323–353; Kenneth Waltz, "The Spread of Nuclear Weapons: More May Be Better," *Adelphi Papers*, no. 171 (London: International Institute for Strategic Studies, 1981).

institutions has been enhanced over the past two or three centuries (and in particular since the end of World War II) by a gradual increase and strengthening in the number of international organizations (such as the United Nations) and norms (such as the inviolability of diplomatic envoys). The development of international institutions, in particular, has been seen as a positive development because they enhance the ability of states, and other strategic actors, to engage in negotiations and seek a peaceful resolution to any conflict of interest that may arise (or discover the underlying harmony of interest that ought to exist). They can serve as channels of communications, aiding the process of diplomacy.

This impressive armature of diplomacy is, however, fraying and becoming less capable of sustaining diplomatic engagements. The clearest example is in the relations between states and non-state groups (tribes, Al-Qaeda), relations that lack an institutional and normative framework. These groups do not participate in any form in international institutions, which therefore cannot abet an environment conducive to negotiations. In other words, international institutions have been established by and for states, and, taking the liberal institutionalist argument as valid, they may improve relations among states. But the modern barbarians do not, and are unlikely to, participate in them. They are outside of the modern international web of institutions.

Moreover, to different degrees, states are poorly set up to start the process of negotiations with such non-state groups. The initial problem that states face is lack of information: barbarians by their very nature arise and function below the radar screen of state bureaucracies in order to avoid being targeted. A state cannot engage in diplomacy with an actor whose existence is unknown until an attack has occurred. Even when these groups are fully operational, conducting attacks and thus becoming more visible, modern states often are confused as to which bureaucracy should try to engage such groups diplomatically. In the case of the United States, the various national security agencies have peculiar strength and advantages, but not a clear mandate or expertise. For instance, the Department of Defense, and in particular the various branches of the military (and even more specifically, the ground commanders directly involved in the region or in the conflict with the non-state group), have the most up-to-date information on the hostile group and most likely the easiest access to its members. Similarly, in other settings, intelligence agencies may be the most effective at engaging the modern barbarians. But diplomacy has been traditionally within the purview of the Department of State, and of analogous ministries of foreign affairs in other states. The point here is that even assuming that the non-state group is interested in starting a process of negotiations, it is not immediately clear which domestic institutions of the state are the most effective and the most appropriate. States have well-honed processes and bureaucratic roles for relations with other states; less so with non-state groups.

Domestic and international institutions are only part of the modern setting that aids diplomatic interactions. The other part, less visible but equally, if not more, important, is composed of the norms of diplomatic interactions. Many of these norms, such as diplomatic immunity, arose in ancient times because of recurrent interactions and quarrels among the various polities (city-states, empires, or nation states). The permanence of these strategic actors and of their interactions spurred the desire to mitigate the recurrent conflict, which in turn led to the mutual acceptance of rules such as the inviolability of envoys.[61] The less recurrent the interactions, the more difficult it is to create and implement such norms because the costs of violating them are lower. If the expectation is that the strategic interaction is short-lived because of the rapid rise and demise, or quick movement, of the barbarian group, there are smaller incentives to figure out such diplomatic norms. It is also less costly to break them because there may be no further interaction in which one could punish the violator. Finally, the cultural and political differences that separate many modern states from modern barbarians also impede the rise of shared norms regulating diplomatic interactions. The resulting fragility of diplomatic norms contributes to the increased difficulty of engaging in a process of negotiations.

The last challenge facing the process of diplomacy is related to the difficulty of implementing whatever agreement may be reached. In order to be able to negotiate it is necessary to have the expectation, or at least the promise, that the potential agreement will be implemented. Diplomats sign an agreement as representatives of a state that has the capability to implement and respect it. In the case of many non-state groups, their nonhierarchical structure makes implementation of an agreement dubious because the various subgroups may challenge the authority of their diplomatic representative or simply reject the final agreement. The institutional weakness of non-state barbarians means that it is relatively easy to disobey the current leadership, which may be engaged in negotiations. Instead of having to follow the negotiating leader, a disaffected cell can splinter away, seeking to continue the conflict. A case in point may be the rise of the Iraqi cell of Al-Qaeda led by Aby Musab al-Zarqawi, who

---

[61] Richard Langhorne, "The Regulation of Diplomatic Practice: The Beginnings to the Vienna Convention on Diplomatic Relations, 1961," *Review of International Studies*, Vol. 18, No. 1 (January 1992), 3–17.

had sworn allegiance to Osama bin Laden but chose to attack Shia targets instead of focusing on American ones. It was clear that it was impossible for the core Al-Qaeda leaders to control outer groups that chose to adopt a different strategy.[62] A decentralized group, in other words, has structural difficulties in engaging in a coordinated strategy and, by extension, in diplomacy.

Second, diplomacy as an outcome, namely, a negotiated settlement of conflicts, is also likely to become more difficult. As many have observed, diplomacy is more likely to succeed among actors that share something in common, whether it is a sense of legitimacy as in the Congress of Vienna or the desire for self-preservation as during the Cold War. It works best within a community of polities, a community that has some underlying unifying feature.[63] But when the actors are fundamentally different and do not share any values (legitimacy or culture) or structural features (that is, they are not states or entities whose main objective is the preservation of their territorial control), diplomatic settlements are less likely to occur. Given their organizational structure and values, it is difficult to imagine what political agreement could be reached with a group such as Al-Qaeda or Hamas. Moreover, it is more arduous to achieve negotiated settlements among states that do not share a similar cultural heritage. Some have observed that diplomacy in Europe has been more effective in restraining its states because they were bound by traditions of unity.[64] The more global international relations become, the less they will be moderated by such traditions and thus the less successful diplomacy will become. Hence, as Martin Wight wrote, "diplomatic standards probably reached their highest level during the century before 1914," declining steadily since then.[65] This is a problem that may be relevant even in the absence of modern barbarians, as relations between states that have culturally little in common are increasing due to enhanced communications, more

---

[62] See Mary Anne Weaver, "The Short, Violent Life of Abu Musab al-Zarqawi," *The Atlantic Monthly* (July/August 2006).

[63] See Nicholson.

[64] "Historically, an effective multilateral diplomatic dialogue within a states system has required more than the chance coexistence of a plurality of independent states with entangled interests. In the past, sustained dialogues developed and flourished between groups of states in a circumscribed geographical area and with a history of close contacts. Such groups of states formed, so to speak, a single magnetic field of political forces. Their identity was determined by membership of, or close contact with, a common civilization. Their diplomatic dialogue was conducted, and the pursuit of their separate interests was mediated, in terms of the concepts of law, honour, morality and prudence which prevailed in that civilization. Even war between them was not indiscriminate violence: it was regulated by the rules of the system." Adam Watson, *Diplomacy* (London: Eyre Methuen, 1982), 16–17.

[65] Wight, *Power Politics*, 120.

intense commercial exchanges, and great power projection capabilities. But it is certainly exacerbated by the rise of groups, such as the various Islamist ones, whose values are fundamentally opposed to those of Western states.

The fact that religious motivations are becoming more salient in political conflicts is contributing to the difficulty of successful negotiations. For instance, in the case of Civil Wars, if the parties in conflict make religious claims, that conflict is much less likely to terminate in a negotiated settlement.[66] Such a religion-infused conflict is also likely to be more violent than other wars, making negotiations more difficult.[67] Religious conflicts in the past have rarely been resolved peacefully, and arguably it was only by taking religion out of international politics, as done fitfully from 1648 on, that diplomatic agreements were made more likely. The pursuit of nonnegotiable objectives *ipso facto* makes diplomacy unlikely.

3.3.2 Deterrence

The second hypothesis about the future character of international relations is that deterrence is less likely to be successful. There are three reasons why this may be the case: a diminishing utility of industrial military force, the rise of stateless actors, the nature of the objectives pursued. All contribute to bringing back features more akin to premodern history.

First, the effectiveness of modern, industrial military force seems to be diminishing. As Klaus Knorr observed, changes in the utility of war and of military power "will occur if there are shifts, uncompensated by shifts in the opposite direction, in the values derived from, or the costs incurred by, the maintenance and use of national military power."[68] Recent conflicts are pointing to such a shift, increasing the costs of using military force by modern, industrial states without corresponding military or political gains.[69] A direct confrontation between two armies, or the threat of destruction of the enemy's industrial centers, or even the actual devastation of the enemy's territory, no longer delivers the strategic outcomes we came to expect in modern times. For instance, the 2006

---

[66] Isak Svensson, "Fighting with Faith," *Journal of Conflict Resolution*, Vol. 51, No. 6 (2007), 930–949.
[67] Monica D. Toft, "Getting Religion? The Puzzling Case of Islam and Civil Wars," *International Security*, Vol. 31, No. 4 (Spring 2007). 97–131.
[68] Klaus Knorr, *On the Uses of Military Power in the Nuclear Age* (Princeton, NJ: Princeton University Press, 1966), 12.
[69] See Rupert Smith, *The Utility of Force* (New York, NY: Knopf, 2005).

Israeli attack on Southern Lebanon did not inflict a decisive defeat on Hezbollah, and did not compel them to change their long-term strategic objective of annihilating Israel.[70] Similarly, the enormous technological advantage of the United States is proving to be of limited value, perhaps even counterproductive, when fighting amorphous groups and tribes in Iraq and Afghanistan.[71] The diminishing utility of force means that the ability of states to threaten, and thus coerce, other actors may be decreasing.

The decrease in the effectiveness of military force has two related components. First, it appears to be increasingly more difficult to impose a decisive military defeat on the enemy, whether a state or non-state group. The wide availability and relative cheapness of many weapons allow the defending party to inflict continued and high casualties on the attacker. The proliferation of violence, described earlier, creates less permissive zones, increasing the costs of victory. An example is the 2014–2015 war between Russia and Ukraine: A limited application of force by Russia has been insufficient to defeat in a decisive fashion a considerably weaker and disorganized Ukrainian military. This forced Russia to escalate by sending in more troops and arming the local separatist militias better. Because of the overwhelming military superiority of Moscow, it is of course entirely plausible to expect a Russian victory, but the costs of invading Ukraine have been and will continue to be high. The point is that the defense has an advantage that is likely to be larger than in the past, catching the offensive actor unprepared.

The second related reason why the application of military force is becoming less effective is that it is becoming more difficult to control territory. This is a trend-reversing development. The modern age has been characterized by territorial control: states fought for it and were defined by it. The most successful states were those that had the technical capabilities to expand and maintain their sway over territory. The imperial age of European overseas expansion was thus possible in part because of the "tools of empire," such as the steamboat, the machine gun, or quinine. These were technological advantages that allowed Europeans to extend their influence and control over vast stretches of

---

[70] Arguably, one reason for the Israeli push to Southern Lebanon was to restore the effectiveness of Israel's deterrent capability. It is still unclear whether the 2006 war achieved this objective. See Anthony H. Cordesman, "Preliminary 'Lessons' of the Israeli-Hezbollah War," CSIS paper, August 2006, 6–7, online at www.csis.org/media/csis/pubs/060817_isr_hez_lessons.pdf.

[71] Noah Shachtman, "How Technology Almost Lost the War: In Iraq, the Critical Networks Are Social – Not Electronic," *Wired*, Issue 15:12, online at www.wired.com/politics/security/magazine/15–12/ff_futurewar.

real estate.[72] This feature of the modern age may be changing. Technological advances allow the less developed and weaker actors to deny control to the stronger counterpart, even if they may not be able to exercise control themselves. A case in point is the growing ability of China to deny access to the littoral. China's A2/AD (anti-access/area denial) capability hinders its rivals' (the United States and its allies in this case) projection of power, but it does not necessarily establish firm control by China. It challenges the control or influence of the existing power, but it does not automatically replace it.[73] While the debate surrounding A2/AD is peculiar to the growing rivalry between China and the United States, the larger point is applicable to other regions and different conflicts. By saturating an area with relatively inexpensive weapons, it is possible to create "no-go zones" on land, air, and sea. And this capability is increasingly within reach of otherwise weak states as well as of non-state groups. These developments have a whole host of consequences for how wars may be waged or what the next arms race may look like. But they also have an impact on the relationship of deterrence that underwrites stability in international relations. The inability of a state to threaten credibly a drastic punishment on the enemy – the conquest and control of its territory – weakens deterrence.

An effective use of violence by small, less powerful, non-state groups is obviously not new, and modern history is replete with cases of insurgencies, asymmetric wars, and guerrillas. We should be careful therefore in heralding the arrival of a fundamentally new era.[74] Nevertheless, because of the diffusion of technology combined with the inherent challenges of such conflicts, non-state actors, whether individuals or groups, may be becoming more effective and capable of inflicting losses to states and even great powers, often forcing them to retreat. Over the past two decades, there has been a long list of setbacks for the forces of industrialized states, incapable of defeating or even mitigating the threat from non-state actors. Russia in Chechnya, the United States in Somalia, Israel in southern Lebanon and Gaza, and currently the United States in Afghanistan represent clear cases where modern, industrialized

---

[72] Daniel R. Headrick, *The Tools of Empire: Technology and European Imperialism in the Nineteenth Century* (New York: Oxford University Press, 1981). For an argument that does not deny but discounts the role of technology in imperial rule, see Paul MacDonald, "Is Imperial Rule Obsolete?: Assessing the Barriers to Overseas Adventurism," *Security Studies*, 18 (2009), 79–114.

[73] Jan van Tol et al., *AirSea Battle: A Point-of-Departure Operational Concept* (Center for Budgetary and Strategic Assessment, 2010); Aaron Friedberg, *Beyond Air-Sea Battle: The Debate Over US Military Strategy in Asia* (London: Adelphi Books, 2014).

[74] See also Hew Strachan and Sibylle Scheipers, eds., *The Changing Character of War* (New York, NY: Oxford University Press, 2011).

powers have encountered stateless groups, and have struggled to find a clear solution to the threat they posed. In the end, most states preferred to retreat, not because of the losses which, albeit tragic, were not devastating to the security of the state, but because of the recognition that the industrial might at their disposal was of little utility to defeat actors that could not be found, did not rely on large and complex infrastructures, and often fought for nonnegotiable objectives.[75]

The second factor that is weakening deterrence is the rise of non-state actors. Many of them are not based on territorial control but prosper in the "empty spaces" of failed states or virtual communities. As described in Chapter 2, the structure of non-state actors does not offer clear targets that can be threatened, and if necessary destroyed, thereby weakening the ability of states to threaten to impose clear costs on them.[76] As former US Secretary of Defense Donald Rumsfeld put it, we are fighting "enemies who have no territories to defend and no treaties to honor."[77] In some current cases, the group in question may simply not put a high value on the cities or population under its control, and may be willing to risk their devastation. For instance, the tactical behavior of Hezbollah in the 2006 war with Israel is an example of the group's willingness to sacrifice vast swaths of land under its own control and impose enormous suffering on its own population. By blending with the civilian population, groups like Hezbollah capitalize on their rival's (Israel in this case) reluctance to cause civilian casualties. Instead of deterring the enemy, the state is self-deterred because it deems the costs of its own retaliation as too high.

A related challenge has to do with the size of the group. The difficulty of targeting a non-state group, a modern barbarian entity, is obviously connected to its nonterritorial nature. But it is also related to its size. Smaller groups are more difficult to locate and track because of their mobility and less visible footprint. In fact, the smaller the grouping, the more difficult it is to deter it – with a single individual on one side of the spectrum who is perhaps the most difficult to deter, and with a large state on the other, being easier to deter. This connection between group size and its imperviousness to discovery and thus to threats has been noted already by Machiavelli. In a famous chapter on conspiracies in his *Discourses*, Machiavelli observed that "to be able to make open war on a prince is granted to few; to be able to conspire against them is granted to

---

[75] Daniel Headrick, *Power over Peoples: Technology, Environments, and Western Imperialism, 1400 to the Present* (Princeton, NJ: Princeton University Press, 2009).
[76] Smith, *Utility*, 273.
[77] Rumsfeld, Testimony, Senate Armed Service Committee, Washington DC, 23 September 2004.

116   The Return of Premodern History?

everyone."[78] This applies to war in general: Few can match a state openly, but many can do so through raids, terrorist attacks, guerilla warfare, and so on. The problem is that the "many" cannot organize and execute conspiracies without being discovered. The size of the group waging asymmetric war is relevant to its success, but in the exact opposite way of a peer competitor: the larger the group, the smaller its chances of success – as opposed to a conflict between states or peer competitors in which the larger (wealthier, with more manpower, and with greater industrial capacity) state has better chances of prevailing.

Finally, the *third* factor that weakens deterrence is the nature of the objectives pursued by the modern barbarians. Such groups seek violent confrontation with a manifestly stronger enemy because such a clash generates solidarity among their members.[79] Threats of an attack, therefore, will not deter such groups, and may have the opposite effect of encouraging the continuation of their behavior, resulting in a violent conflict.[80] In fact, as in premodern history, individuals join groups (in our times, terrorist groups) that are on the frontline of wars. Scores of Europeans have traveled, for instance, to Syria to join Islamist groups.[81] Violence attracts and breeds social cohesion. An attempt to deter such groups, that is, to threaten retaliation and violence, is welcome, rather than feared by the targeted actors.[82]

The modern faith in deterrence, reinforced by the development of nuclear weapons since the mid-twentieth century, may be therefore unjustifiably strong.[83] The decline of deterrence is not due to the fact that some actors are no longer rational, and thus incapable of calculating the potential repercussions of their actions. On the contrary, they are rational and their calculation is that their attacks will remain unpunished

---

[78] Niccolò Machiavelli, *Discourses*, trans. Harvey Mansfield and Nathan Tarcov (Chicago, IL: The University of Chicago Press, 1998), III:6, 226.
[79] For this dynamic in Hezbollah, see Cordesman, 6–8.
[80] Furthermore, it is difficult to deter against an enemy whose main tactic is to shock and surprise. See Thérèse Delpech, "The Imbalance of Terror," *The Washington Quarterly*, Vol. 25, No. 1 (Winter 2002), 38.
[81] Griff Witte, "Europeans are flocking to Syria. What happens when they come home?", Washington Post, 29 January 2014; Barak Mendelsohn, "Foreign Fighters—Recent Trends," *Orbis*, Vol. 55, Issue 2 (2011), 189–202.
[82] Max Abrahms, "What Terrorists Really Want," *International Security*, Vol. 32, No. 4 (Spring 2008), 100–101.
[83] In fact, nuclear weapons are not a source of deterrence. Rather, the apparatus of deterrence is erected in order to deal with nuclear weapons. If, as I suggest, deterrence is more difficult to achieve for a variety of reasons, the presence of nuclear weapons only makes the consequences more devastating. As Leon Wieseltier put it, "Nuclear weapons are not there to create deterrence. Deterrence is there to cope with nuclear weapons." Leon Wieseltier, "When Deterrence Fails," *Foreign Affairs*, Vol. 63, Issue 4 (Spring 1985), 829.

or that the punishment will bring more benefits than costs. Either because of technological changes or the nature of the strategic actors involved, it is simply more difficult to engage in a relationship of deterrence.

3.3.3 Likelihood and Levels of Violence

If diplomacy and deterrence lose some of their effectiveness, international relations are likely to become more violent. Diplomacy mitigates existing conflicts of interests, and in some cases it can resolve them. Deterrence maintains the status quo when there is little possibility to reach a negotiated settlement. To be effective, both demand certain prerequisite conditions, described earlier. When these conditions are absent, it becomes arduous to mitigate violence between strategic actors through diplomacy and deterrence. Another way to put this is that when diplomacy and deterrence do not work, states and all other strategic actors involved in political relations are more likely to revert to violence to resolve their claims and try to achieve their goals.[84]

The reduction in the effectiveness of diplomacy and deterrence can tell us merely that violence is more likely to erupt. But on the basis of existing trends it is also plausible to speculate about more precise characteristics that a resurgence of violence may take. First, violence is likely to be constant, and not, as in modern times, be a moment of great devastation followed by protracted periods of peace. Second, it is also likely to be more pervasive, geographically diffuse, and not limited to a more or less well-defined frontline as over the past two or three centuries. Third, violence also may be increasingly more devastating, perhaps causing greater casualties or perhaps simply being more disruptive of the economic and political life of states.

First, it is plausible to posit that future conflicts will be lengthy and resolvable only through force. Instead of periods of relative stability punctuated by large, increasingly more industrialized wars (think of the Napoleonic Wars, the Crimean War, the American Civil War, World War I, and World War II), the next decades may be more similar to the constant struggle and violence that characterized Roman-Germanic or

---

[84] Also, as it becomes clear that a confrontation cannot be solved by diplomacy and cannot be stopped by deterrence, preventive wars are more appealing. If the strategic parties expect a conflict, there is a premium on choosing to fight on one's own terms and timing. The premium put on prevention then exacerbates instability and tensions. David S. Yost, "NATO and The Anticipatory Use of Force," *International Affairs*, No. 83, 39–68; Colin Gray, "The Implications of Preemptive and Preventive War Doctrines: A Reconsideration," Strategic Studies Institute, US Army War College, July 2007; Peter Dombrowski and Roger Payne, "The Emerging Consensus for Preventive War," *Survival*, Vol. 48, No. 2 (June 2006), 115–136.

Chinese-Mongol relations, or the Middle Ages, or the protracted conflict between Byzantium and Arab tribes.[85] As in the past, conflicts infused by religion, wars *sub specie aeternitatis* so to speak, will likely be lengthy, perhaps even "timeless."[86] Even for traditional, modern states war is becoming increasingly less about territorial conquest. For instance, military interventions by the United States of the past two decades have not been to hold territory, but rather to alter the political conditions in the target region.[87] Territorial conquest can be finite, clearly delimited in time and space, whereas the alteration of political conditions is often endless and requires open-ended occupation or recurrent interventions. Finally, as military force becomes less capable of achieving decisive victories (a feature described earlier, one that affects negatively the ability of strategic actors to coerce), it will likely be employed for protracted periods of time. The war against Islamist groups has so far lasted fifteen years, longer than World War I and World War II combined. This is a paradoxical situation when the inability of force to deter leads to more violence as well as longer conflicts. Ineffective violence will thus be protracted.

Second, violence will be more pervasive, geographically diffused and not limited to a well-defined frontline or battlefield. The monopoly of violence of the modern state is being challenged, as mentioned earlier, by several trends, including the widespread availability of weapons and the concurrent resurgence of non-state and sub-state actors. The proliferation of violent actors, often detached from territorial concerns and capable of delivering violence to places far beyond the region of their origin, is lengthening, or rather muddling, the security frontier. Al-Qaeda gave us a sense of this, but other groups, such as Hezbollah, may be capable of fighting on what has been termed as the "global battlefield."[88]

The absence of distinct and secure frontlines also means that, as in much of premodern history, areas interior to states and empires will be increasingly vulnerable to disruptive attacks. It will be insufficient to fortify borders because, as in the past, many security threats arose from the ability of groups to overwhelm frontier defenses through rapidity, mass, and, what a

---

[85] Another term to describe this situation is a "forever war," following the title of a book on the wars in Afghanistan and Iraq. Dexter Filkins, *The Forever War* (New York, NY: Knopf, 2008).

[86] Smith, *Utility*, 291–4. Also, on how religious motivations affect the length of conflict, see Michael Horowitz, "Long Time Going: Religion and the Duration of Crusading," *International Security*, Vol. 34, No. 2 (Fall 2009), 162–193.

[87] Smith, *Utility*, 272.

[88] Stephen Biddle and Jeffrey A. Friedman, "The 2006 Lebanon Campaign and the Future of Warfare: Implications for Army and Defense Policy," Strategic Studies Institute (Carlisle, PA: US Army War College), September 2008, xv. Available on line at www.strategicstudiesinstitute.army.mil/pubs/display.cfm?pubID=882.

historian of Rome called, "seepage."[89] In the past, the walling of cities was a sign of the geographic spread of instability and violence. So it may be that now and in the future we will have to harden potential targets (cities, infrastructure, etc.) inside, rather than on the border of, the territory of states.[90] The slew of terrorist attacks in European cities over the past few years, for example, have resulted in a visible presence of military forces patrolling streets and armored vehicles blocking potential avenues of attack. The conflict is not something that happens "out there," along a distant front, but on the streets of cities inside the state.

Third, there is an ongoing debate on whether wars in the future will be more or less destructive than in the past. Some argue that wars are causing increasingly smaller levels of casualties for three reasons. First, medical advances allow greater chances of surviving battlefield wounds; second, wars are small-scale, fought by smaller armies over a geographically limited battlefield; and third, many of today's wars are accompanied or quickly followed by humanitarian activities that reduce wartime casualties even further.[91] These arguments are by no means widely accepted and have been contested in large measure because of the difficulty of measuring war casualties.[92] In fact, some argue that the numbers of post-1945 war casualties are vastly underestimated and it is at best unclear whether there is a downward trend in the destructiveness of wars.[93]

A hypothesis can be made, however, that the future security environment will be analogous to ancient history also in how destructive and disruptive conflicts may be. This hypothesis is based on four observations, derived from a reading of premodern history and of the premodern traits reappearing in current international relations.

---

[89] Averil Cameron, *The Mediterranean World in Late Antiquity, AD 395–600* (London: Routledge, 1993), 56.
[90] Christopher Dickey, *Securing the City* (New York, NY: Simon & Schuster, 2009).
[91] B. A. Lacina, N. P. Gleditsch, and B. M. Russett, "The Declining Risk of Death in Battle," *International Studies Quarterly*, Vol. 50, No. 3, 673–80; M. Spagat, A. Mack, T. Cooper, and J. Kreutz, "Estimating War Deaths: An Arena of Contestation," *Journal of Conflict Resolution*, Vol. 53, No. 6 (December 2009), 934–950; Human Security Report Project, *Human Security Report 2009 – The Shrinking Costs of War* (Simon Fraser University: 2009), online at www.humansecurityreport.info/2009Report/2009Report_Complete.pdf.
[92] See, for instance, the debate about World War II casualties in the Soviet Union. Michael Haynes, "Counting Soviet Deaths in the Great Patriotic War: a Note," *Europe-Asia Studies*, Vol. 55, No. 2 (2003), 303–309; Mark Harrison, "Counting Soviet Deaths in the Great Patriotic War: Comment," *Europe-Asia Studies*, Vol. 55, No. 6 (2003), 939–944; Michael Haynes, "Clarifying Excess Deaths and Actual War Deaths in the Soviet Union During World War II: A Reply," *Europe-Asia Studies*, Vol. 55, No. 6 (2003), 945–947.
[93] Z. Obermeyer, C. Murray, and E. Gakidou, "Fifty Years of Violent War Deaths from Vietnam to Bosnia: Analysis of Data from the World Health Survey Programme," *British Medical Journal*, Vol. 336, No. 7659, 1482–1486.

120   The Return of Premodern History?

First, the enemy is becoming increasingly more personal rather than abstract. We are fighting less against states and more against individuals and groups; these conflicts are also increasingly more caused by identity differences rather than power differentials or territorial disagreements.[94] Wars of territorial adjustment or of balance of power tend to end when the desired adjustment has been achieved, whereas conflicts of identity (and thus religion) end only with the assimilation or annihilation of the opponent.[95] In fact, according to a study, territorial wars result in the lowest percent of civilians being killed (47 percent of total casualties), while ethnic or religious conflicts kill the most civilians (76 percent).[96]

Second, as observed earlier, weapons are widely available, and their lethality is increasing. The parallel with premodern history is that technological differences between states and non-state groups are becoming smaller or at least easier to overcome.[97] Statelessness allows for great lethality. Now it has to be added that the capacity for destruction of modern weapons has increased exponentially. A "super-empowered" individual or group can cause destruction that until a few decades ago was feasible only at the hands of a state.

Third, violence organized by states can be ended by a decision of a central authority. But violence brought about by multiple, small, and often decentralized actors will not end by *fiat*. Like in premodern history, conflicts are less likely to end in treaties and peace agreements, and will wreak destruction until the complete exhaustion or destruction of the parties involved. The length of conflicts, even if low-intensity, means greater devastation and disruption.

Fourth, the attempt to limit both military and civilian casualties in war is a peculiarly Western and relatively new preoccupation, made more salient by the imperatives of population-centric counterinsurgency warfare.[98] It is unlikely to be widely accepted outside of the West, as

---

[94] See Mary Kaldor, *New and Old Wars* (Malden, MA: Polity Press, 2006).

[95] See also Louis Halle, "Does War Have a Future?" *Foreign Affairs*, Vol. 52, No. 1 (October 1973), 20–34; John Mueller, *Retreat from Doomsday: The Obsolescence of Modern War* (New York, NY: Basic Books, 1989); John Mueller, *The Remnants of War* (Ithaca, NY: Cornell University Press, 2004); Michael Mandelbaum, "Is Major War Obsolete?" *Survival*, Vol. 40, No. 4 (Winter 1998–99), 20–38.

[96] William Eckhardt, "Civilian Deaths in Wartime," *Security Dialogue*, Vol. 20, No. 1 (1989), 91.

[97] Headrick, *Power over Peoples*.

[98] Harvey M. Sapolsky and Jeremy Shapiro, "Casualties, Technology, and America's Future Wars," *Parameters*, Summer 1996, 119–127; Colin H. Kahl, "In the Crossfire or the Crosshairs? Norms, Civilian Casualties, and US Conduct in Iraq," *International Security*, Vol. 32, No. 1 (Summer 2007), 7–46; Thomas W. Smith, "Protecting Civilians ... or Soldiers? Humanitarian Law and the Economy of Risk in Iraq," *International Studies Perspectives*, Vol. 9, Issue 2, 144–164.

recent wars in Syria, Chechnya, or Sri Lanka have indicated.[99] Moreover, paradoxically, the sensitivity to civilian casualties may be decreasing the West's ability to coerce antagonistic states, and the realization of this can lead to a gradual reversal of this Western norm.[100] Again, the result will be that conflicts will be less discerning between civilian and military targets, and ultimately more destructive.

In the end, and again this is only a hypothesis, the future security landscape may be very similar to the premodern state of things, when international relations were characterized by "religio-political hostility, erupting in acts of extreme violence."[101] Unmitigated by deterrence and diplomacy, exacerbated by nonnegotiable objectives, and pursued by multiple types of actors, international relations in the future may be more like those of premodern history.

If the security challenges facing states carry some premodern traits, then it is reasonable to expect analogous strategies adopted to cope with them. In the chapters that follow, three broad approaches will be examined: altering the state to deal with the barbarian threat, altering the enemy to match state strengths, and altering the environment to undermine and constrain the enemy.

---

[99] See, for instance, Russia's counterinsurgency approach in Chechnya or Sri Lanka's war against the Tamil. Mark Kramer, "The Perils of Counterinsurgency: Russia's War in Chechnya," *International Security* Vol. 29, No. 3 (Winter 2004/05), 5–63; Robert Kaplan, "To Catch a Tiger," *The Atlantic Monthly*, July 1, 2009, at www.theatlantic.com/doc/200907u/tamil-tigers-counterinsurgency.

[100] Daniel Byman and Matthew Waxman, "Defeating US Coercion," *Survival*, Vol. 41, No. 2 (January 1999), 107–120.

[101] Riley-Smith, 79.

4 Altering the State
Decentralization

Charles Tilly's pithy phrase that "war made the state, and the state made war" succinctly described the rise of the modern nation state.[1] The needs of modern industrialized war drove the formation of the modern state. To survive, states had to embark on a gradual centralization of fiscal administration and of military force, resulting in the preeminence of the modern state. But modern states are a particular response to a particular security challenge, namely, fellow modern industrial states. They may not be the most effective way of dealing with a premodern type of threat, the barbarian menace, which tends to be ubiquitous, relatively small, and localized. A persistent barbarian threat can initiate a dynamic of decentralization within the targeted polity because a localized threat demands and generates a local response.

The case of the Roman Empire, facing barbarians along their frontier, points to this dynamic. The continued assaults by barbarian groups forced the most affected local authorities to take security in their own hands, resulting in a gradual decentralization of the empire. In some cases, this was a conscious decision of central authorities, but in many it was simply the result of the inability (and unwillingness) of imperial forces to defend the city or region directly targeted by a barbarian group. Such dynamic of decentralization may be applicable to other cases, including today's strategic landscape. Localized, small, and unpredictable attacks that disrupt everyday life but do not necessarily threaten the existence of the state as a whole are an increasingly common occurrence, particularly in Europe. The 2008 terrorist attack on Mumbai, the 2013 Boston marathon bombing, the 2015 Charlie Hebdo assault followed a few months later by a series of attacks in Paris, the 2016 bombings in Brussels, the attack in Berlin, and the 2017 attacks in London – to name the most tragic ones – were dramatic and very violent but also

---

[1] Charles Tilly, "Reflections on the History of European State-Making," in Charles Tilly, ed., *The Formation of National States in Western Europe* (Princeton, NJ: Princeton University Press, 1975), 42.

very localized and small, and are examples of what the future may hold. A centralized state not only may be more vulnerable to a well-aimed, localized attack, but also may be poorly suited to respond quickly and effectively to many "Mumbai-style" assaults. And as it proves too slow or incapable of preventing and quickly responding to such attacks, it will gradually lose legitimacy, forcing local communities to fend for themselves. The reality is that so far such attacks have not resulted in security decentralization in the Western world. But the decentralizing pressure will intensify as local communities do not feel well served by the state security apparatus. I do not suggest here that the Roman past will be the Western future, but only that there are analogous dynamics at work that may also have at some point analogous outcomes.

The starting premise of this chapter is that the external security environment shapes the organizational principle of states. Then, I lay out the conditions that may facilitate state decentralization. I illustrate these dynamics with the case of the late Roman Empire, and end with some thoughts on the general factors that affect how such decentralization occurs.

4.1 The Security Environment as the Demiurge of Polities

War shapes states because the primary purpose of the state is to provide security to its citizens. The legitimacy of states is thus, at least in part, derived from their ability to protect the safety of their population. A polity that fails to do so, or one that claims it does not need to pursue this task, will quickly lose its main *raison d'être*. As a historian of the Middle Ages points out, the main "test was whether rulers could protect their peoples and keep the peace. For in reality little else mattered."[2] As the political appeal of the polity wanes because it proves unable to pass this test, its élites and population will search for alternative sources of security. Therefore, states, modern and ancient alike, must adapt to the demands of war. The security environment is the demiurge of polities, and war is a powerful creative force.

This logic is most often applied to modern history.[3] But the causal mechanism linking the character of war with the organization of the state

---

[2] Bisson, 30.
[3] As historian Michael Howard observes, it is "hard to think of any nation-state, with the possible exception of Norway, that came into existence before the middle of the twentieth century which was not created, and had its boundaries defined, by wars, by internal violence, or by a combination of the two." Michael Howard, *The Lessons of History* (New Haven, CT: Yale University Press, 1991), 39. See also Bruce D. Porter, *War and the Rise of the State* (New York, NY: The Free Press, 1994).

has equal validity for ancient times.[4] As the nature of the threat changes, so do polities, which are forced to adapt in order to provide security effectively. As Gianfranco Poggi writes, "major changes in the modalities of warfare, and in the structure of military forces, have from time to time induced equally significant changes in political arrangements."[5]

The barbarian threat is more decentralized than that presented by another state. Barbarians are nonterritorial and decentralized, composed of tribes or clans coalescing temporarily around a leader. They materialize in unexpected places because of their high mobility, creating a geographically diffused threat along a long frontier. While such groups can penetrate deep inside a state's territory, they present a localized danger because of their relatively small size. They can bring devastation to a region or a city, but rarely can they singlehandedly topple the whole state.

Given the different nature of the security threat, it is plausible to suggest that a decentralized and diffused external threat may lead to a decentralized state. More specifically, *a decentralized and geographically diffused threat forces the state to decentralize some of its functions.* A centrally organized state is, in fact, poorly equipped to respond to small-scale incursions along a lengthy frontier.

4.2   Decentralization at the Tactical Level: *Spargere Bellum*

Pressures to decentralize are most visible at the tip of the spear, on the frontier where imperial or state forces meet barbarians. To match the barbarian enemy, the polity needs to adapt its military forces. Large imperial armies, in premodern and in modern times, are concentrated in large bases and dependent on long logistical lines. Consequently, such a military force tends to move slowly, is vulnerable to disrupted supply lines, and can protect only a few possible targets of enemy attack. An army like this can respond to a threat of a similarly organized force, slow in its movements and large in its manpower. But a small, quick attack on a distant city or outpost along the frontier is likely to remain unanswered if the defending army is not placed precisely along the vector of the assault. Concentration of forces, a fundamental military principle, is an ineffectual posture in front of widely dispersed, localized attacks. It is not surprising therefore that throughout history military clashes between imperial forces and barbarians did not follow established "rules of military

---

[4] Ramsay MacMullen, *Corruption and the Decline of Rome* (New Haven, CT: Yale University Press, 1988), 172–173.
[5] Gianfranco Poggi, *The State: Its Nature, Development and Prospects* (Stanford, CA: Stanford University Press, 1990), 111.

Decentralization at the Tactical Level

theory."[6] Unlike imperial armies, barbarians moved quickly. As Tacitus succinctly summed up, it was often "easier to set whole armies in motion than avoid the lone killer."[7]

In a conflict with barbarians, tactical prowess required some form of decentralization. Smaller military formations placed along the frontier or in defense of the many potential targets were likely to be more effective in defending against, and mitigating the effects of, dispersed attacks perpetuated by mobile tribal forces. The ubiquity of small security detachments also had an important effect on the domestic audience of the polity because it demonstrated the commitment of the central authorities to the protection of disparate local communities, thereby maintaining the legitimacy of the state.

The tactical and operational difficulty of fighting decentralized and small tribal forces was a recurrent problem facing premodern empires, and colonial ones in more recent times. The conflict on the American Plains, for instance, was not between two large armies engaging in battles, but a war "of great distances, sudden incursions, and rapid flight on horseback." As the attacking Indians were dispersed, highly mobile, and difficult to stop as well as to catch, US forces had to adapt by being "on horseback with an organization equally mobile."[8] To be effective, armed forces had to match the enemy, acquiring some of their characteristics.

A similar challenge was presented by the relatively small but worrisome threat of a Numidian rebel, Tacfarinas, in Roman North Africa in the first century AD.[9] Like many other lethal enemies of Rome (notably, a Germanic leader Arminius, a Roman citizen and soldier, who tricked a Roman commander, Varus, and three of his legions into marching into a disastrous ambush in the Teutoburg forest in 9 AD), Tacfarinas had

---

[6] Julius Caesar: "The battlefront was not formed according to rules of military theory but as necessitated by the emergency and the sloping ground of the hillside. The legions were facing different ways and fighting separate actions, and thick hedges obstructed their view." Julius Caesar, *The Conquest of Gaul* (New York, NY: Penguin, 1982), II, 22, 67.

[7] Tacitus, *Histories* (New York, NY: Penguin, 1972), II:75, 127.

[8] Walter Prescott Webb, *The Great Plains*, 166.

[9] Tacfarinas' story is in Tacitus, *Annals*, book 3 and 4. For book 3, see Tacitus, *The Histories and Annals*, trans. John Jackson, Loeb Classical Library (L249) (Cambridge, MA: Harvard University Press, 1931), and for book 4 see Tacitus, *Annals*, trans. John Jackson, Loeb Classical Library (L312) (Cambridge, MA: Harvard University Press, 1937). For a description of Roman North Africa, as well as an overview of Tacfarinas' rebellion, see C. R. Whittaker, "Roman Africa: Augustus to Vespasian," in Alan. K. Bowman et al., eds., *Cambridge Ancient History* (Cambridge: Cambridge University Press, 1996), Vol. X, 586–618; Adrian Goldsworthy, *The Roman Army at War: 100BC–AD200* (Oxford: Clarendon Press, 1996), 93–95; Ronald Syme, "Tacfarinas, the Musulamii, and Thubursicu," in E. Badian, ed., *Roman Papers* (Oxford: Oxford University press, 1979), Vol. 1, 218–231.

learned martial skills in one of the many indigenous or auxiliary units that fought alongside Roman legions. Intimately familiar with Roman tactics and operations, he turned this expertise against his former ally. But initially, he tried to mimic the Roman method of war and sought a decisive battle in which to test his strength. It is likely that he thought that the inferior Roman numbers – after all this was the periphery of Roman power – would either result in a clear military defeat or in a preventive retreat of the Romans, both amounting to a strategic victory for him. He organized his own forces into formations and units, probably mimicking Roman legions, but was defeated several times.

Having learned the painful lesson that a direct clash with imperial legions was not the most effective approach, Tacfarinas changed tactics. He adopted an approach more attuned to the methods of local Numidian tribes. In Tacitus' evocative phrase, Tacfarinas *spargit bellum*;[10] he began to "scatter war," sowing terror and disruption here and there, retreating and advancing, moving to the front and then to the rear of Roman forces. Instead of limiting the war to a series of pitched battles along a clearly delimited front or on a set piece of real estate, Tacfarinas spread the war everywhere. A relatively small rebellion became therefore a ubiquitous war, engulfing a whole region and creating a series of challenges for the defending Roman army. Such a *spargere bellum* tactic, in fact, stretches the defending imperial forces, tiring and frustrating them. It took some time (the war lasted almost a decade) for the Romans, tired and demoralized because of their ineffectiveness, to learn that it was impossible to defeat a *hostem vagum* – a wandering enemy – in a traditional way.[11]

Perhaps more importantly because it belittled their reputation and thus diminished their ability to maintain political control, the Romans were ridiculed or mocked with impunity (*impune ludifacabatur*).[12] Tacfarinas realized that he did not need to kill Roman soldiers to defeat the Roman Empire; he did not need tactical victories in order to achieve political ones. He could simply chip away at Rome's reputation of power and its authority by mocking its forces militarily, showing that its mighty legions could not win against an enemy that they could not fix in place.

The threat was troublesome for Rome. Surprising, plentiful, and yet small attacks threaten the order established by the imperial power in that distant frontier region. Such attacks empty this order of meaning (the legal rules, the property rights, the system of taxation, and the commercial systems) even though they leave its armature (the legions) intact. They make the security environment unpredictable, weakening the authority of Rome and then requiring an even larger and more costly intervention.

[10] *Annals*, III:21.   [11] *Annals*, IV:24.   [12] *Annals*, III:21.

That is why, when rebellions occurred, Romans preferred to risk a military defeat early on (and often suffering one in the process) in the attempt to forestall the spiral of rebellious violence and a war with an enemy that could metastasize and grow, constantly reappearing in new places. Once the seeds of violence have been spread, more and more tribes would join the rebellion, widening the belt of instability and demanding ever-greater commitment and resources from the empire.[13]

To win, the Romans had to abandon some of their well-drilled tactics and fight Tacfarinas on his terms.[14] They decentralized their forces by dividing their army into three groups: a mobile force to chase the marauding enemy, a more defensive group sent to protect the villages of local populations, and an elite group of soldiers whose task was to occupy strategic chokepoints, passes, and roads. But even these three groups were subdivided into smaller companies led by experienced centurions. The broad goal was to make the Numidians as afraid of a raid as the Romans were, while at the same time limiting their mobility by fortifying potential targets and roads. In effect, the Romans decentralized their forces, dispersing them around the region to counter Tacfarinas' spreading of war. An analogous situation is described by Tacitus in his *Histories*. Under Vitellius' brief reign in the "year of four emperors" 69 AD, the Danube region was in the midst of a prolonged rebellion and the local commander decided to spread the army in the provinces (*spargere per provincias*), a wise move that would instill a modicum of peace.[15] If the enemy makes war ubiquitous, the defender has to bring ubiquitous war back to him (with a corresponding effort to establish ubiquitous safety to the locals). When the enemy is decentralized, the defense has to decentralize too; *spargere bellum* calls for *spargere legiones*.

There are, however, serious risks when an imperial army, trained to fight together, is spread out in order to chase an elusive enemy or to

---

[13] Virgil, in the *Aeneid*, suggests a similar thought, using the same verb (*spargere*) adopted by Tacitus. The Fury Allecto, whose task was to push the Trojans away from Italy and prevent them from establishing a foothold in Latium, claims that
"With rumors I will draw the border towns into war, ignite their hearts with a maddening lust for battle. They'll rush to the rescue now from every side – I'll sow their fields with swords" (Virgil, *Aeneid*, VII, #638–641 in Virgil, *Aeneid*, translated by Robert Fagles (New York, NY: Penguin, 2006)).
Like Tacfarinas who was sowing war in North Africa (*spargere bellum*), Allecto would scatter arms around the fields of Latium (*spargam arma per agros* – *Aeneid*, VII, #551 in Latin). Such spreading of ubiquitous violence, an ancient and effective way of challenging the monopoly of violence and thus the authority of existing powers, was rightly feared by the Romans because a response to it required painful adaptation and a lot of time.

[14] *Annals*, III:73.

[15] Tacitus, *Histories*, trans. Clifford Moore, Loeb Classical Library (Cambridge, MA: Harvard University Press, 1925), III:46, 404.

protect the many potential targets. Julius Caesar during his conquest of Gaul became keenly aware of these risks, and of the trade-offs associated with them. The demands of pacification and political control clashed then – as they continue to do now – with the requirements of force protection when confronting barbarian rivals. Facing the risk of revolts four years into his Gallic campaign, Caesar decided to spread his forces across the region. In part, this decision was driven by the necessity of finding sufficient victuals and quarters for his soldiers during the off-season (winter) when military campaigns were effectively unfeasible. But he could not withdraw his legions completely from the region because the local population was far from being pacified and did not readily accept Roman authority. The risks were clear: By dividing his forces and placing them in various camps and towns throughout the region, he also put each individual group of his soldiers at risk of a surprise concentrated attack from the locals. In 54 BC, a legion plus fifteen cohorts (so, roughly, a legion and a half) under the command of Sabinus and Cotta was placed near the Rhine, far from potential reinforcements, to keep order in the region – a form of military decentralization. A rebellious tribe, the Eburones, quickly took the opportunity to attack the isolated Roman forces and surrounded the fortified camp. Contrary to the advice of wiser men, Sabinus decided to attempt to break the siege of the Roman camp and march toward the nearest friendly force. Outnumbered and poorly led, the Romans were annihilated. The Eburones, led by the ambitious Ambiorix, then assaulted another camp, commanded by Quintus Cicero (younger brother of Marcus Tullius Cicero), but were repelled after Caesar managed to join the fight.[16]

A year later, Caesar chose to keep his troops together when chasing the same Eburones led by Ambiorix. Caesar's desire to put force protection above the potential victory over the enemy was understandable because Sabinus and Cotta's defeat, despite his attempt to blame his subordinates, was clearly a blemish on his record and diminished his political capital back in Rome.[17] The unified troops "were in no danger from a panic-stricken and scattered enemy; but losses severe enough to weaken the army might easily be sustained by the waylaying of individual soldiers." Of course, this meant that the Romans could not hurt the hostile

[16] *The Conquest of Gaul*, V:24–37, 115–122. See also J. F. C. Fuller, *Julius Caesar: Man, Soldier, and Tyrant* (New Brunswick, NJ: Rutgers University Press, 1965), 129–132; Matthias Gelzer, *Caesar: Politician and Statesman* (Cambridge, MA: Harvard University Press, 1968), 143–144.

[17] Adrian Goldsworthy, *Caesar* (New Haven, CT: Yale University Press, 2006), 300.

tribes.[18] But "Caesar thought it better to let the enemy off comparatively lightly, in spite of the men's burning desire for revenge, than to punish them severely at the cost of serious loss to his own troops."[19] He chose to let Ambiorix go – suggesting that the hostile leader was hiding "in a wood or raving, and under the cover of night would make off in some new direction, escorted only by four horsemen" – rather than risk another embarrassing loss.[20]

4.3 The Political Organization

The Tacfarinas episode and Julius Caesar's troubles in Gaul were examples of a momentary rebellion by barbarian tribes in a frontier region not yet under full control of a rising Rome. A revolt called for tactical adjustments that were temporary for good reasons: Empires like Rome faced at the same time enemies of different natures, including peer competitors that had to be deterred or repelled with regular formations. Once an uprising such as the one led by Tacfarinas in North Africa had been pacified, a speedy reorientation of attention to these other frontiers and a return to mass military formations was necessary. The organizational change affected only the military directly involved in the quelling of the rebellions and thus forced to adapt to battlefield realities.

The changes were much deeper and longlasting when the threat was not a relatively brief outburst of disaffected populations but a persistent menace. When such a long-term barbarian presence threatened the

[18] Ambiorix had dispersed his tribe to the point, according to Julius Caesar, that they no longer presented a strategic threat. "Some fled into the Ardennes, other into a continuous belt of marshes, while those who lived nearest the sea hid in places cut off from the mainland at high tide. Many left their own country and entrusted their lives and all their possessions to complete strangers." (*The Conquest of Gaul*, 148) Nevertheless, they continued to pose a threat to Romans. "Each man had installed himself in any remote glen, any wooded spot, or impenetrable morass, that offered a chance of protection or escape. These hiding-places were known to the natives living in the neighborhood, and great care was needed to ensure the safety of the Roman troops." *The Conquest of Gaul*, VI, 34 148–149).

[19] *The Conquest of Gaul*, VI:34, 149.

[20] *The Conquest of Gaul*, VI:43, 154. To restore some of his *dignitas*, diminished by the frustrating chase of Ambiorix, Caesar ravaged the territory of the Eburones (in a way reminiscent of his "slash and burn" approach to the Germans' lands beyond the Rhine). As Ramsay MacMullen points out, "What Caesar wants to assert through total war is a certain perception of himself ... He must be seen as capable of ruthless and effective action." Such a *vastatio* was, however, a testament of the inability to defeat the enemy without the risk of incurring unacceptable casualties. It was a sign of frustration as much as an attempt to keep a reputation of power for domestic and foreign audiences. Ramsay MacMullen, "Personal Power in the Roman Empire," *American Journal of Philology*, Vol. 107, No. 4 (Winter 1986), 516.

frontier of an empire, the organizational alterations affected much more than just the tactical posture of military forces. The sheer perseverance of the barbarian threat was an affront to the claim of the targeted empire or state to be bringing order to its territories. Consequently, the imperial authorities could no longer take for granted the allegiance of the frontier populations who were under the constant shadow of the barbarian threat.

The obstinacy of the barbarian threat was in large measure due to the difficulty, examined in Chapter 2, of defeating or deterring these groups. It was effectively impossible to eliminate the threat once and for all, and therefore frontier security was a long-term process of managing barbarians. The security conditions led to structural adjustments along the frontier. Broadly speaking, the presence of a barbarian threat resulted in the rise of local forces, geared to respond to localized threats, often bringing greater power down to local political centers. Barbarians tend to target narrowly defined locations, destabilizing particular and mostly small areas rather than menacing the existence of the entire state or empire. The populations living in the targeted regions are therefore the ones that have the greatest incentives to respond to those attacks, while for the decision-makers in the capital the threat is too far away to warrant attention and too small to commit large resources. Localized threats create incentives for local solutions, and local defense is difficult to manage from a distant central court. In other words, a long-term military decentralization is not simply a matter of tactics but has political implications on how the state is structured.

Absent such a military (and most likely, political) decentralization, states need to prioritize what to defend with their larger centralized army. The large force has to be deployed in towns or locations deemed to be at greatest risk of a barbarian attack or to be most valuable to the empire because of their geographic position, commercial importance, or political significance. Amassing imperial forces in a limited number of places along the threatened frontier can certainly protect those locations from a direct attack but it also may redirect barbarian forays toward less defended, softer targets. Moreover, the sheer act of defense prioritization undermines the appeal and legitimacy of the state in those locations that are considered less at risk or unworthy of military defense. As a result, the cities and regions that are not defended by the state tend to seek their own security arrangements, either by surrendering to the enemy or by developing local forces. Local élites will gradually wrest control over tax extraction and military power from the central state administration, shoring up their own legitimacy based on their ability to provide security to the local populations.[21] In many cases, this fragmentation of power is simply an outcome of state weakness. It is a sign of decay, rather than of a well-thought-out defensive posture. Such fragmentation, a result of preexisting structural weakness, leads to profound and often irreversible changes in the political and military structure of the state – indeed, it results in a new entity, which in modern parlance is often associated with the broad concept of "failed states." Decentralization can lead to fragmentation and ultimately to the end of the state in question.

The point here is that there are different ways in which the devolution of security provision can occur: an empire can seek to decentralize security willingly, keeping control over the local commanders and political leaders, or local authorities can wrest power and resources away from the state because of indigenous pressures to stabilize the frontier. When faced with a barbarian threat, states do not automatically decentralize

[21] State decentralization is the subject of a vast literature, which, however, does not link external threats to the internal structure of the state. In fact, decentralization is studied especially in the context of internal strife, as a solution or as a cause of Civil Wars and armed clientelism, rather than as a response to external threats. Decentralization is tied to domestic processes, and is often pursued in order to mitigate ethnic tensions. The empowerment of regions and local leaders through elections and fiscal devolution is seen, in fact, as a strategy to maintain the unity of a state torn by existing centrifugal forces. The challenge is that it often leads to the breakdown of the state and to a higher degree of violence. As Kent Eaton writes, decentralization "has played into the hands of illicit armed groups who have used their control of decentralized resources to reinforce and expand their domination of vast stretches of the national territory. Decentralization has fed the problematic rise of armed clientelism, the private appropriation of public goods through violence or the threat of violence." Decentralization becomes then a prelude to a failed state. A decentralized state often ends up as a mosaic of warlords and armed gangs, rather than a more efficient and peaceful polity. See Kent Eaton, "The Downside of Decentralization: Armed Clientelism in Colombia," *Security Studies*, Vol. 15, No. 4 (October–December 2006), 535. See also Barbara Walter, "Designing Transitions from Civil War: Demobilization, Democratization and Commitments to Peace," *International Security* Vol. 24, No. 1 (1999), 127–155; David Lake and Donald Rothchild, "Containing Fear: The Origins and Management of Ethnic Conflict," *International Security*, Vol. 21, No. 2 (1996), 41–75; Dawn Brancati, "Decentralization: Fueling the Fire or Dampening the Flames of Ethnic Conflict and Secessionism," *International Organization*, Vol. 60, No. 3 (July 2006), 651–685.

My argument does not deny that decentralization can have negative connotations and result in some cases in a collapse of a centralized authority. But it is not necessarily always a top-down process, initiated by the central government in response to a particular challenge (internal, in the above mentioned literature; external, in my argument). Rather it can be simply an outcome of the failure of central authorities to provide security and other public goods. Decentralization, that is, is a strategy pursued by local leaders and authorities who fill the void left by the state, and should be seen as an attempt to restore the order already missing rather than a source of violence and turmoil. Moreover, and this is the biggest difference between my argument and the literature, decentralization of state functions can be a factor of external threats, and not only of domestic processes. I argue that the nature of the external threat plays a crucial role in shaping the internal arrangement of a state.

security provision, the same way that armies do not immediately divide their forces to respond to a geographically dispersed rebellion. But some form of decentralization may be the outcome of such a threat anyway, because the populations most affected by the barbarian threat may demand greater control over their own security.

4.4 The End of the Roman Empire

Because processes of domestic change have multiple causes, it is difficult to point to a single cause of state decentralization. The presence of an enemy that attacks along a lengthy frontier but with localized effects does not automatically cause decentralization because a combination of other internal factors, ranging from economic and social problems to ethnic tensions, also influences the decisions of the central authorities. The best one can do is to show that this argument – namely, that geographically diffused attacks can result in a decentralized state, either because of a strategy implemented by the central authority or because of local authorities taking over security provision – is plausible.

The example of the late Roman Empire (fourth to fifth centuries AD) is illustrative of how decentralization can occur when a polity faces a barbarian threat. The Western Roman Empire ended in a catastrophic form of decentralization, with the splintering of regions, the creation of new kingdoms, and the overall localization and privatization of political authority, military force, and economic life. There is certainly no disagreement regarding the outcome of this decentralization, which resulted in the end of the Western Roman Empire and sowed the seeds of the medieval period. The Roman Empire did collapse.

But historians do not agree on what caused the withering away of a central imperial authority over the Western Mediterranean and Western Europe. The key question for the argument of this chapter is whether the political and security decentralization of the Roman Empire was caused by the assaults of foreign groups crossing the Rhine and Danube, or whether internal factors, ranging from social cleavages to cultural changes, were decisive in splintering the empire. I lean toward the former explanation.

There are two schools of thought regarding the end of the Roman Empire, the "internalist" and the "externalist." This distinction has characterized studies of political decline since ancient times and it has been succinctly presented by Polybius, who argued that the decline of Rome, as of any other polity, can be attributed to either external enemies or internal (cultural and social) factors. While the latter followed a regular and inevitable cycle, the former, the external threats, were not predictable but perhaps more manageable.[22] He was hence pessimistic about the ability of Rome to withstand the internal decay associated with states, and in particular with expanding empires. Centuries later, St. Ambrose of Milan (340–397 AD) similarly indicated the existence of two enemies, internal (the moral degradation of society) and external (the barbarian hordes), that caused the weakening of the Roman Empire.[23] And these two sets of arguments continue to characterize much of the debate among modern historians.

On the one side, some argue that the Roman Empire collapsed because of internal disarray (social, economic, cultural, and/or political), and the fifth-century barbarian assaults were migrations of people who gradually and mostly peacefully were accommodated on imperial territories. By then, the Roman Empire was already weakened because of structural problems, and the new arrivals from the east simply filled a vacuum left by imperial degradation.

On the other side, a more recent group of historians reiterates the violent nature of the political changes in "late antiquity." The barbarian groups that from the late fourth century kept tramping through Roman territories brought with them enormous devastation, undermining the economic wellbeing of the empire, decreasing tax revenues, disrupting trade, and stretching Roman military forces to their limit (and in fact, in some cases defeating them in a spectacular fashion). What brought Rome down was the relentless and devastating pressure of external actors, rather than inherent domestic problems.[24] As French historian André Piganiol famously put it at the end of his book on the third-century Roman

---

[22] The internal cycle was the following: "When a state, after warding off many great perils, achieves supremacy and uncontested sovereignty, it is evident that under the influence of long-established prosperity life will become more luxurious, and among the citizens themselves rivalry for office and in other spheres of activity will become fiercer than it should... The principal authors of this change will be the masses, who at some moments will believe that they have a grievance against the greed of other members of society, and at others are made conceited by the flattery of those who aspire to office." Polybius, *The Rise of the Roman Empire* (New York, NY: Penguin, 1979), Book VI:57, 350. For a detailed discussion of Book VI and its contradiction between the natural and inevitable cycle of political life and the ability of Rome to overcome it, see also C. O. Brink and F. W. Walbank, "The Construction of the Sixth Book of Polybius," *The Classical Quarterly*, Vol. 4, No. 3/4 (July– October 1954), 97–122.

[23] See Santo Mazzarino, *The End of the Ancient World* (New York, NY: Alfred A. Knopf, 1966), 44–57; Arnaldo Momigliano, "La caduta senza rumore di un impero nel 476 D.C.", *Annali della Scuola Normale Superiore di Pisa*, Serie III, Vol. 3, No. 2 (1973), 409.

[24] Strong proponents of the "internalist" version are Edward Gibbon, *The Decline and Fall of the Roman Empire*, introduction by Hugh Trevor-Roper (New York, NY: Everyman's Library, 1993); Walter Goffart, *Barbarian Tides: The Migration Age and the Later Roman Empire* (Princeton, NJ: Princeton University Press, 2006); Guy Halsall, *Barbarian Migrations*. The externalist view is represented by, among others, Bryan Ward-Perkins, *The Fall of Rome and the End of Civilization* (New York: Oxford University Press, 2006);

Empire, "La civilisation romaine n'est pas morte de sa belle mort. Elle a été assassinée."[25] Rome has been assassinated. Without the continued assaults by groups from across the Rhine and Danube, the Roman Empire would not have fallen apart by the second half of the fifth century.

There is ample evidence to indicate that the barbarian invasions were a truly catastrophic event. The arrival of Gothic tribes on the Danube in 376 was followed by their victory over Roman legions in the battle of Hadrianople (378), where the Roman emperor also met his demise. More importantly, this episode signaled the intensification of several decades of barbarian movements across the Rhine and Danube frontiers. In some cases, such as that of the Vandals, foreign groups moved across thousands of miles of Roman territories, sailing to North Africa, from where they launched raids on the Italian peninsula. Most of these groups came uninvited and were met with military force, often with great Roman success but still at great expense of resources and manpower. Imperial frontiers were more permeable and less defined than modern state borders, but there is no indication that Roman authorities did not seek to prevent movements of people across them. While fixed fortifications such as Hadrian's Wall in Britain were exceptional, the Rhine and Danube served as an approximate line marking the limits of imperial territories in central Europe. They were not demarcated land borders of the empire, but any crossing of them by external actors was considered threatening and demanded a defensive response.[26]

The barbarian incursions had a direct impact on the political structure of the empire. Most spectacularly, by the second decade of the fifth century, some of the barbarian groups managed to wrest from Rome control over large swaths of territory, from Aquitania to Spain and North Africa. They tore, quite literally, the empire apart. But they also forced the central imperial authorities either to abandon certain regions (starting from Britain) because of the need to prioritize defense or to relax their monopoly over military force in order to allow local communities to

---

Arther Ferrill, *The Fall of the Roman Empire* (London: Thames and Hudson Ltd., 1986); Peter Heather, *The Fall of the Roman Empire* (London: Pan Macmillan, 2006). For a summary of these views, see Peter Heather, "Why Did the Barbarians Cross the Rhine?" *Journal of Late Antiquity*, Vol. 2, No. 1 (Spring 2009), 3–29. See also Mazzarino, *The End of the Ancient World*, 44–57, 184–189.

[25] André Piganiol, *L'Empire Chrétien, 325–395* (Paris: Presses Universitaires de France, 1947), 422.

[26] Benjamin Isaac argues that the term *limes* has been used incorrectly to indicate a defended border with manmade fortifications. Benjamin Isaac, "The Meaning of the Terms 'Limes' and 'Limitanei'," *Journal of Roman Studies*, Vol. 78 (1988), 125–147; Benjamin Isaac, *The Limits of Empire: the Roman Army in the East* (Oxford: Oxford University Press, revised edition 1992). See also C. R. Whittaker, *Frontiers of the Roman Empire* (Baltimore, MD: The Johns Hopkins University Press, 1994).

defend themselves. The nature of the external threat, in fact, was such that it encouraged a gradual decentralization of military, fiscal, and ultimately political functions, resulting by the late fifth century in a political landscape that is unlikely to have come into being otherwise. In the following two sections, I examine, first, the nature of this external threat and, second, the effects of this threat on the Roman Empire.

4.5 The Barbarians

As examined in Chapter 2, the barbarian threat facing premodern states in general, and Rome in this case, was different from that presented by other states. In the case of the late Roman Empire, six features distinguished this threat from the menace presented by a peer competitor, such as Persia. These features have been described in broad terms in Chapters 2 and 3, and here I examine them in greater detail as applied to this specific case.

First, Roman intelligence of the barbarian groups was very limited. The Romans had some knowledge of the political realities on the other side of their frontier in Europe but it was often vague and incomplete, and above all, tinted by a strong belief in the cultural and material inferiority of the barbarians. Furthermore, the mobility of the barbarian groups of the fourth and fifth centuries deprived Rome of neighbors that had temporal and geographic permanence. Many of the groups that arrived on the frontier in the fifth century, pushed westward by the Huns, were new and unknown to Rome. Whatever the reason for this imperfect intelligence of barbarian movements, it seems clear that Roman authorities had considerably fewer sources of intelligence and thus less information of imminent attacks by barbarian groups across the northern frontier.[27] As a result, the scope for uncertainty was much larger on the Rhine and Danube than on the frontier with Persia in the east, making it more difficult for central authorities to tailor defensive measures to specific areas.

Second, unlike an invasion by a peer competitor, barbarian attacks were often raids, rapid and in-depth penetrations of small groups seeking booty, rather than full-scale territorial conquests.[28] Raids devastated targeted regions, and with the later barbarian attacks of the fifth century, even walled cities, but none of these groups appeared to want, or to have the capability, to replace the empire and its authorities. For instance, the

---

[27] A.D. Lee, *Information & Frontiers* (Cambridge: Cambridge University Press, 1993), 128–139.
[28] Ward-Perkins, 52.

410 AD sack of Rome by Alaric's Goths was a direct attack against the by-then former administrative capital and it was considered a shocking sign of the catastrophic collapse of Roman power, but it was perpetuated more out of a desire for gold and glory than by a conscious decision to take over the Roman Empire. The threat presented by these rapidly moving groups was undoubtedly very serious and resulted in great loss of life and material wellbeing over the course of several decades. Writing in 396 AD, St. Jerome bemoans that "for twenty years and more the blood of Romans has every day been shed between Constantinople and the Julian Alps" and such devastation could not but lead to a feeling that the "Roman world is falling."[29] And in the end the relentless incursions of various barbarian groups weakened irreparably the economic base of the empire, especially after the Vandal takeover of North Africa. But from the late fourth century on, each individual barbarian threat was individually too small to topple the empire. It was a localized menace, spreading gradually from the frontier regions to areas increasingly deeper inside the Roman Empire.

The third feature of the barbarian threat was related to the previous one, namely, the relatively small size of each group. Given the lack of definitive information, the numbers are highly speculative but there seems to be a broad consensus that at most some of these groups fielded 20–30,000 fighting men.[30] Often much smaller groups crossed the Rhine and the Danube, and while some of them were either defeated or assimilated by Rome, it appears that barbarians gradually moved into imperial territories. As a historian puts it, it was a "seepage of barbarian peoples" that undermined the security of imperial territories; they were small but numerous groups that kept entering at the same time into several territories from Gaul to Noricum and Thrace.[31] The military advantage of the Roman armies, which were still a formidable force by the late fourth century, was by and large useless when facing such a threat. The impressive logistical capabilities, combined with a well-trained infantry and a growing number of cavalry, made Roman forces quite capable of winning large battles that, however, were becoming rare occurrences.

---

[29] Jerome, *Select Letters* (Cambridge, MA: Harvard University Press, Loeb Classical Library, 1933), Letter LX, 301 and 303. See also Stefan Rebenich, "Christian Asceticism and Barbarian Incursion: The Making of a Christian Catastrophe," *Journal of Late Antiquity*, Vol. 2, No. 1 (Spring 2009), 49–59.

[30] Herwig Wolfram, *The Roman Empire and its Germanic Peoples* (Berkeley, CA: University of California Press, 1997), 7; Walter Goffart, *Barbarians and Romans* (Princeton, NJ: Princeton University Press, 1980), 5 and 231–234; Heather, *Fall of the Roman Empire*, 446.

[31] Averil Cameron, *The Mediterranean World in Late Antiquity, AD 395–600* (London: Routledge, 1993), 56.

The story of barbarian incursion is not a story of large battles, but of raids, skirmishes, and rapid and deep penetrations along a lengthy frontier. The 378 AD battle of Hadrianople, lost by the Romans, was an exceptional event, both because it occurred and because the Romans were defeated. As Ward-Perkins observes, the "West was lost mainly through failure to engage [militarily] the invading forces successfully and to drive them back."[32]

Fourth, while each assaulting party was relatively small, there were many groups or tribes concurrently pressuring the frontier. After successful raids, many groups unified into larger entities, joining the leading tribe. Yet, even such larger groupings were often led by multiple leaders whose allegiance to, and alignment with, other tribes was constantly shifting.[33] The strategic landscape on the European frontier of the Roman Empire was, therefore, an ever-changing mosaic of highly mobile groups. In such circumstances, it was difficult to develop diplomatic interactions with these hostile actors and to enforce agreements that may have been reached with them. There was simply not enough knowledge and not enough time to establish a pattern of diplomacy.

Fifth, the time and place of conflict was often not of Roman choosing. The length of the frontier allowed the barbarian groups to cross at multiple locations, making their assaults unpredictable and difficult to prevent. Unlike the armies of a peer competitor, barbarian forces were sufficiently small and mobile not to require lengthy and large logistical preparations. As a result, it was difficult to foresee where and when they were preparing a penetration of imperial territories. As a historian puts it, in the fifth century "it must often have been difficult to know exactly not only who was defending and who was attacking but also what was being threatened."[34]

Sixth, the early invaders were technically inferior to Roman forces, often arming themselves with the battlefield spoils of the defeated Romans. Most importantly, lacking logistical and technical skills, they could not put walled cities under siege. This gradually changed, and the Huns, who arrived after the Goths, had some ability to assault cities and possessed a tactical advantage in cavalry. But the early technical inferiority meant that the barbarians left cities, the core of Roman civilization, alone and focused on devastating the countryside. The result was the growing solitude of cities, increasingly fortified with walls and severed

---

[32] Ward-Perkins, 40.
[33] Mark Humphries, "International Relations," in P. Sabin, H. Van Wess, M. Whitby, eds., *The Cambridge History of Greek and Roman Warfare*, Vol. 2 (Cambridge: Cambridge University Press, 2007), chapter 7, 240.
[34] Cameron, *The Mediterranean World*, 54.

from the rest of the Roman community because of unsafe roads. Trade decreased and cities became increasingly more detached from the imperial economic and political system. Life in all of its aspects became more and more localized.

In brief, from the fourth century on, the Roman Empire faced a security environment that was characterized by multiple, often concurrent, attacks of varying strength and across a long frontier. The groups that were threatening Rome were neither peer competitors nor similarly organized polities, and their rapid and unexpected movements across the frontier combined with their small sizes made Roman military superiority in large battles irrelevant. Individually, these groups were no match for the Roman security apparatus but precisely because of this, and their avoidance of set battles, they presented a novel and resilient threat that demanded, and in the end caused, a very different political entity on former Roman lands.[35] In a nutshell, Rome had a tactical advantage against barbarian threats (that is, it could defeat the hostile groups in a direct military clash), but had strategic disadvantages because its centralized nature made it arduous to defend against multiple, diffuse, localized assaults.

This was a relatively new security situation for the Roman Empire. Single barbarian groups have appeared on the radar screen of Rome since its founding but never with the frequency and intensity that characterized the fourth century on, when Roman authorities had to deal with the "needs of constant defence against a multiplicity of enemies from an ever diminishing pool of fiscal and military resources."[36]

4.6 Roman Responses and Decentralization

How did Rome respond to this security environment? It is difficult to draw univocal conclusions on the policies pursued by Roman authorities due to the paucity of information. We know, for instance, that emperors communicated with foreign leaders and that provincial governors and commanders exchanged information and instructions with Rome, but we

---

[35] Concerning Roman superiority, Bryan Ward-Perkins sums up: Rome had "well-built and imposing fortifications; factory-made weapons that were both standardized and of a high quality; an impressive infrastructure of roads and harbours; the logistical organization necessary to supply their army, whether at base or on campaign; and a tradition of training that ensured disciplined and coordinated action in battle, even in the face of adversity. Furthermore, Roman mastery of the sea, at least in the Mediterranean, was unchallenged and a vital aspect of supply. It was these sophistications, rather than the weight of numbers, that created and defended the empire, and the Romans were well aware of this fact." Ward-Perkins, 34.
[36] Humphries, "International Relations," 238.

have very few surviving documents.[37] As a result, we can only speculate whether Roman authorities had a clear idea of the nature of the threat they were facing, whether they were aware of their own resource constraints, and whether they tried to formulate and implement a coherent plan to deal with it. Some historians even doubt that Roman authorities thought in grand strategic terms, namely, that they related their objectives to the available resources in a systematic way.[38] Many arguments about what happened and why it happened must be therefore made "from silence."[39]

We have, however, some inkling of the political and economic processes that occurred in the late Roman Empire from the fourth century on. Perhaps the most striking change was a gradual de-urbanization of Western imperial territories. The city was the center of Roman life, where the powerful lived, conducted their business, and made their political careers, and where the highest expression of human activity occurred. The city was the place where the most revered and indispensable traditions of political life sustained themselves: It was more than the accumulation of magnificent buildings as long as it preserved the social order. Tacitus described such splendid buildings as "dumb, lifeless things – their collapse or restoration means nothing." The source of the domestic and international order resided in the "continued preservation of the senate."[40] Cicero, in the famous "dream of Scipio," similarly affirmed a deeply held Roman belief that to god nothing is more welcome than "those companies and communities of people linked by justice that are

---

[37] See Fergus Millar, "Emperors, Frontiers, and Foreign Relations, 31 BC to AD 378," *Britannia*, Vol. 13 (1982), 1–23; Fergus Millar, "Government and Diplomacy in the Roman Empire during the First Three Centuries," *International History Review*, Vol. 10, No. 3 (August 1988), 345–377.

[38] The debate on whether there was a Roman "grand strategy" revolves in large measure around Edward Luttwak's book, *Grand Strategy in the Roman Empire from the First Century A.D. to the Third* (Baltimore, MD: The Johns Hopkins University Press, 1976). His argument that Rome pursued a clear grand strategy that could be also broken down into three distinct periods spurred a large critical literature. See Benjamin Isaac, *The Limits of Empire: The Roman Army in the East*, rev. edn. (Oxford: Oxford University Press, 1992); Whittaker, *Frontiers of the Roman Empire*; Everett Wheeler, "Methodological Limits and the Mirage of Roman Strategy," Part I and Part II, *Journal of Military History*, Vol. 57, No. 1 (January 1993) and No. 2 (April 1993), 7–41 and 215–240; Susan Mattern, *Rome and the Enemy: Imperial Strategy in the Principate* (Berkeley, CA: University of California Press, 1999). For a summary of the arguments and a defense of the study of grand strategy, see Kimberly Kagan, "Redefining Roman Grand Strategy," *Journal of Military History*, Vol. 70, No. 2 (April 2006), 333–362; Adrian Goldsworthy, "War," in P. Sabin, H. Van Wess, M. Whitby, eds., *The Cambridge History of Greek and Roman Warfare*, Vol. 2 (Cambridge: Cambridge University Press, 2007), chapter 3, 76–121, in particular 108–111.

[39] Millar, "Emperors, Frontiers, and Foreign Relations," 3.

[40] Tacitus, *The Histories* (New York, NY: Penguin, 1972), I:84, 70.

140   Altering the State

called cities (*civitates*)."[41] In fact, the running of the Roman Empire was centered on cities, which always had some autonomy, both as a result of a deep belief that the cities were an indispensable locus of law and political life and of a recognition that the sheer size of the imperial territories required local decisions. Central authorities and forces could not be everywhere at the same time, naturally leading Rome to rely on local authorities located in cities to administer everyday life and to raise taxes.[42] The Mediterranean world, and Western Europe in particular, under Roman rule was an overwhelmingly urban society, with a hierarchy of cities linked by an extensive network of maritime and land routes.[43] The weakness of this political system was the security of this communication network. Even though barbarians by and large could not conquer cities, they made safe passage on the roads rarer, curtailing trade. As trade diminished, so did the wealth and size of cities.[44] Moreover, the difficulty of linking the cities with each other and with the imperial center further contributed to their autonomy, which, as made clear by the story of Sidonius described in Chapter 5, was not always desired.

From the fourth century on, these cities became increasingly smaller and were walled for defense. Once the barbarians had pierced the outer frontier of the empire, they could roam through most of the Roman territory, terrifying rural areas, making travel unsafe, and threatening civilized centers.[45] Orosius, a student of Saint Augustine, described how the various barbarian tribes "were roaming wildly through Gaul."[46] Zosimus, a historian observing the end of the Western Roman Empire from his perch in Constantinople at the turn of the sixth century, noted

[41] Cicero, *Republic*, book 6:13, online at www.classicitaliani.it/dante1/somnium.htm. Greg Woolf writes: "The city was conceived of as a community of citizens united by laws and the worship of the gods, the natural environment of men, in other words that in which they could best realize their moral potential. Beyond the civilized world of cities, the classical writers described men living in villages, scattered through the countryside, or else as nomads, wanderers with no fixed abode eating raw flesh like animals, drinking only milk." Greg Woolf, *Becoming Roman* (New York, NY: Cambridge University Press, 1998), 106.

[42] Chris Wickham, *The Inheritance of Rome* (New York, NY: Viking, 2009), 24; Peter Brown, *The Rise of Western Christendom* (Malden, MA: Blackwell Publishing, 2003, original 1996), 55.

[43] "For the Romans, cities were first of all parts of a structure of power, "small fatherlands" inside the "common fatherland," rings linking the central authority of the empire and the various local realities." Lellia Cracco Ruggini, "Città tardoantica, città altomedievale: permanze e mutamenti," *Anabases*, No. 12 (2010), 106, translated by the author.

[44] MacMullen, *Corruption*, 37.

[45] Chester G. Starr, *The Roman Empire: 27 B.C.-A.AD. 476* (New York, NY: Oxford University Press, 1982), 142.

[46] Paulus Orosius, *Seven Books of History Against the Pagans: The Apology of Paulus Orosius*, trans. by Irving Raymond (New York, NY: Columbia University Press, 1936), VII:40, 390.

that Alaric in 408 could wander around Italy as if on a festival or on a vacation.[47] It is not surprising therefore that even large and previously safe cities such as Rome and Constantinople developed impressive layers of fortifications. Rome's Aurelian wall, built toward the end of the third century AD, "was a sign of changed times," characterized by increasing levels of insecurity deep inside imperial territories.[48] If the key cities of the empire needed walls – if Rome needed ramparts, smaller towns in Western Europe and in the Balkans were even more vulnerable to the roaming bands of barbarians and erected their own defensive stockades. Some walls appear to have been built in a hurry, indicating perhaps an unexpected degeneration of their security.[49] Probably as a result of local initiative, fortified positions on strategic hilltops, called *oppida*, began to appear, a sign of "the increasing remoteness of a centralized authority that could be relied upon to respond with sufficient speed or strength in times of crisis."[50] The retreat of populations to such *oppida* began along the Rhine and the Danube, the most vulnerable regions, but it expanded to Gaul, Northern Italy, modern day Tuscany, and the southern Balkans by 400 AD.[51]

A similar process occurred a few centuries later, in the tenth to eleventh centuries, when local political or religious authorities fortified their places at least in part because of the external threat of Magyars, Muslims, and Normans, even if those fears in many places did not materialize. This process of *incastellamento* was driven, at least in part, by security concerns analogous to those faced by the late Western Roman Empire.[52] The fact

---

[47] Zosimus, *New History* (London: Green and Chaplin, 1814), book 5, www.tertullian.org/fathers/zosimus05_book5.htm.

[48] Michael Whitby, "War," in P. Sabin, H. Van Wess, and M. Whitby, eds., *The Cambridge History of Greek and Roman Warfare*, Vol. 2 (Cambridge: Cambridge University Press, 2007), chapter 9, 312.

[49] Whitby, 313. Some historians dispute, at least in part, the security-based explanations of these walls. First, they suggest that it is difficult to date with great precision the construction of walls and thus assert without doubt that most had been erected in this period. Second, they suggest alternative explanations, such as the need to regulate commerce, the desire to distinguish one's own city from others, or perhaps the aspiration to make the city more beautiful and majestic. See Michael Kulikowski, *Late Roman Spain and Its Cities* (Baltimore, MD: The Johns Hopkins University Press, 2004), 101–109; A. D. Lee, *From Rome to Byzantium AD 363 to 565* (Edinburgh: Edinburgh University Press, 2013), 210.

[50] William Bowden, "The fourth century," in E. Bispham, ed., *Roman Europe* (New York, NY: Oxford University Press, 2008), 290.

[51] MacMullen, *Corruption*, 24.

[52] John Howe, *Church Reform and Social Change in Eleventh-Century Italy* (Philadelphia, PA: University of Pennsylvania Press, 1997), 11–12; Pierre Toubert, *Les Structures du Latium Medieval* (Paris: Ecole Francaise de Rome, 1973), Vol. 1 and Vol. 2; Étienne Hubert, "L'incastellamento dans le Latium: Remarques à propos de fouilles récentes," *Annales*, 55e Année, No. 3 (May-June 2000), 583–599.

that some fortified places were truly castles, but the vast majority seemed to be simply fortified houses (*case forti*), points to the low-intensity nature of the threat.[53] The menace was not another large state invading and certainly not one capable of keeping a place under lengthy siege, but a quick, surprising, and yet small attack by a group of barbarians.

Going back to the late Roman Empire, another effect of the decline of urban areas was the movement of the more affluent citizens to rural areas. The wealthy probably thought they were better off in their increasingly fortified rural estates, which until then tended to be their sources of wealth and secondary homes and now became their primary places of residence.[54] As a small anecdotal evidence confirms, in a city in Pannonia, mosaics are no longer laid after 350 AD and coins disappear after 370 AD – suggesting that people no longer saw many reasons to beautify urban areas and were probably hiding their money under ground.[55] Many of those estates developed local security forces for their own protection and sought special legal arrangements freeing themselves from the larger imperial administration. As a historian notes, many "landlords obtained an exemption from the jurisdiction of the local authorities and began themselves to exercise some jurisdictional functions on their estates. They fortified their residences and provided for their protection."[56]

The provision of security gradually became a local responsibility because a centrally administered military apparatus could no longer counter multiple localized threats.[57] And, further diminishing the empire's ability to maintain large forces, the landowners stopped paying the land tax because they were no longer receiving security in exchange for it.[58] Local defense – in fact, private defense in some cases – became more appealing than the hope of an increasingly more distant and weaker

---

[53] For an overview of the types of fortified places, see Benoit Cursente and Claudio Rosso, "La casa forte nel Medioevo," *Studi Storici*, Vol. 28, No. 3 (July–September 1987), 779–784.

[54] On de-urbanization in Late Antiquity, see W. Liebeschuetz, "The End of the Ancient City," in J. Rich, ed., *The City in Late Antiquity* (London: Routledge, 1992), 1–49.

[55] MacMullen, *Corruption*, 20.

[56] Richard Gerberding, "The Later Roman Empire," in Paul Fouracre, ed., *The New Cambridge Medieval History* (New York, NY: Cambridge University Press, 2005), Vol. I, chapter 1, 29.

[57] In the eastern part of the empire, there is also some level of local "spontaneous opposition": the "Athenian historian Dexippus pulled together enough military strength to check the Heruli in central Greece; in Asia Minor the Sassanian incursion was also limited by another leader, Callistus, an imperial military official who rallied local forces." Starr, *The Roman Empire*, 143.

[58] Peter Heather, "State, Lordship and Community in the West (*c.* A.D. 400–600)," in A. Cameron et al., eds., *The Cambridge Ancient History* (New York, NY: Cambridge University Press, 2000), Vol. XIV, 437–468, 441–444, in particular.

imperial army. Such defense, a pocket of "concentrated coercion," was also more effective against dispersed and small bands of barbarians.[59]

While a lot of towns disappeared, especially in Britain and the Balkans, those that survived in Italy, France, and Spain did so as quasi-independent entities.[60] Some cities, such as Cordoba and Seville in the sixth century rejected any central administration and acted as independent entities for twenty years.[61] This devolution of power was a result of imperial withdrawal or inability to protect individual cities and regions, and there is no evidence that it was a conscious policy of the central authorities to cede power to the regions most likely to be affected by barbarian incursions. The central government was simply incapable of protecting every region under assault. As historian J. B. Bury writes, the "task of ubiquitous defence" was beyond the abilities of the imperial authorities.[62] For instance, the historical record points to a Roman withdrawal from Britain in the first decade of the fifth century, in part perhaps because of the need to move troops to defend the Rhine and in part because an imperial usurper (Constantine III) took the remaining Roman troops in Britain across the Channel to claim the throne for himself.[63] Interestingly, the official letter announcing Roman withdrawal was addressed to cities, not local Roman leaders, probably because no legitimate and clearly recognizable Roman authorities existed there.[64] Other regions, such as southern and central Gaul in the second half of the fifth century, experienced similar military withdrawals.

The vacuum left by the central imperial government – incapable of providing security because of internal weakness and because of the nature of the threats – was filled by local authorities that in the fifth century became increasingly more self-sufficient and separated from the imperial capital. Indeed, in some cases, the head of the city, the *defensor*, was elected by local people who sought him as a replacement of the governor

---

[59] Michael Mann, *The Sources of Social Power* (New York, NY: Cambridge University Press, 1986), Vol. I, 391.
[60] J. H. W. G. Liebeschuetz, "Administration and Politics in the Cities of the Fifth to the Mid Seventh Century: 425–640," in A. Cameron et al., eds., *The Cambridge Ancient History* (New York, NY: Cambridge University Press, 2000), Vol. XIV, 229. C. R. Whittaker, "Landlords and Warlords in the Later Roman empire," in John Rich and Graham Shipley, eds., *War and Society in the Roman World* (London: Routledge, 1993), 292.
[61] Heather, *CAH*, 455.
[62] J. B. Bury, *The Invasion of Europe by the Barbarians* (New York, NY: W.W. Norton & Company, 1967), 161.
[63] Peter S. Wells, *Barbarians to Angels* (New York, NY: W. W. Norton & Co., 2008), 109.
[64] Michael E. Jones, *The End of Roman Britain* (Ithaca, NY: Cornell University Press, 1996), 249.

appointed by the central government.[65] These cities also took over the provision of security, and the army became attached to them rather than to the imperial center. At least in part, from the end of the fourth century on, the decreased mobility of the army and its reliance on cities for supplies was due to the degeneration of the logistics system, made unreliable by the lack of security of the Roman road network.[66] In part to solve the logistical challenges, troops were placed in small fortified camps or walled towns, but as a result they gradually became separated from the rest of the imperial infrastructure and turned into local defense forces incapable of complex movements and bold projections of power. As Ramsay MacMullen observes, these forces "became civilianized; assigned to guard duty behind the walls of fortlets or small cities, they knew nothing of maneuvers or exercises and could only stand on the defensive. For the savings in their cost there was thus a high price to be paid."[67]

The geographic contraction of imperial power and its focus on Italy from the mid-fifth century on created the space necessary for local elites to assume the responsibilities until then fulfilled by the central authorities. Yet, this process of decentralization was not smooth because local armies could not fill quickly the security vacuum left by the imperial forces. In fact, the barbarian groups that entered the Roman Empire encountered overall very little local resistance. The fact that local populations were unable to counter militarily the barbarian raids and movements was a symptom of the novelty of the security situation. The British historian A. H. M. Jones, in his classic history of the later Roman Empire, suggests that this

> was probably in large part due to the fact that for generations the population had been accustomed to being protected by a professional army. The civilian population was in fact, for reasons of internal security, forbidden to bear arms. More important than this legal prohibition was the attitude of mind which it reflected. Citizens were not expected to fight, and for the most part they never envisaged the idea of fighting.[68]

It is true that some regions had always maintained small local armies for security purposes. Even at the peak of the empire's power, Roman authorities had to rely on local governments to maintain a modicum of safety on the roads and in cities, across the large expanses of territories that lacked a persistent presence of imperial soldiers. Hence, as P. A. Brunt observes,

---

[65] A.D. Lee, *From Rome to Byzantium*, 204.
[66] Whittaker, "Landlords and Warlords," 294. [67] MacMullen, *Corruption*, 176.
[68] A. H. M Jones, *The Later Roman Empire, 284–602* (Baltimore, MD: The Johns Hopkins University Press, 1986), Vol. 2, 1062.

it was "desirable for loyal local governments to have armed men at their disposal ... It is indeed quite clear that throughout Spain and Gaul communities as such were not disarmed."[69] But these were mostly small forces for policing purposes. Moreover, the broader challenge remained: Local populations, and local elites in particular, expected the empire to provide for their security. In a sense, they contracted their safety from external threats to professional imperial forces and authorities, and when these became either unwilling or incapable of supplying the promised security, the most threatened locals could not immediately replace them. The remilitarization of provinces that until then had been peaceful and thus insouciant of security needs was slow and difficult.[70] Unlike a few centuries later when local landowners in the Carolingian empire had already "their own ready-made armies ... Roman landowners, by contrast, were civilian, and had to struggle to put together enough of a force in their locality to defend themselves from predation from the centre" and later from external groups.[71] The danger of any empire and state that exercises a monopoly of force is that devolution of security roles, whether willing or not, takes time and presents a substantial adjustment to the structure and culture of the affected society. It is a reality that is not too dissimilar from our modern one because we too have come to rely on our states, and the military forces they maintain, to deliver security.

By the mid-fifth century, Roman emperors were willing to relax the imperial monopoly over arms production by, for instance, providing armories to cities. And in 440 when Italy was being targeted by Vandal seaborne raids, Valentinian III formally repealed the law banning civilians from carrying arms.[72] The law, entitled "The Restoration of the Right to Carry Arms," permitted and encouraged individual citizens to use any arms in their possession to defend their city, in particular along the coasts, as long as needed before the arrival of imperial forces.[73] The centrality of Italian lands, where also the emperors felt less threatened by potential local usurpers, made decentralization of security provision much more appealing than in strategically less important regions that were also more at risk of generating local challengers to the imperial throne (as proven, for instance, by the self-declared emperor Constantine III in Britain). The trade-off was that in regions where a strong local leadership existed,

---

[69] P. A. Brunt, *Roman Imperial Themes* (Oxford: Clarendon Press, 1990), 259.
[70] Michael Whitby, "Armies and Society in the Later Roman World," *CAH*, Vol. XIV, chapter 17, 469.
[71] Heather, *Fall of the Roman Empire*, 449. See also Whitby, *Cambridge Ancient History*, Vol. XIV, chapter 17, 481, and Whitby, *Cambridge Ancient History*, Vol. XIV, chapter 11, 297.
[72] Ward-Perkins, 48; Whitby, *Cambridge Ancient History*, Vol. XIV, chapter 17, 481.
[73] Penny MacGeorge, *Late Roman Warlords* (New York, NY: Oxford University Press, 2002), 170.

the devolution of imperial power resulted in centers more capable of defensive actions but also in the end less interested in staying within the Roman orbit. The least Romanized regions of the empire, such as Brittany, Western Britain, Northern Spain, and parts of Gaul, were those that resisted barbarian incursions the longest. In these areas, in fact, the Roman Empire never succeeded in replacing completely the existing tribal structures on which the populations, facing the various Gothic and Hunnic groups, relied to organize their defense. The militarization of local populations was easiest then in places where Roman imperial influence had been least successful.[74] Similarly, the revolts of the Bacaudae in the early fifth century, often interpreted as slave rebellions, were more likely local rebellions against central authorities that failed to provide security. The large number of slaves who participated in these uprisings was probably due to the fact that they were the most skilled warriors, as many came from barbarian tribes.[75]

The political success of the empire was therefore a mixed blessing when the barbarian – that is, small, local, mobile, and frequent – threats materialized in the late fourth century. The sophistication of Roman society, which encouraged labor specialization that led local populations to buy manufactured products from distant markets and security from a professional army, made it vulnerable to a disruption of the system. As a historian observes, the ability to buy pots from skilled workers and superior security from imperial legions was beneficial because people "got a quality product – much better than if they had had to do their soldiering and potting themselves. However, when disaster struck and there were no more trained soldiers and no more expert potters around, the general populations lacked the skills and structures needed to create alternative military and economic systems. In these circumstances, it was in fact better to be a little 'backward'."[76]

Finally, a decentralized empire could defend itself as a unified polity as long as local elites felt they were Roman. Perhaps unavoidably, the population writ large had little desire to defend the "empire," the world under Roman control. As A. H. M. Jones notes, "Rome was ... a mighty and beneficent power which excited their admiration and gratitude, but the empire was too immense to evoke the kind of loyalty which they felt to their own cities."[77] There was little or no sense of patriotism as we understand it now, affecting the large masses of people that lived within

---

[74] Van Dam, *New Cambridge Medieval History*, Vol. I, chapter 8, 222.
[75] Ward-Perkins, 47–48; Ian N. Wood, "The North-Western Provinces," in A. Cameron et al., eds., *Cambridge Ancient History* (New York, NY: Cambridge University Press, 2000), Vol. XIV, 497–524, and 502–504, in particular.
[76] Ward-Perkins, 49.   [77] A. H. M. Jones, 1062.

the boundaries of the empire. The élites were culturally Roman; most of them were educated in classical literature and were well versed in Roman law and tradition; and many had extensive contacts as well as residences in Rome, and often came from the senatorial class. But they were also very small in number relative to the population. At the time of Augustus, there were about 200 officials to administer the entire empire, with a population of around 50 million, of which less than 10 percent were Roman citizens.[78] They were the ones who picked up the task of defense when the barbarians began their raids and attacks, and assumed positions of administrative and military responsibility in the late fourth century in their respective cities because they were interested in preserving the civilization associated with the empire. They saw themselves as defending Roman civilization and power by protecting their own city or region. Very rarely they seemed to be seeking separation from the empire. As the barbarians kept attacking and weakening the empire, the outcome was a "world of 'Romans' without a Roman empire."[79] Gradually, however, from the late fifth century on, the connection to a Roman Empire withered away and the political outlook of the leaders shrunk to their own province. With each new generation of local leaders, Rome was becoming an increasingly distant and abstract authority.

This bottom-up decentralization of power required the presence of élites who had the authority and popular following necessary to demand money and manpower to protect their cities and regions. Many of them were or became bishops who were locally elected, and thanks to the authority derived from the Church, they rallied populations around them and became the new local leaders.[80] Bishops, in a manner similar to successful barbarian warriors, had the ability to attract and mobilize manpower. Writing in the sixth century, Gregory of Tours would mention several armed bishops, such as Hilary of Arles and Cantinus of Auvergne.[81] As will be described later, a case in point is Sidonius Apollinaris, bishop of Clermont in Gaul, who defended the city against the Goths in the late fifth century. While ultimately unsuccessful

---

[78] Ruggini, 106.   [79] Peter Brown, *The Rise of Western Christendom*, 98.
[80] Liebeschuetz, 230. Peter Brown argues that the rise of the bishops as political authorities was also due to the Roman tradition of patronage and friendship. The "emergence of men and women who claimed intimate relations with invisible patrons ... meant that yet another form of 'power' was available." The point here is that the changes of Late Antiquity relied on the existing traditions and structures: Bishops reflected the tradition of patronage while the devolution of imperial power and security provision to cities and their leaders was possible because cities were the legal and administrative centers of the empire at its peak. Peter Brown, *The Making of Late Antiquity* (Cambridge, MA: Harvard University Press, 1978), 64.
[81] Whittaker, "Landlords and Warlords," 291.

148   Altering the State

militarily, Sidonius maintained his position as a bishop, insisting on the ability of the Church to be independent from the Goths' (who were Arian and therefore heretic) interference.[82] Bishops then became the representatives of the population and of Roman culture, negotiating the best deal possible with the new barbarian leader that dominated their regions.[83] In fact, bishops became judges of civil cases, a task that occupied an enormous amount of time and that made this position of authority undesirable to many.[84] As historian Peter Brown put it, "walls and bishops went together."[85] Religious leaders became the defenders of the towns and provinces against the barbarians, the guardians of Roman culture at the imperial frontier, and in the end, the protectors of their populations under the Germanic conquerors. But at the same time a renewed sense of civic participation developed: The defense of the empire was no longer a task limited exclusively to the emperor and the legions under his command.

4.7   Western vs. Eastern Roman Empire

The historical record is clear: The Western Roman Empire collapsed, and by the sixth century various barbarian kingdoms took its place. It was a "a victory of the parts over the whole, of the periphery over the weakened centre."[86] Rome as a central authority simply could not cope with the multiple localized threats, and had to abandon some regions and relax its monopoly of violence over others. The decentralization of the Western Roman Empire was gradual and it was undertaken by Roman élites. The fact that the new local leaders who opposed the barbarians were Romans made it difficult for the contemporaries to notice the dramatic changes. The 476 AD deposition of Romulus Augustulus, the last emperor in the West, lacked the dramatic ending of a massive military defeat or

---

[82] Eric J. Goldberg, "The Fall of the Roman Empire Revisited: Sidonius Apollinaris and His Crisis of Identity," *Essays in History*, Vol. 35 (1995), 1–15.

[83] Massey Hamilton Shepherd, Jr., "The Effect of the Barbarian Invasions upon the Liturgy," in J. T. McNeill et al., eds., *Environmental Factors in Christian History* (Chicago, IL: The University of Chicago Press, 1939), 168. On the decentralization of the Church as part of its adaptation to the larger political environment, see also John Thomas McNeill, "The Feudalization of the Church," ibid., 187–205. The argument is that the Church reflected the wider political conditions to survive.

[84] Saint Augustine, for example, assiduously avoided towns that had no bishop because of his fear of being elected as one and thus of having to curtail his life of prayer and study. See Possidius, *The Life of Saint Augustine*, trans. Herbert Weiskotten (Merchantville, NJ: Evolution Publishing, 2008), 3–4; Henri Marrou, *Saint Augustine and His Influence through the Ages* (New York: Harper and Brothers, 1957), 33.

[85] Peter Brown, *The Rise of Western Christendom*, 107.

[86] Mazzarino, *The End of the Ancient World*, 40.

a physical destruction of a capital: It was a silent fall.[87] The "piecemeal destruction" of the empire, as Byzantine historian Zosimus put it, could be clearly seen only after the damage had been accomplished.[88]

Arguably, this imperial fragmentation was influenced by diminishing material capabilities as well as by the unstable internal political scene. But it is certainly plausible to argue that the external threat had an enormous impact on the internal structure of the attacked state. The case of the Eastern Roman Empire is instructive because Byzantium in the fourth to sixth centuries faced the barbarian threats in the north and a peer competitor, Sasanian Persia, on its southern frontier. Unlike its Western counterpart, Byzantium had to face the powerful Persian state, capable of fielding a large army that relied on extended logistics, could hold the territories it invaded, and presented a fixed threat from across the southern frontier.[89] The barbarians in the north could raid a region or damage a city, but an invasion of a Sasanian army could result in a territorial loss that would have required enormous military efforts to reverse.[90] To deter and, if need be, to defeat such a hostile army Byzantium needed a comparable force, led by a central authority that could direct it to where it was most needed. While regional forces, in some cases private armies or retinues of local individuals and commanders, developed in this period, all were ultimately under imperial control, and the emperor could decide how to use them. There was certainly a distinction between border troops (*limitanei*) and a field army (*comitatenses*) but it should not be interpreted as a sign of the development of local and quasi-independent militias along the frontier.

The recognition by Byzantine authorities that their resources were not infinite also resulted in a greater drive to keep tight central control over the military capabilities. For instance, Byzantine strategy stressed the

---

[87] Arnaldo Momigliano, "La caduta senza rumore di un impero nel 476 D.C.", *Annali della Scuola Normale Superiore di Pisa*, Serie III, Vol. 3, No. 2 (1973), 397–418.

[88] Walter E. Kaegi, *Byzantium and the Decline of Rome* (Princeton, NJ: Princeton University Press, 1968), 103. Zosimus was really the first historian to observe the outcome of the collapse of Rome and, unlike writers before him, he did not limit himself to a list of depredations committed by barbarians or to a *cri du coeur* of regret about the end of a centuries-old order, but sought to examine the roots of it – and for him, contrary to Saint Augustine, the fundamental cause was the abandonment of the pagan gods. As Walter Goffart observes, "[t]hough he lived in a state that called itself the Roman Empire, Zosimus in his own mind already stood where Poggio, Gibbon, and we ourselves stand: in the age following the fall of the world empire of Rome." Walter Goffart, "Zosimus, The First Historian of Rome's Fall," *The American Historical Review*, Vol. 76, No. 2 (April 1971), 413.

[89] Beate Dignas and Engelbert Winter, *Rome and Persia in Late Antiquity* (Cambridge: Cambridge University Press, 2007).

[90] Edward Luttwak, *The Grand Strategy of the Byzantine Empire* (Cambridge, MA: Harvard University Press, 2009), 50.

need to avoid set battles with the enemy in order to protect the dwindling imperial military resources.[91] But to implement such a strategy, centralized control over the military forces had to be maintained because otherwise local armies might have chosen to engage enemy forces approaching a city or region that they were expected to protect. As a historian observes, "Warfare against the Persians usually entailed the deployment of an imperial army which could repress separatist tendencies ... and there was little hope that a city or region could sustain an independent existence in the face of Persian might ... The direct clash of the two great powers of an ancient world helped to ensure that their common frontier was an area of strong central control, not of disintegration."[92]

The power of the Eastern Roman Empire remained firmly seated in Byzantium. Byzantium maintained wealthy taxable lands that provided the money necessary to pay for the armies. Taxes continued to flow directly to the capital, and not to local commanders as it had gradually become the norm in the West in the fifth and sixth centuries.[93] To be powerful meant to be part of the state apparatus, and not to possess large estates from which one could draw taxes and manpower or to administer a city. The privatization and localization of security provision that characterized the late Roman period in the West did not occur in the East – or at least it did not occur with the same speed.[94] Similarly, as noted earlier, the decentralization of political authority in the West was made possible by the local Church hierarchy, which assumed increasingly larger roles as protectors of cities, as the example of bishop Sidonius in Gaul indicates. In the East, bishops preferred to reside in Byzantium, where the seat of all power remained.[95]

When and where Byzantium faced a more decentralized, mobile, and localized threat, a process of political and military devolution did occur. For instance, starting in the seventh century, the southern frontier came under the threat of Arab raids and the centralized system of security provision became inadequate for dealing with rapid and unpredictable assaults on border regions and cities. The challenge was that local populations were left exposed to raids but were also woefully unprepared to defend themselves because Byzantium had maintained a prohibition on private individuals possessing and producing arms. There are some cases

---

[91] Luttwak, passim; John Haldon, *Warfare, State and Society in the Byzantine World, 565–1204* (London: UCL Press, 1999), 278–279.
[92] Whitby, *Cambridge Ancient History*, Vol. XIV, chapter 17, 484.
[93] Also, the Eastern Empire did not lose revenue-generating regions, unlike the Western part, which lost the mines of Spain and a few years later, with the Vandal southward movement, the wealthy and relatively stable North Africa. See also Harries, 245.
[94] Mark Whittow, *The Making of Byzantium, 600–1025* (Berkeley, CA University of California Press, 1996), 106.
[95] Wickham, 353.

Conclusion   151

where local individuals attempted to lead the defense of their cities, but most of Syria and Palestine, recognizing that armed resistance would have been futile in the long run, gradually surrendered to Arab invasions.[96] But in the fifth century the Eastern Empire simply did not face the same level of violence that the Western part had to cope with.

The case of Byzantium, therefore, appears to strengthen the broad argument that the nature of the external threat has a great impact on the internal structure of the state. It also confirms the more particular argument that a decentralized threat encourages and in some cases forces decentralization of state functions, including that of security provision. Byzantine history points to the fact that a threat by a peer competitor, a similarly structured state or empire, increases the pressure to keep a centralized fiscal, political, and military apparatus to be able to maintain deterrent and defensive capabilities.

4.8   Conclusion

The story of Late Antiquity suggests that there are four factors that influence the dynamic of decentralization when a barbarian threat arises.

First, the more internally secure and legitimate is the central government or ruler, the more likely it will pursue decentralization as a conscious strategy. Any decentralization involves a degree of devolution of power, and consequently it is seen with suspicion and preoccupation by the central authorities. A ruler or a government that has limited legitimacy, an unsupportive domestic base, or a fragile hold over the levers of power is less likely to support a strategy of decentralization – of giving some responsibility for security to the local authorities – because of fears of losing power. The rise of powerful local military commanders with local armies and with local legitimacy is in fact a threat to any central government, especially one that has a shaky hold over its own population. In brief, the more insecure the central government, the less likely it will devolve power and security provision to local elites.

Fear for its own survival or at least its political power may even lead a central government or ruler to prefer abandoning a distant frontier city rather than allowing local initiatives to take hold or letting a commander

---

[96] Benjamin Isaac, *The Eastern Frontier*, A. Cameron et al., eds., *The Cambridge Ancient History*, Vol. XIII, chapter 14, 437–460, 456–458, in particular; Walter E. Kaegi, *Byzantium and the Early Islamic Conquests* (Cambridge: Cambridge University Press, 1992), 47–51. George Ostrogorsky argues that from seventh century on, the Byzantine army was essentially a peasant army, supported freely by local populations. This theory has been abandoned and most historians argue the armed forces continued to be managed by the imperial center. Andrew Louth, "The Byzantine Empire in the Seventh Century," *CMH*, Vol. I, chapter 11, 291–316.

be successful in its defense. The success of such a commander may, in fact, give him incentives to challenge the emperor. Decentralization, therefore, is more likely to arise out of local frustration, rather than out of a strategy pursued by the center. In any case, the level of legitimacy and internal security of the central government will impact its decision on whether, and how, to protect against a barbarian threat.

Second, the concurrent presence of a peer-competitor threat along a different frontier will dampen the drive to decentralize. A decentralized security posture makes the state vulnerable to a large-scale attack by a well-organized army that could easily break the small frontier outposts and penetrate deep inside the territory, unless opposed by an equally potent army. In other words, an extremely decentralized state with no central army has a hard time deterring, and defending against, a state fielding a large, trained, and well-armed army. It can perhaps produce extended guerilla warfare based on the dispersed forces, shoring up deterrence by denial, but it is a risky strategy that promises long-term costs to the invader but also to the defender. Consequently, by decentralizing forces, and more broadly, security provision, a state may increase the incentives for a peer rival to invade. Hence, the greater the threat of a hostile peer-competitor, the weaker the incentive to decentralize.

Third, the strategic and economic value of the frontier locations that are most likely to be attacked affects the government's decision whether and how to decentralize. In some cases, such locations, deemed unimportant, may simply be abandoned to their own fate, resulting in a *de facto* devolution of power likely to be permanent. In other cases, the regions under threat may be of great strategic value and the government may decide to devote resources to protect them. This is likely to be a form of defense prioritization, rather than devolution of power. But it must involve a commitment to local defense, and hence it may have an impact on local politics, favoring a specific set of leaders or groups most needed to shore up the security of the place. It will therefore result at least in a mild form of decentralization, characterized by local elites receiving greater attention and more resource from the capital. It is also a decentralization that may be likely to be permanent as the central authorities can withdraw their support and armed forces, depriving the local elites of a key source of their power and legitimacy.

The fourth factor that affects the ability of a state to decentralize security provision is related to the previous point and is an important caveat to the idea that decentralization can be "turned on or off" with great ease. The prior existence of local elites and local ability to extract and administer resources and to organize local defenses can make decentralization more effective. If local elites exist, decentralization is more

Conclusion

feasible but also more centrifugal. Local leaders have the interest to protect their cities or regions, and can draw on fiscal and military support of the local populations. Yet, the risk is that devolution of power to the local authorities may generate greater aspirations for independence from the central government or court, fueling a separatist movement. The question then becomes one of identity, namely, of how much the local elites identify themselves with being part of a larger entity (say, the Roman Empire or the United States) and act in defense of local populations but in the name of this larger community. A strong "central" identity mitigates the centrifugal drift of empowered local authorities, and thus makes a willful strategy of decentralization more palatable to the state capital and more effective.

The absence of local elites upon which the central government can rely makes a strategy of decentralization more difficult to implement but easier to control and reverse. In such cases, decentralization needs to be manned by leaders and forces sent from the center, who depend fully on the central authorities for supplies, money, manpower, and legitimacy. While there is the risk that the leaders and forces detached to a region go "native" and aspire to greater independence from the center, their dependence on the state for financial and political benefits dampens their ability to turn against the capital. In some ways, this is a tactical decentralization, affecting mostly the placement of state military units, rather than devolution of power to the lowest possible political level. Such decentralization is shallow and more transient, as military forces can be easily withdrawn from frontier areas, and it also may be less effective because the facility with which troops can be moved away diminishes the credibility of the commitment of the central authorities to that region.

The case of the late Roman Empire does not prove that political fragmentation is unavoidable when a state is assaulted by multiple small groups that present localized threats. But it does indicate that a centralized polity is not always the most effective way of approaching security matters, especially when facing barbarians. Because of the unpredictable and localized nature of this threat, a polity may be better served by decentralizing some of its authority and allowing local forces and leaders to provide for their own security. Such devolution of power is likely to occur anyway, because a centralized state is poorly prepared to deal with militarily small and geographically diffuse assaults. It is more provident, therefore, to establish the conditions, such as local leaders with strong roots in the idea of the state and a population with skills and capabilities to defend itself, that would allow pursuit of a strategy of decentralization. A centralized state that arrogates to itself all the functions of security provision may undermine its own safety.

5 Three Saints and the Barbarian Threat

> *Why place we our hearts in the earth, when we see that the earth is being turned upside down?*
>
> Saint Augustine, Sermon 55[1]

The decentralization of security provision is gradual, occurring over generations. It is also dangerous because it can weaken the bonds uniting the polity. As barbarian groups nibble on the frontiers of a targeted empire, and then roam with relative impunity inside of it, the provision of security slowly becomes a task for local forces, authorities, and individuals. Their immediate surroundings, their closest political grouping, their region and city – rather than the wider political entity – become the sources of civic mobilization. Decentralization leads to a narrowing of horizons.

This dynamic of security decentralization – of the growing role of local authorities and of the weakening of their commitment to the wider polity – is well illustrated through the experiences of three individuals in their respective and very different regions affected by barbarian attacks: Saint Augustine in North Africa, Saint Sidonius Apollinaris in Gaul, and Saint Severinus of Noricum along the Danube. With Vandals invading North Africa, Saint Augustine of Hippo (354-430 AD) sought the military support of an imperial commander, Boniface, who, albeit vying for great personal power and clashing with Roman imperial authorities, was still a Roman commander. In Gaul, effectively abandoned by imperial forces, Sidonius Apollinaris (430–490 AD circa) took over the command of his city and nourished the hope, in the end in vain, that the empire would back him up. Finally, Severinus of Noricum (410–482 AD) on the Danubian frontier was alone, with no tangible signs of Rome or a possibility of a rescue by Roman legions.

None of them expected, nor hoped for, a demise of the empire. There is no nascent nationalism or anti-imperialism in their writings and actions.

---

[1] Saint Augustine, Sermon 55 on the New Testament, #11 online at www.newadvent.org/fathers/160355.htm.

But there is an unpleasant realization that the central government was unable, and unwilling, to devote attention and resources to the protection of individual outposts of Roman civilization. The result is a "growing provincialization" or decentralization: "Augustine thought in terms of the whole empire ... But Sidonius was definitely a Gaul."[2] And Severinus' concern was a number of small cities or villages where the most he could do was to assuage the devastation of barbarian attacks.

5.1 Saint Augustine of Hippo

Saint Augustine was a product of the Roman Empire and of the culture that flourished in it. His education and early career were a testament of the strength of Roman culture, capable of unifying the vast Mediterranean world through a common intellectual heritage and language. Born in Thagaste in North Africa, probably of Berber descent, Saint Augustine moved to Carthage, then Rome, and then Milan, the capital of the Western Empire, in search of education and of a public career as a teacher. His was an impressive path for somebody who probably always spoke with an African accent.[3] In Milan, because of Saint Ambrose's influence and most importantly through his mother's intercession, Augustine became a Christian and applied his intellect to the defense of his faith. One of the key questions characterizing his thought concerned the role of the Roman Empire in history and of its relationship to the advent of Christianity. This became even more timely as anti-Christian propaganda became more pronounced, blaming the political and military disasters of the late empire on the wrath of pagan gods.[4]

Like other Christian leaders in the late fourth century, Saint Augustine in his early writings seemed to treat the now-Christianized empire as a welcome congruence of political and Christian orders. But as the barbarians advanced, and as he returned to North Africa from Italy, he separated the two orders: The particular form of the polity, and indeed, the very existence of the Roman Empire, was not necessary to attain salvation. The empire after all, even at the peak of its forces, could never fulfill the promise of peace because it had been, like all polities, an imperfect human product. In his *City of God*, Saint Augustine mentions Emperor Augustus

---

[2] Chris Wickham, *The Inheritance of Rome* (New York, NY: Viking, 2009), 91. See also Pietro Vaccari, "Dall'unità romana al particularismo medioevale," *Annali di scienze politiche*, Vol. 4, No. 1 (March 1931), 1–24.

[3] Henri Marrou, *Saint Augustine and His Influence through the Ages* (New York, NY: Harper and Brothers, 1957), 20–22; Agostino Trapé, *Saint Augustine: Man, Pastor, Mystic* (New York, NY: Catholic Book Publishing, 1986), 16–19.

[4] R. P. C. Hanson, "The Reaction of the Church to the Collapse of the Western Roman Empire in the Fifth Century," *Vigiliae Christianae*, Vol. 26, No. 4 (December 1972), 275.

who had "pacified the world" (*orbe pacato*), expressing a momentary sentiment of appreciation for the political achievement of Octavian.[5] But that accomplishment was fleeting at best, and its importance was overshadowed by that other great event – namely, the birth of Jesus – that occurred under the emperor's tenure. Moreover, Rome had been far from a just city: It had created an order but through violence. "How many great wars, how much slaughter and bloodshed, have provided this unity! And though these are past, the end of these miseries has not yet come."[6] The pacification of the world was not the same as peace.

Seeing the faults of the empire, made more visible by the barbarians battering the *limes* and the city of Rome itself, Saint Augustine did not bestow some sacred task or role on the polity in which he lived. "Augustine's theological mind was happily concentrated by Roman weakness as well as Roman unreliability."[7] The empire, like all political entities, was a transient form of temporal order; the empire comes and goes, polities augment their power and they decay. "The Empire has become no more than a historical, empirical society with a chequered career, whose vicissitudes are not to be directly correlated with the favour of the gods, pagan or Christian, given in return for services rendered. It is theologically neutral."[8] And in fact, the decay of Rome had nothing to do with the advent of Christianity, a charge that he refuted at length in his *City of God*, but rather stemmed from the corruption of the ancient virtues that allowed the rise and survival of the empire. Citing Sallust, Augustine wrote in a letter to a friend: "The moment that the decline of the Roman commonwealth began is clear enough. Their own literature tells of it. Long before the name of Christ shone out on earth, someone [Sallust] had said, 'O venal city, ripe for destruction, if only it finds a buyer'."[9]

His criticism of the empire of his day did not lead him, however, to an anti-imperial position or, to be more precise, to rejecting the necessity and desirability of political order. Augustine was still a Roman, and in North Africa, a bishop in charge of a Roman city in a frontier region of the Roman Empire. The empire was not the fulfillment of mankind's

---

[5] Saint Augustine, *The City of God* (New York, NY: The Modern Library, 2000), translated by Marcus Dods, XVIII:46, p.656; for the Latin version of this phrase, see Saint Augustine, *City of God* (Cambridge, MA: Harvard University Press, 1960), Loeb, translated by William Chase Greene, 46.
[6] Saint Augustine, *City of God*, XIX, 7, 683.
[7] John. M. Rist, *Augustine: Ancient Thought Baptized* (New York, NY: Cambridge University Press, 1994), 228.
[8] R. A. Markus, *Saeculum: History and Society in the Theology of St. Augustine* (Cambridge University Press, 1970), 55.
[9] Letter 138, #16, in *Augustine: Political Writings*, E. M. Atkins and R. J. Dodaro, eds.(New York, NY: Cambridge University Press, 2001), 39.

aspirations nor of God's plan, but it was still a source of order and security. Political order was a good, and was necessary to live here and now. But it was not a good in itself, representing the pinnacle of human achievement and thus used to justify every conceivable sacrifice and means deemed necessary to defend it. It was conceivable that the empire could collapse, and political order could be supplied by some other form of polity. That is why Saint Augustine was not as alarmed as Saint Jerome, the "excitable hermit of Bethlehem," by the 410 AD fall of Rome.[10] Rome, like all empires and cities, was a temporary device in an inscrutable plan of God, the architect who builds a lasting house through transient tools.[11] It was natural and desirable for political leaders and citizens alike to be actively involved in the building and the protection of their city or empire, but it was equally vital to understand that these actions were not ends in themselves. The temptation of the secular leader, or even of the politically engaged citizen, was to elevate the political entity, such as the Roman Empire, to a position it did not deserve. As French historian Henri Marrou put it,

[t]he artist will idolize his art, the lover his love, the man of action the city which it is his duty to build. It is well that all should remind themselves that man is not in the world for himself, nor yet for the world, but for God, that man is not just an animal species whose function is to build civilizations, one after the other, like ants and termites endlessly labouring to build and rebuild their wonderful but fragile dwellings.[12]

Saint Augustine distances himself from the classical – and traditional Roman – view that the political life was the supreme achievement of man.[13] But he does not embrace the opposite view, suggesting a complete detachment from the vicissitudes of the state and from public duties. Because of our fallen condition, there is simply no way of withdrawing from the world, and pride, the search for glory, or the desire of domination will always intrude on our lives even in the most remote and peaceful monastery. Moreover, even monastic life, to which Saint Augustine was drawn his entire life, requires a wider political order that allows it to prosper and survive: Security is a necessary and desirable good.

---

[10] Rudolph Arbesmann, "The Idea of Rome in the Sermon of St. Augustine," *Augustiniana*, Vol. 4 (1954), 309.
[11] "*Architectus aedificat per machinas transituras domum manentem.*" Sermon 362, 7. Quoted in Ernest L. Fortin, *Classical Christianity and the Political Order* (Lanham, MD: Rowman & Littlefield, 1996), 121.
[12] Henri Marrou, *Saint Augustine and His Influence through the Ages* (New York, NY: Harper and Brothers, 1957), 80.
[13] Linda C. Raeder, "Augustine and the Case for Limited Government," *Humanitas*, Vol. 16, No. 2 (2003), 95.

The order provided by the empire in the form of its laws and implemented by its judges and legions was worth defending.[14] It was a bulwark against the forces of disintegration from within, as men will always tend to "devour each other like fish."[15] More importantly and more timely in the first half of the fifth century, whatever was left of the empire was the last bastion of security, protecting populations against the barbarian attacks and the violence, the depredations, and the following chaos that engulfed the wider Mediterranean.

In 429 AD North Africa, where Saint Augustine was a bishop, became a target of the Vandals. In the previous decades, the various barbarian groups that spread over the Western Roman Empire had two serious limitations; they lacked the capacity to maintain sieges around fortified towns and had no naval skills. The Vandals, led by Genseric, proved instead to be capable of crossing the Gibraltar strait from Spain, penetrating a Roman province that had until then been protected by the Mediterranean waters. It was a reminder of a geopolitical reality that the ancient Romans recognized in their early years: The Mediterranean had never hindered the flow of populations. On the contrary, throughout history it served as a highway, rather than a barrier, allowing intense commercial interactions and political integration but also destabilizing movements of people and bold projections of power. The security of one shore was tied to the security of the opposite one. When Rome was growing, the threat was from North Africa. The Punic assaults in the third and second centuries BC presented the greatest threats to Roman power in Italy, and the response was to extend Rome's control over the North African shore of the Mediterranean. In the fifth century AD, the situation was reversed: The European shores (Spain to be precise) were the source of instability and threat, and North Africa could not remain immune for long.

When the Vandals crossed the straits of Gibraltar *en masse*, they disrupted the life of the North African region. Unrest, devastation, weakening of civil authority, and war were the result, ruining the wealthiest and until then safest part of the late Roman Empire. As Edward Gibbon put it eloquently:

War in its fairest form implies a perpetual violation of humanity and justice; and the hostilities of barbarians are inflamed by the fierce and lawless spirit which incessantly disturbs their peaceful and domestic society. The Vandals, where they found resistance, seldom gave quarter; and the deaths of their valiant countrymen were expiated by the ruin of the cities under whose walls they had fallen.[16]

---

[14] Rist, 206–208.   [15] A line by Irenaeus, quoted in Markus, *Saeculum*, 98.
[16] Edward Gibbon, *The Decline and Fall of the Roman Empire* (New York, NY: Alfred A. Knopf, 1993), Vol. 3, chapter 33, 381.

The Vandal flood of North Africa was the outcome of petty infighting among Roman administrators and just plain stupidity of imperial authorities. The barbarians had been invited by Boniface, the local Roman commander, who felt threatened by the imperial authorities in Italy who were eager to curb his ambition to become the supreme leader in the region. He probably had even greater aspirations, being one of those recurrent cases in history of a huge mismatch between ambition and capabilities. It is likely that Boniface thought that he could strike a deal with the Vandals, trading some control over the region for their manpower that then he could use for his own personal purposes. By the time he realized that the Vandals were too powerful to accept a deal and that the emperor was after all positively inclined toward him, it was too late. As Procopius puts it, Boniface "repented of his act and of his agreement with the barbarians, and he besought them incessantly, promising them everything, to remove from Libya."[17] Gibbon added in his inimitable style that the "generous mind of Count Boniface was tortured by the exquisite distress of beholding the ruin which he had occasioned, and whose rapid progress he was unable to check ... The military labours and anxious reflections of Count Boniface were alleviated by the edifying conversation of his friend St. Augustine."[18] Of course, by then, the Vandals were quite aware they had the advantage and showed no intention of withdrawing from North Africa, and the entire political structure in the region went up in flames.

Whatever the reasons for the Vandals' southward push, one thing was certain: The existing political order was threatened. Roman military presence was scant while local barbarian tribes that until recently were on the imperial payroll turned unreliable. As Saint Augustine observed in a letter, the stability of the Roman Empire had been sustained by fragile agreements with tribal forces: "For not only on the frontier, but throughout all the provinces, the security of peace rests on the oaths of barbarians."[19] These oaths were easily broken.

As the Vandals advanced eastward along the North African coastline, cities and communities surrendered without putting up much of a fight. As Possidius, the bishop of Cama and friend of Saint Augustine, put it, "a great host of savage foes, Vandals and Alans, with some of the Gothic tribe interspersed, and various other peoples, armed with all kinds of weapons and well trained in warfare, came by ship from the regions of

---

[17] Procopius, *History of the Wars*, Vol. 2, trans. by H. B. Dewing, Loeb Classical Library (Cambridge, MA: Harvard University Press, 1916), III:iii:30–31, 33.
[18] Edward Gibbon, *The Decline and Fall of the Roman Empire* (New York, NY: Alfred A. Knopf, 1993), Vol. 3, chapter 33, 382.
[19] Saint Augustine, Letter 47, www.newadvent.org/fathers/1102047.htm.

Spain ... [And] they completely devastated everything they could by their pillage, murder and varied tortures, conflagrations and other innumerable and unspeakable crimes ... "[20] The barbarians did not want to become shareholders of the existing political and social order; they wanted to wreck it and establish their own.

The security situation, then, posed a big question to Saint Augustine. Why defend a political order that was clearly corrupt and led by half-witted pompous hedonists? And how could one do it given the absence of strong imperial authorities and capable leaders? Some locals were surely tempted not to oppose the Vandals, seeking some accommodation, or simply running away and abandoning their positions of responsibility, high and low. After all, they probably rationalized that a new social order would surely arise, underwritten by the Vandals, and it was futile to stand athwart this mass movement. Perhaps, their thinking went, people should simply accept changes in who ruled and should adapt to the inexorable movement of history.

Saint Augustine thought otherwise, and in his writings he suggested a two-prong response. First, he gently reprimanded fellow bishops and church leaders who seemed unwilling to stay in the cities on the Vandal path and to share the fate of their flocks. In a letter written in the early months of the Vandal invasion, he addressed the thorny question of what the clergy ought to do when their towns were under attack. In typical Augustinian fashion, he does not give a clear-cut simple answer but goes through several possibilities. For instance, Saint Augustine writes that,

> on the one hand, those who desire to remove, if they can, to fortified places are not to be forbidden to do so; and, on the other hand, we ought not to break the ties by which the love of Christ has bound us as ministers not to forsake the churches which it is our duty to serve.[21]

In the end, priests and bishops have an obligation to stay with their people, and ought not to deprive them of the spiritual support they need. Were the people themselves to decide to flee, then the bishop was freed from the bonds that tied him to the place. But if for whatever reason they did not flee, the church leader had the duty to stay with them and avoid contributing to the collapse of social order, underwritten in part by the unity and succor provided by spiritual leadership. Saint Augustine concluded the letter by reminding his correspondent that a position of authority in the Church did not bestow a greater claim to survival. "Let no

---

[20] Possidius, *The Life of Saint Augustine*, trans. by Herbert Weiskotten (Merchantville, NJ: Evolution Publishing, 2008), chapter XXVIII, 40–41.

[21] Saint Augustine, Letter 228 to Bishop Honoratus, #1, at www.newadvent.org/fathers/1102228.htm.

one hold himself in such esteem because of apparent superiority in any grace as to say that he is more worthy of life than others, and therefore more entitled to seek safety in flight. For whoever thinks this is too self-satisfied, and whoever utters this must make all dissatisfied with him."[22] In similar terms, he defined the role of the bishop in book 19 of *City of God*. The position of a bishop was serious work, not an honor, and this work was to take care of those under him. The word *episkopos* (bishop), he writes, is Greek for "superintendent," meaning that a bishop was supposed to oversee or look out for those under him.[23]

This letter does not describe a military strategy to be employed against the Vandals, but it clarifies the role of the bishop in a political order collapsing under the barbarian pressure. The towns that were abandoned by imperial forces and authorities were not to be deserted by the bishops, whose duty was to remain with their people. As the secular order of the empire retreated or was unable to provide the security it promised, the vacuum was gradually filled by the bishop. The principal obligation of the bishop was to his own community, the people who lived in the town and region under his authority – and not necessarily to the empire writ large. As in all human societies, there are limits to the ability and responsibility of individuals: for a man, "his own household are his care, for the law of nature and of society gives him readier access to them and greater opportunity of serving them."[24] For the bishop, it was his city and his immediate community of the faithful. Unsurprisingly, in peacetime bishops spent most of their time administering justice in their towns, a task that Saint Augustine dreaded but fulfilled out of love for his "flock."[25]

From a purely secular perspective, the bishop had a different set of considerations from those of the imperial center. Imperial authorities

---

[22] Letter 228, #12.   [23] *City of God*, XIX:19, 698.
[24] *City of God*, XIX:14, 693. Elsewhere, Saint Augustine writes: "After the state or city comes the world, the third circle of human society – the first being the house, and the second the city. And the world, as it is larger, so it is fuller of dangers, as the greater sea is the more dangerous. And here, in the first place, man is separated from man by the different of languages ... a man would more readily hold intercourse with his dog than with a foreigner." *City of God*, XIX:7, 683. Following Cicero, Saint Ambrose of Milan similarly argued that there was a hierarchy of obligations: "first toward God; secondly, towards one's own country; next, towards parents; lastly, towards all ... From the beginning of life, when understanding first begins to be infused into us, we love life as the gift of God, we love our country and our parents; lastly, our companions, with whom we like to associate." Saint Ambrose, *On the Duties of the Clergy*, Book 1, Chapter 27, #127, online at www.newadvent.org/fathers/34011.htm. Cicero did not pretend that we should care about "all" and his hierarchy of duties went from the gods to the country and then to lower forms of social associations: *prima dis immortalibus, secunda patriae, tertia parentibus*. Cicero, *De Officiis* (Cambridge, MA: Harvard University Press, 1913), LCL 30, trans. by Walter Miller, I:45:160, 164.
[25] Trapè, 147–148.

might have to weigh the protection of a particular town against some larger security consideration, allowing a small sacrifice for the greater good of the empire. Such a trade-off was especially likely when the region or towns under attack were at the frontier, distant from the imperial center, and the loss of which was not deemed catastrophic to the wider imperial structure. Moreover, if the attack was led by barbarian groups, whose reach may have been limited, the imperial authority was even less likely to expend resources to parrying it. In the end, there was a divergence between the interests of the bishop and those of the imperial authorities. For the bishops, the local community trumped the wider empire and the horizons narrowed.

For Saint Augustine, there was still, however, the imperial option to protect his local community. This is the second prong of the Augustinian approach to the insecurity brought by the barbarians. On top of advising his fellow bishops to remain with the populations, Saint Augustine put some hopes on the local Roman commander, Boniface. Perhaps this general was confused and lacking strategic acumen (as his initial cozying up to the Vandals indicated – followed quickly by a panicked recognition of his mistake), but he still had forces at his disposal and, despite his tensions with the emperor and his court, he represented the remnants of imperial power. Saint Augustine did not appeal to the imperial court for help, in part because of the distance separating North Africa from it, but in part perhaps because he understood that the defense of Hippo and other adjacent cities would have never been very high on the emperor's list of strategic concerns. Hence, the most he could expect from the empire was the attention of the local commander, an imperfect man but the best hope for maintaining security in the region.

In a series of letters to Boniface, the Saint of Hippo argued in no uncertain terms that secular authorities had the obligation to protect the social order and the populations entrusted to them. In fact, citizens had the duty to accept, if offered, a public position out of love of the others.[26] There is recognition in Saint Augustine's letters to Boniface that war is often inevitable because it is imposed by violent enemies – and in fact, war can never be eradicated on this earth.[27] "For it is the wrong-doing of the opposing party which compels the wise man to wage just wars."[28] War is

[26] Quinto Tosatti, "Agostino e lo stato Romano," *Studi Romani* (September 1955), 545.
[27] John East writes that "the student of Augustine has no illusions about the utopia of the world state. He is prudent, cautious, and restrained. As with Augustine, he is braced for the interminable conflicts of world politics, for pressure, tension, and 'power politics' are inherent in the nature of things human, and no panacea of human construction, including world government, can eliminate those realities." John P. East, "The Political Relevance of St. Augustine," *Modern Age* (Spring 1972), 174.
[28] *City of God*, XIX:7, 683.

therefore not a lesser evil – in fact, Saint Augustine does not accept the idea of a necessary lesser evil – but an imposed necessity, testament to the misery of man.[29] That is why, as he writes in letter 189, being a soldier was not incompatible with being a good Christian: "Do not think that it is impossible for anyone to please God while engaged in military service."[30] It is certainly true that social life is enveloped in darkness (*in tenebris vitae socialis*) and leads good men to engage in otherwise despicable actions, but a wise public official will recognize the misery of human life and will continue to serve in his position because the requirements of human society compel him to this duty.[31]

Sometime before the Vandal invasion, Boniface had been tempted to abandon his active life and retreat into some sort of monastic, even eremitic, lifestyle. He respected Saint Augustine's wisdom and must have asked him for counsel. The answer was surprising, coming from somebody who, as one of the first actions when he returned to North Africa from Italy, established a monastery for himself and his followers. The Saint replied in one of his letters by praising the diversity of vocations. Abandoning earthly preoccupations was always a noble cause but not all were called to do that in their daily life. "There are some who by praying for you fight against your invisible foes, while you by fighting for them are striving against the visible barbarians."[32] *Contra visibiles barbaros* – these were visible, tangible, real enemies to eliminate, and Saint Augustine is clear that they needed to be thwarted. War should be waged against them, in the hope and with the purpose of achieving peace. Harmony – or a *tranquillitas ordinis* – is not of this earth.[33] A political order, like the one North Africa enjoyed under the remnants of Roman authority, was a blessing, but, as a scholar put it, "All human order was fragile, poised over an abyss of chaos. It needed the best that men – Christian and non-Christian alike – could give to its preserving and fostering."[34] The preservation of such order was not automatic, and therefore it did not allow all to retreat to the prayerful solitude of monastic life. Later on, Saint Augustine praised Boniface for remaining in his post as a commander and not engaging in the "sacred leisure" or retirement of the

---

[29] "Augustine occasionally speaks of a 'lesser justice' (*iustitia minor*) as an object of choice, but, to my knowledge, never of a lesser evil, small as it may be. The nuance was not unimportant to him. He had not read Machiavelli, did not anticipate him, and would doubtless have rejected him if he had known him." Ernest L. Fortin, "Review: The Why, Not the What," *The Review of Politics*, Vol. 59, No. 2 (Spring 1997), 367.
[30] Saint Augustine, Letter 189, #4, online at www.newadvent.org/fathers/1102189.htm.
[31] *City of God*, XIX:6, 682; Rist, 214–216.   [32] Saint Augustine, Letter 189, #5.
[33] "Peace between man and man is well-ordered concord ... The peace of all things is the tranquility of order. Order is the distribution which allots things equal and unequal, each to its own place." *City of God*, XIX, 13, 690.
[34] Markus, *Saeculum*, xi.

servants of Gods, that is, of monks.[35] By staying, Boniface allowed others, including monks, to be "protected from all disturbance by barbarian hordes" and "live 'a quiet and peaceful life', as the apostle says, 'in all godliness and honesty'."[36]

War therefore is often a necessity, and has to be waged by the proper authority. It is imposed by the enemies and should not be sought. One even ought to pray to be freed from this necessity of war.[37] When possible, war should be avoided and the hostility of men should be mitigated by negotiations. In a letter to a Roman envoy, Darius, who had been sent to North Africa to negotiate with the rebellious Boniface, Saint Augustine suggests that "greater glory still is merited by killing not men with swords, but war with words, and by acquiring or achieving peace not through war but through peace itself. For those who fight, if they are good men, are certainly aiming for peace, but still through bloodshed." Negotiations are preferable to war, but this does not imply that when war is imposed it ought not to be fought. It is a "necessity."[38]

When the enemies were at the door, there was no doubt in Saint Augustine's mind that the political authorities had the duty to fight them – and that there was a role for the "vigilance of the authorities" in inspiring fear in those who threatened order and Christianity (like the heretical Donatists).[39] "Let necessity, therefore, and not your will, slay the enemy who fights against you. As violence is used towards him who rebels and resists, so mercy is due to the vanquished or the captive,

---

[35] Saint Augustine, Letter 220, #3, online at www.newadvent.org/fathers/1102220.htm.
[36] Saint Augustine, Letter 220, #3. Saint Augustine understood perfectly the desire to live a quiet monastic life and, upon his return to North Africa from Italy, avoided towns that had no bishop, in fear of being asked to become one. Unfortunately for him, in Hippo Regius, people seized him and asked the sitting vetust bishop to ordain him. Augustine "wept floods of tears" but did not escape this duty. See Possidius, 4:2; Trapè, 125–126.
[37] Markus, *Saeculum*, xiii.
[38] Letter 229 to Darius, in *Augustine: Political Writings*, E. M. Atkins and R. J. Dodaro eds. (New York, NY: Cambridge University Press, 2001), 226.
[39] In the treatise, *The Correction of the Donatists*, addressed to Boniface, Augustine describes the benefits of a forceful intervention of the authorities against the heresies that threatened Christian unity. Later, in his *Revisions*, he reinforces the point by arguing that his early opposition to using force against schismatics was mistaken because he "did not as yet realize all the evil things they would do with impunity, or all the improvement that the vigilance of the authorities could inspire in them." There was an important role, therefore, for the use of force and the establishment of fear of punishment. See Trapè, 224–225. Similarly, a war fought with justice in mind will direct the enemy toward the proper course of action. As he wrote to Marcellinus, the "aim [of such wars] will be to serve the defeated more easily by securing a peaceful society that is pious and just. For if defeat deprives the beaten side of the freedom to act wickedly, it benefits them." Letter 138, #14 in *Augustine: Political Writings*, E. M. Atkins and R. J. Dodaro eds. (New York, NY: Cambridge University Press, 2001), 38. See also Phillip Wynn, *Augustine on War and Military Service* (Minneapolis, MN: Fortress Press, 2013), 178–179.

especially in the case in which future troubling of the peace is not to be feared." The purpose was to protect the existing order, which, even if imperfect because human, was preferable to the destruction, the killing, and the upheaval that would surely be brought by the enemies. "For peace is not sought in order to the kindling of war, but war is waged in order that peace may be obtained. Therefore, even in waging war, cherish the spirit of a peacemaker, that, by conquering those whom you attack, you may lead them back to the advantages of peace."[40]

In another letter to Boniface, Saint Augustine wrote in a tone of great worry and urgency. "The barbarians of Africa are succeeding here without meeting any resistance so long as you are in your present state, preoccupied with your own needs, and are organizing nothing to prevent this disaster." Nobody thought, he continued, that with Boniface as commander (*comes*) "the barbarians would have become so bold, have advanced so far, have caused so much devastation, have plundered so widely, have made deserts of so many places that were full of people."[41] He admitted that perhaps Boniface felt mistreated by the imperial court, jealous of his success, or simply fearful of his ambition. But the fact that his service at the frontier was unrequited by the emperor did not mean that he was justified to sit on his hands and not oppose the Vandals. The "Roman empire provides you with good things, even if they are ephemeral and earthly (for it is an earthly, not a heavenly, institution and can only provide what is in its power)."[42] Those good things – social order and absence of physical threats – are worth defending.[43]

Therefore, Saint Augustine reiterated in several places that the duty of the commander was to man the walls while controlling his worst impulses. In particular, Saint Augustine reprimanded Boniface for his lascivious lifestyle (he was on his second wife and surrounded by concubines), betraying a lack of discipline that could not but diminish his ability to fight the barbarian enemy. "It is certainly shameful if someone who is undefeated by another human being is defeated by lust, or undefeated by iron, but overwhelmed by wine."[44] The most important fight is always internal, against the corruption arising from vice, but the physical conflict with enemies who are threatening the stability of one's own political order should not be ignored. Secular leadership, in this case represented by Boniface, has a heavy responsibility.

---

[40] Saint Augustine, Letter 189, #6.
[41] Saint Augustine, Letter 220, #7, at www.newadvent.org/fathers/1102220.htm.
[42] Saint Augustine, Letter 220, #8.
[43] He does not share the view of those who advocated shunning the secular order and the polity in which they lived, deriving joy from its hatred. See Markus, *Saeculum*, 56.
[44] Saint Augustine, Letter 189, #7.

Saint Augustine was careful in not offering operational or policy advice in his letters. Boniface had the political experience, a trained military mind, and the ability to assess the state of the forces at his disposal, and thus, it was his task to figure out the most effective way of defending the North African cities. Saint Augustine writes to Boniface: "Are you asking me to give advice in the light of this world on how to safeguard this ephemeral security of yours ... ? If so, then I am unable to answer you. There is no secure advice to give for purposes that are so insecure."[45] Military victory, like material wealth and political success, was given to the good as much as to the impious, paralleling the fate of polities, temporal entities that rose and fell. The role of the bishop was to encourage the commander to pray and to be free from vice, that is, to attend to his own eternal salvation. But, again, Saint Augustine did not advocate that Boniface retreat to a monastic life of prayer: the barbarians were coming, action was needed. The fragile political and social order needed to be defended, and not sacrificed for personal vanity or for an abstract and utopian harmony.

Saint Augustine's philosophy straddles between ancient thought and modern theory, making it often difficult to comprehend. His body of work is a "gigantic effort to integrate Christian faith and the principles of the Greek-Roman philosophy."[46] The intellectual challenge stems in part from the fact that he does not develop a theory of the state and of regimes, and, in particular, he is unconcerned about the level of power of rulers as long as they do not force citizens to commit immoral acts.[47] His arguments sometimes can be frustrating, as in the case of his letters to Boniface. On the one hand, he argues, the empire, or rather the security of the small community in North Africa, ought to be defended because, however fragile and ephemeral, order and absence of violence was preferable to the alternative, the barbarian onslaught. On the other hand, the empire was not a good in itself and were it to collapse for one reason or another the possibility of salvation would remain unaffected.[48] He is a loyal Roman citizen, a product of the deep and wide culture of the empire,

---

[45] Saint Augustine, Letter 220, #9.
[46] E. L. Fortin, "Idéalisme politique et foi chrétienne dans la pensée de saint Augustine," *Recherches Augustiniennes*, Vol. 8 (1972), 232.
[47] Quentin P. Taylor, "St. Augustine and Political Thought: A Revisionist View," *Augustiniana*, Vol. 48, Issue 3 (1998), 287–303.
[48] In Sermon 105, Saint Augustine calls Virgil, the poet of Roman imperial glory, that "poet of theirs," separating himself from the empire, a political construction that was doomed to end. Referring to Virgil (Book 1 of the Aeneid in particular), he wrote: "They who have promised this to earthly kingdoms have not been guided by truth, but have lied through flattery. A certain poet of theirs has introduced Jupiter speaking, and he says of the Romans;

To them no bounds of empire I assign,
Nor term of years to their immortal line.

and a detached observer of the political vicissitudes of a temporal political reality. In fact, it is clear that Saint Augustine is no longer a staunch defender of the Roman Empire writ large – a "cesspool of evil characters, where the ancient ethos has been abandoned"[49] – choosing only to advocate vigorously for the defense of his immediate region, a symptom of the decentralization and provincialization of the fifth century. He did not favor the breakup of the empire because the church community after all lived within the polity, but he severed the connection between the fate of the Roman polity and that of the Church.[50]

In the end, the barbarians won in North Africa. Saint Augustine died during the siege of Hippo Regius in 430 AD and Boniface was utterly defeated by the Vandals. North Africa fell under the barbarian attacks, and Saint Augustine witnessed most of the cities turned into rubble (only three, Carthage, Cirta, and his own Hippo, were still standing before his death). As his biographer Possidius recalls, Augustine "was consoled by the thought of a certain wise man who said: 'He is not to be thought great who thinks it strange that wood and stones should fall and mortals die'."[51] Meanwhile Boniface retreated to Italy, rejoined the regent Galla Placidia, defeated the rebellious Aetius (Procopius calls both Aetius and Boniface the "last of the Romans"[52]) near Rimini (432 AD) but died after receiving a mortal wound there. This

---

Most certainly truth makes no such answer. This empire which thou hast given 'without term of years,' is it on earth, or in heaven? On earth assuredly. And even if it were in heaven, yet 'heaven and earth shall pass away.'(15) Those things shall pass away which God hath Himself made; how much more rapidly shall that pass away which Romulus founded! Perhaps if we had a mind to press Virgil on this point, and tauntingly to ask him why he said it; he would take us aside privately, and say to us, 'I know this as well as you, but what could I do who was selling words to the Romans, if by this kind of flattery I did not promise something which was false? And yet even in this very instance I have been cautious, when I said, "I assigned to them an empire without term of years," I introduced their Jupiter to say it. I did not utter this falsehood in my own person, but put upon Jupiter the character of untruthfulness: as the god was false, the poet was false.'" Saint Augustine, Sermon 105, #10 at www.ewtn.com/library/PATRISTC/PNI6-10.TXT. For an analysis of this sermon, see also Rudolph Arbesmann, "The Idea of Rome in the Sermon of St. Augustine," *Augustiniana*, Vol. 4 (1954), 305–324.

[49] Saint Augustine, Letter 138, #17, 40.

[50] As an African bishop, Ottatus of Milevi, wrote: "the republic is not in the church, but the church is in the republic" (*non enim respublica in ecclesia, sed ecclesia in republica est*). Cited in Paolo Brezzi, "Impero romano e regni barbarici nella valutazione degli scrittori cristiani alla fine del mondo antico," *Studi Romani* (May 1961), 260. Saint Augustine preferred unity over particularism in the Church (and was agnostic on the empire) – and this explains his strong position against the various heresies that threatened to break up the unity of Christians. On the rise of particularism or separatism in late antiquity, see Vaccari, 9–11.

[51] Possidius, 42, ch. XXVIII.

[52] Procopius, *History of the Wars*, Vol. 2, trans. by H. B. Dewing, Loeb Classical Library (Cambridge, MA: Harvard University Press, 1916), III:iii:15, 27.

infighting only allowed further consolidation of Vandal control over North Africa.[53]

5.2 Sidonius Apollinaris of Clermont-Ferrand

Saint Augustine was concerned about the security of Hippo Regius and less so of the empire, but his intellectual horizons were still wide. He thought about the empire, its place in history, and the role of secular authority in maintaining order. A "Latin rhetorician turned Christian bishop,"[54] he wrote freely and beautifully, and his style spoke of a learned Roman well versed in history and literature. The political and cultural horizons of Sidonius Apollinaris (430–490 AD) were instead much narrower, reflecting a further imperial retrenchment and decentralization. He "turns his mind to Aquitaine and to the small country of the Clermont-Ferrand and not to the wide Roman world."[55] Sidonius was a Roman Gaul, and for him the empire was a source of a prestigious political position (briefly) and then of a great betrayal. The imperial court of the mid-fifth century was incapable of, and not interested in, protecting the small frontier communities and cities. The bishop, as Sidonius would become, was the local leader, protecting his city from the rapaciousness of imperial administrators and from the attacks of barbarians alike. Augustine was still a Roman; Sidonius was a Roman Gaul.

The provincialization of the outlook was evident from Sidonius' writings. A prolific writer who had a greater facility than skill at writing,[56] Sidonius addressed not a vast global audience like Augustine, but a more limited Gallic readership. He wrote for a small circle of Roman friends, often located near him rather than on the other side of the Mediterranean, and claimed to be satisfied with this smaller audience.[57] His letters are peppered with references to classical writes from Cicero to Pliny, still read by well-educated Romans, but his style is overly elaborate, often in search of a difficult or obscure phrase, as if he were trying desperately to maintain Latin literacy.[58] It is also a writing that, unlike Saint Augustine's, carries

---

[53] J. B. Bury, *History of the Later Roman Empire* (Minneola, NY: Dover, 1958), Vol. 1, 248; the entire story of Boniface is on pages 244–248.

[54] Albert C. Outler, "Augustine and the Transvaluation of the Classical Tradition," *The Classical Journal* 54 1959), 213.

[55] Vaccari, 6.

[56] "*Cui scribendi magis est facilitas quam facultas*," Sidonius, trans. by W. B. Anderson, *Letters III-IX* (Cambridge, MA: Harvard University Press, 1965), Loeb, Letter III:7:1, 30–31.

[57] "*Dictio mea, quod mihi sufficit, placet amicis*" – it is sufficient for me that my words please my friends. Sidonius, trans. by W. B. Anderson, *Letters III-IX* (Cambridge, MA: Harvard University Press, 1965), Loeb, Letter 8.16.5, 498.

[58] Philip Rousseau, "In Search of Sidonius the Bishop," *Historia*, Bd. 25, H. 3 (3rd Qtr., 1976), 356–357.

no hope nor aspiration to shape public opinion or engage in important debates, perhaps because it was more a form of escapism in difficult times.[59]

Furthermore, Sidonius was writing in times of great insecurity, arising from unstable Roman politics and barbarian attacks. He remained often silent on important historical episodes of his life to avoid the wrath of imperial authorities.[60] He wrote to a friend in a dispirited tone that "our account of things past is profitless, that of things present is only half-complete; and while it is shameful to utter falsehoods, it is dangerous to tell the truth; for it is an undertaking in which any reference to the good brings but scant favour, and any allusion to the infamous brings great offense."[61] The politics of the imperial court were, however, a luxury preoccupation that faded in importance as the security conditions in Gaul deteriorated. In the last years of his life, when Gaul fell under control of Euric's Visigoths, Sidonius became even more circumspect in his writings because it was common for private missives to be intercepted. In a letter, Sidonius wrote that the roads were "insecure by the commotions of peoples" and couriers could not "pass the guards of the public highroads without a strict scrutiny." Thus, he continued, it was safer to "renounce our rather too busy pens, putting off for a little our diligent exchange of letters, and concerning ourselves rather with silence."[62] The art of keeping silent was a symptom of the increasing insecurity of Gaul.

A diminished volume of letter-writing was the least traumatic outcome of barbarian attacks. The insecurity of the region created also political uncertainty and an absence of law enforcement that awakened the rapaciousness of small-town administrators. In a letter to his brother-in-law, Sidonius describes in scathing terms a certain Seronatus, a Roman official in charge of contacts with the Visigoths. He lists numerous nasty qualities of tyrannical stamp and even suggests that this official was betraying Rome (and indeed, later on, Seronatus was put to death for treason): "he brags to the Goths and insults the Romans, mocks the magistrates and plays tricks along with the public cashiers; he tramples on the laws of

---

[59] "Writing well becomes thus a rite that is celebrated in a small world, closed on itself, in the contemplation of a past, the glory of which is turned into a myth and is enjoyed with pride and regret." Isabella Gualandri, *Furtiva Lectio: Studi su Sidonio Apollinare* (Milan: Cisalpino-Goliardica, 1979), 27.

[60] Ralph W. Mathisen, "Sidonius on the Reign of Avitus: A Study in Political Prudence," *Transactions of the American Philological Association*, Vol. 109 (1979), 165–171; J. D. Harries, "Sidonius Apollinaris, Rome and the Barbarians: A Climate of Treason?", in John Drinkwater and Hugh Elton, eds., *Fifth-century Gaul: A Crisis of Identity?* (New York, NY: Cambridge University Press, 1992), 298–308.

[61] Letter to Leo, Ep. IV.22.5 in Sidonius, *Letters III-IX* (Cambridge, MA: Harvard University Press, 1965) 148–149.

[62] Ep. IX:3:1–2, 509.

Theodosius and issues laws of Theodoric."[63] The continued barbarian attacks weakened the resolve and the capacity of the empire to respond, but left in place administrators who thought they had the power without the imperial oversight and abused it.

More interestingly, in the same letter, Sidonius offers a clear rationale for a certain form of decentralization. "If the state has neither strength nor soldiers, if... the Emperor Anthemius has no resources, then our nobility has resolved under your guidance to give up either its country or its hair."[64] That is, Roman aristocrats in Gaul were ready to abandon their country or in any case to give it up to the barbarians pressuring with increasing vigor. Or, the second option, they were ready to cut their hair, namely to accept the tonsure that came with becoming clergy.

The latter approach was seen as a way of remaining Roman – namely, to defend Roman culture and tradition in their own region, regardless of who the emperor was or what new political order arose. There was no desire to separate Gaul from the empire. Sidonius was not a proponent of a nascent Gallic separatism; he does not hark back to Vercingetorix, the Gallic rebel defeated by Julius Caesar.[65] In fact, there are only two examples in this period of regions or areas in the Roman Empire that unify in some form and seek to separate from the empire: Britain in 409 and the movement of the Bacaudae in the 430s. In both cases, the absence of imperial forces allowed (or forced) the rise of local forces, perhaps peasants in the latter case.[66] But this was not the case of Clermont-Ferrand and Sidonius. He saw himself as a descendant of Rome, with a growing sense that he may have been one of the last ones (and, in fact, his son ended up serving the Visigoths, proving perhaps his worst fears). Rather he, like his correspondents in Gaul, wanted to participate in the empire (that is why the Roman nobles in Gaul had elevated Avitus as emperor) in order to protect his region and his own possessions. Later on at the end of the century, as we will see with Sidonius, when the security situation degenerated even further, they simply wanted not to be abandoned by the empire and its authorities.[67]

The doubt that the empire was not as interested in or capable of protecting Gaul created an opportunity – and a necessity – for the aristocratic families in Gaul to take over some power. For many, including

---

[63] Ep. II:1:3, 415–417.   [64] Ep. II:1:3, 417.
[65] Arnaldo Momigliano, "La caduta senza rumore di un impero nel 476 D.C.," *Annali della Scuola Normale Superiore di Pisa*, Serie III, Vol. 3, No. 2 (1973), 406–407; C. E. Stevens, *Sidonius Apollinaris and His Age* (Oxford: Clarendon Press, 1933), 38–39.
[66] E. A. Thompson, "Britain, A.D. 406–410," *Britannia*, Vo. 8 (1977), 303–318.
[67] Jill Harries, *Sidonius Apollinaris and The Fall of Rome: AD 407–485* (Oxford: Clarendon Press, 1994), 80.

Sidonius, an active engagement in the empire to defend Gaul was seen as a duty. The pillaging of Rome by Geiseric in 455 was a signal that even the heart of the empire was no longer safe, and certainly its capacity to protect its core areas was greatly diminished. And the frequent changes of emperor demonstrated a political confusion that hindered any ability of the empire to respond in a consistent fashion to the barbarian threat, a reality that invited further and more decisive Gothic incursions from 469 on.[68] The frontier regions, such as Gaul, therefore, were even less likely to be defended, unless the locals took a much more vigorous role. And Sidonius, together with many of his aristocratic friends, pooled money to raise a small militia to protect Clermont-Ferrand. It was a small force but the barbarian groups were also puny. In one case, Sidonius' brother-in-law broke through Gothic lines that encircled the city during the recurrent siege in 470–474 AD with less than twenty men "in the middle of the day [and] in the middle of an open plain."[69]

Noble Romans in Gaul had also a personal interest in figuring out how to maintain order because they risked losing their vast land properties. Possession of land tied the senatorial families to specific regions and very few could abandon their properties in Gaul to retreat to Italy or elsewhere in the shrinking empire.[70] "As their horizons narrowed, the holding of episcopal chairs became an increasingly attractive option for noble families, as one means of perpetuating their dominance of their local communities."[71] The barbarians, in fact, gradually translated their military strength into political leverage, taking over the lands owned by wealthy members of the Roman senatorial class. Gibbon described the situation in vivid terms:

Injuries were aggravated by insults; the sense of actual sufferings was embittered by the fear of more dreadful evils; and as new lands were allotted to new swarms of barbarians, each senator was apprehensive lest the arbitrary surveyors should approach his favourite villa, or his profitable farm. The least unfortunate were those who submitted without a murmur to the power which it was impossible to resist. Since they desired to live, they owed some gratitude to the tyrant who had spared their lives; and since he was the absolute master of their fortunes, the portion which he left must be accepted as his pure and voluntary gift.[72]

It is probably around this time, in the mid-fifth century, that Sidonius entered civil service.[73] His first approach was to support an emperor and seek to shape policies through a position at the imperial court. He married

[68] Peter Heather, *The Fall of the Roman Empire* (London: Pan Macmillan, 2006), 416.
[69] Ep. III:3:3, 15.   [70] Heather, 422.   [71] Harries, 103.
[72] Edward Gibbon, *The Decline and Fall of the Roman Empire* (New York, NY: Alfred A. Knopf, 1993), Vol. 3, chapter 36, 526–527.
[73] Stevens, 29–30.

the daughter of Emperor Avitus, who, however, had a very short reign (455–456). He also wrote three tedious panegyrics over the course of a decade, seeking the good graces of the emperors. The first one, for Avitus, "seems to contain a very moderate proportion either of genius or of truth," in Gibbon's scathing opinion.[74] A second one for Majorian in 458 was followed by the last one in 468 for Anthemius, a piece that, again in Gibbon's words, "rewarded [Sidonius] with the prefecture of Rome; a dignity which placed him among the illustrious personages of the empire, till he wisely preferred the more respectable character of a bishop and a saint."[75] Sidonius' desire to ingratiate himself with the emperor of the day was not merely a symptom of his shallow ambition but it was motivated by a desire to help Gaul. In his second panegyric, he wrote: "my land of Gaul hath even till now been ignored by the lords of the world, and hath languished in slavery unheeded."[76] If the emperors were ignoring the frontier province, then the provincial leaders had the duty to try to change their minds.

Sidonius' career in Rome was short-lived for unknown reasons. But it is likely that his return to Gaul had to do with the recognition that Rome, or what was left of the imperial apparatus, was no longer interested in defending frontier regions such as Gaul.[77] Rome was corrupt not as much financially but intellectually, having lost its sense of identity, whether in the form of the ancient virtues of Roman ancestors or by letting poorly assimilated barbarians run the affairs of the state. In a letter written probably in the 460s to a friend, a Roman *vir illustris*, Sidonius bemoans the difficult times they were witnessing. The ancient republic was characterized by greater virtue, he writes, but it was still possible to find good men: a "Brutus or Torquatus" – the former played a role in the expulsion of the Tarquins while the latter in the defense of Rome against the Gauls in the fourth century BC – could always be found. Sidonius probably considered himself and his friend as potential successors to these great men and citizens of early Rome, even though he was born and bred in Gaul. Sidonius saw himself as a descendant of Rome with a growing sense that he was one of the increasingly few. But the problem was that the Roman polity of their day no longer seemed to appreciate the service and the valor of these few men. The reason was simple: "it is no great wonder,

---

[74] Gibbon, *Decline and Fall*, 478. A modern historian agrees with this judgment: "This is very uninspired writing. It is worse than mere padding, it is very bad padding." Stevens, 32.
[75] Gibbon, *Decline and Fall*, 499.
[76] Panegyric on Maiorianus, *Sidonius, Poems, Letters I-II* (Cambridge, MA: Harvard University Press, 1936), #356–357, 93.
[77] Harries, 180.

at a time when a horde of Federates is not only controlling the resources of Rome in a tyrannous spirit but even destroying them at their foundations."[78]

If the imperial court had no role for true Romans, then the alternative was to stay close to Gaul, Sidonius' native land. In one of his letters to his brother in law (474 AD), Sidonius writes that a man's native soil "rightly claims the chief place in his affection."[79] To defend Rome – the Roman civilization, not the capital city or the entire empire – meant to defend the Romans, the few wherever they were left; it was a "world of 'Romans' without a Roman empire."[80] And in the fifth century it was becoming clear that seeking tonsure, that is, becoming a clergyman and a bishop, was not only a religious vocation but a form of political service, a civic duty for those who wanted to protect and defend the crumbling order. Sidonius was probably more eager than Saint Augustine to become a bishop, having demonstrated a desire for positions of authority and influence. But we have no reason to doubt that he was only interested in social advancement or in the protection of his senatorial status. Given his devotion to his province and the local population, Sidonius had no choice but to become a bishop.

The role of Sidonius, like of bishops in general in the second half of the fifth century, was to be the advocate of the local population. As mentioned earlier, the fraying of imperial authority meant that provincial governors often became more rapacious, and "an emperor might listen to the complaints of a bishop when he would not listen to any one else."[81] Sidonius describes the role of the bishop in a speech he gave in support of a particular candidate to an episcopal seat. The bishop, when necessary, must be a "spokesman of this city before skin-clad monarchs or purple-clad princes."[82] The state must admire him, the Church love him.[83] The bishop, that is, was not merely a spiritual leader, a protector of the souls of his flock, but also a defender of his people in front of secular authorities.

Moreover, bishops were judges of sort, dealing with the time-consuming and difficult task of adjudicating small quibbles among the locals, because the Roman legal system, like the rest of the state apparatus, was no longer capable of fulfilling its duties.[84] But, and this was particularly true at the imperial frontier that was most immediately threatened by barbarian advances, the role of the bishop was also to organize the defense

---

[78] Ep. III:8:2, 35.   [79] Ep. III:3:1, 13.
[80] Brown, *The Rise of Western Christendom*, 98. And the bishops "looked their part. We see them in the mosaics of the time, which represented saints and former bishops. With their quiet eyes, solemn stance, and weeping, silken robes, they are recognizably 'last Romans'." Brown, 113.
[81] Stevens, 115.   [82] Ep. VII:9:19, 351.   [83] Ep. VII:9:16, 349.   [84] Harries, 209–211.

of the population under him. The bishop thus became not only a mediator, but also a military leader, shoring up defenses, in some cases even going to battle, and certainly keeping the populations in their beleaguered towns and provinces united.[85]

The moral authority of the bishop was the main source of unity and strength of the local population, even when, as in Sidonius' case, he did not deem it appropriate to take military command.[86] Sidonius sees the role of the bishop as the guarantor of social unity, tested by continued barbarian attacks, weakness of imperial authority, and a variety of religious sects. There were in fact divisions even among the ranks of the Roman aristocrats, as Sidonius himself attested in his letters (and as, later on, his own son would join the forces of the Visigoths).[87] Every action of the bishop, including his homilies, was meant to shore up this unity.[88] In a moving letter to Mamertus, a fellow bishop in Gaul, Sidonius recounts how before the fall of his town, Clermont-Ferrand, to the Goths, the inhabitants' resolve to resist the siege and constant attacks (471–475 AD) was strengthened by prayers, which he, Sidonius, led. He wrote:

> the Goths have moved their camp into Roman soil; we luckless Arvernians are always the gateway to such incursions ... As for the surrounding country, its whole length and breadth has long since been swallowed up by the insatiate aggression of that threatening power. But we have little confidence that our reckless and dangerous courage will be supported by our hideously charred walls, our palisades of rotting stakes, our battlements worn by the breasts of many a sentinel; our only comfort is in the aid of the Rogations which we introduced on your advice ... it is because of these rogations that they [the inhabitants of Clermont-Ferrand] are not yet retreating from the terrors that encircle them.[89]

The Visigothic siege of Clermont-Ferrand between 471 and 475 AD was a series of annual incursions that gradually cut off the city from the rest of the empire and made the region unstable, dangerous, and poor. A few years earlier, it was already evident that the area surrounding Clermont-Ferrand was no longer secure. Visiting a friend in 469, Sidonius observes

---

[85] Stevens, 115.
[86] "Moral leadership and the support of his friends were the main weapons available to the bishop Sidonius as leader of the Clermont resistance. He had never been a military man and his status now precluded direct military activity." Harries, 227.
[87] On the internal divisions, see Heather, 419–420.
[88] Ugo Dovere, "La Figura del Vescovo tra la Fine del Mondo Antico e l'Avvento dei Nuovi Popoli Europei," *Archivum Historiae Pontificiae*, Vol. 41 (2003), 29.
[89] Ep. VII:1:1–2, 287. The Rogations, introduced a few years earlier by bishop Mamertus, were days of prayer and fasting. For Mamertus this was a way of shoring up his community after a natural disaster or some personal tragedy, whereas for Sidonius the Rogations were meant to unite the population against the barbarian threat. Stevens, 153; Harries, 227–228; Brown, *The Rise of Western Christendom*, 108; Rousseau, 364.

that the roads were hazardous and his friend moved to a "castellum," a fortified building, surrounded by Alpine cliffs.[90] This Visigothic threat, combined with the weakness of imperial forces, led also to the rise of petty Roman warlords, interested in booty and private promotion, rather than in keeping Roman traditions alive. They plundered to enrich themselves and their bands, and in the process further increased the instability and insecurity of the region.[91] Such a chaotic situation could not but increase the reliance of the population on their bishop.

Finally in 475, Italian forces under Emperor Julius Nepos came over the Alps to Gaul. The authorities of the Western Roman Empire feared that the Visigoths would not have stopped in Gaul, but instead of fighting the barbarians in battle, they entered into negotiations with the Gothic leader, Euric. Sensing perhaps that Clermont-Ferrand would be officially abandoned, as it had been de facto for years, and resentful that he was not asked to be part of the high-level meetings, Sidonius wrote to one of the bishops, Basilius of Aix, who participated in the negotiations. The letter carries a tone of desperation. Euric was indeed powerful and winning, Sidonius acknowledged, but not because he was right. "With all his military might, his ardent spirit, and his youthful energy, he labours under one delusion: he imagines that the success of his dealings and plans comes from the genuine orthodox of his religion, whereas it would be truer to say that he achieves it by earthly good-fortune."[92] Moreover, an Arian, Euric was forcing Catholic bishops out of their positions, with the result of "spiritual ruin" or devastation.[93] Gregory of Tours recounted later on that Euric was persecuting Catholics: "he cut off the heads of all who would not subscribe to his heretical opinions, he imprisoned the priests, and the bishops he either drove into exile or had executed. He ordered the doorways of the churches to be blocked with briers so that the very difficulty of finding one's way in might encourage men to forget their Christian faith."[94] At this point, probably aware that militarily there was little that could be done to reverse the Gothic onslaught, Sidonius wanted to carve out some autonomy and to protect Catholic bishops and their congregations under the likely new political regime.[95]

The empire signed a treaty with the Visigoths from a position of weakness, and Sidonius' Clermont-Ferrand was sacrificed in the hope of

---

[90] Ep. IV:15:3, 122–123. [91] Harries, 223–224. [92] Ep. VII:6:6, 319.
[93] Ep. VII:6:7, 319.
[94] Gregory of Tours, *The History of the Franks* (New York, NY: Penguin, 1974), 138.
[95] Clermont was probably successful in resisting for four years because of modest help from Burgundians, interested in hindering the growth of the Visigoths, rather than because of its own strength or imperial aid. Harries, 236.

preserving Italy.[96] When he found out about the deal, Sidonius penned a bitter letter to another bishop, Graecus of Marsilia (one of four bishops who signed the treaty). Clermont-Ferrand, Sidonius wrote, had opposed the common enemy of the Roman Empire, the barbarian Visigoths, and fought alone. And "yet when their arms had any success their triumph benefited you, whereas if they were worsted it was only they who were crushed by the blow."[97] He continued: "If necessary, it will be a joy to us still to endure siege, still to fight, still to starve. But if we are surrendered, we who could not be taken by force, it is undeniably you who devised the barbarous expedient which in your cowardice you recommended."[98] Sidonius and his town were still willing to hold out, to defend Rome at the frontier, but it was Rome – not the Roman people in Gaul – that abandoned the fight. "Our freedom has been bartered for the security of others."[99] The larger strategic consideration of the emperor was that the landlocked regions of Clermont-Ferrand were not as valuable as the southern coast of Gaul, with ports such as Arles and Marseille.[100] To make his feelings perfectly clear, he added: "We pray that you and your colleagues may feel ashamed of this fruitless and unseemly treaty."[101]

Sidonius at this point was very aware that he had lost: His political project of protecting Gaul and of keeping Roman civilization alive had failed. And he experienced firsthand the dramatic need to separate the fate of Christianity and Christians like himself from the fate of the Roman Empire. Even under hostile political leaders, it had to be possible to maintain the culture and religion. Sidonius' quest, therefore, after 475 AD was to be free under the rule of tyrants (*liber sub dominantibus tyrannis*).[102]

But he also continued to care for his people and asked his episcopal correspondent, Graecus, to save those who could escape the Visigothic rule. "If you cannot save us in our extremity, at least secure by unceasing prayer that the blood of those whose liberty is doomed may still survive; provide land for the exiles, ransom for the captives-to-be, and aid for the refugees on their way. If our walls are opened to admit our foes, let not yours be closed to exclude your friends."[103]

This 475 AD letter was the "epitaph of the Western Empire."[104] A year later, the last emperor, Romulus Augustulus, was deposed by Odoacer, a Germanic military leader in Italy. After the fall of Clermont-Ferrand, Sidonius was arrested because of his role in shoring up resistance against

---

[96] Stevens, 159.   [97] Ep. VII:7:2, 327.   [98] Ep. VII:7:25, 329–331.
[99] Ep. VII:7:2, 325–327.
[100] Vincent Burns, "The Visigothic Settlement in Aquitania: Imperial Motives," *Historia*, Bd. 41, H. 3 (1992), fn. 58, 372.
[101] Ep. VII:7:4, 329.   [102] Ep. III:12:12, 46.   [103] Ep. VII:7:6, 331.   [104] Stevens, 160.

the Visigoths. Released some time later, he died between 480 and 490 AD.[105] The empire failed to protect Gaul and, in particular, Clermont-Ferrand because of military weakness followed by a diplomatic deal – an appeasement attempt – that traded the outer frontier region for Italy. The empire also failed Sidonius, who tried to defend his "native land" first, by joining the imperial court; second, by returning to Gaul and engaging in local political life; and third, by becoming a bishop and assuming a position of authority in his town.

His career was emblematic of an inward turn in the regions most threatened by barbarian raids. The imperial center was unable to protect them, forcing local élites to assume a greater role in providing security and maintaining social order (and, when everything else failed, to accept the new Gothic overlords, as Sidonius' son did). Sidonius' professional and personal path was one of decentralization out of necessity, but he was never tempted to break away from the empire. He remained a Roman, even when the empire cut him and his region off.

5.3 Severinus of Noricum

Sidonius never thought the empire would collapse and worked ceaselessly to protect his native land, gradually moving away from the imperial center to the confines of his town. Only in his last years, when Clermont-Ferrand could no longer resist the barbarian attacks alone, his attention switched to what we now refer to as humanitarian concerns. As security conditions deteriorated, his outlook gradually narrowed, focusing more and more on his province rather than on the wider empire. Sidonius could in the end still survive, even if no longer in a position of authority, and reach some sort of agreement with the new barbarian overlords, however unpleasant and uncomfortable that deal must have been. In a more exposed frontier region, along the Danube, it was much more difficult to reach a settlement with the barbarian warlords, who were more aggressive, more divided, and more aware of the vacuum created by the withdrawing empire. There, a mysterious monk, Severinus, took responsibility for some villages and small towns, organizing them, striking deals for them with the barbarians, and strengthening their resolve.

Unlike Saint Augustine or Sidonius, Severinus (*c.* 410–482 AD) did not write anything and, as far as we know, did not say much about himself either. He probably came from a Roman family because he was well educated, and had experience with eastern desert monasteries. But all we know with certainty is that he appeared on the Danube shortly after

---

[105] On the date of Sidonius' death, see Stevens, Appendix G, 211–212.

178   Three Saints and the Barbarian Threat

Attila's death in 453 AD. This imperial frontier separated a tenuous Roman order from barbarian lands to its north. The barbarian lands, as far as we know, were shaken by various tribal forces, unleashed after Hunnic dominance had quickly disintegrated with Attila's death (of a nosebleed induced by heavy drinking on his wedding night). Attila's sons demanded to have the various tribes of their empire divided among themselves. The various tribal leaders naturally resented such treatment, rebelled, and gradually tore the Hunnic Empire apart. As sixth-century historian Jordanes commented, "in their rash eagerness to rule they all alike destroyed [Attila's] empire."[106] As a result of this barbarian infighting, the Roman settlements along the Danube were placed between a frail empire and a gaggle of raiding barbarians.

Severinus did not solve the security problem facing the Roman towns. But he helped them to manage this dangerous condition. A man of great faith – indeed the "saint of the open frontier,"[107] as the historian of late antiquity Peter Brown calls him – Severinus devoted the last decades of his life to Noricum, the region roughly congruent with modern-day Austria. In those frontier outposts, the locals had to make difficult decisions based on an assessment of how resilient their empire was, how persistent and dangerous the enemy appeared, and how strong their own will to resist was.

Severinus moved from city to city on the right bank of the Danube – a string of small villages with terrified populations sheltering behind walls *(castella)*, targeted by small barbarian raids, sustained by sporadic commerce, and mostly abandoned by imperial troops. The might of Rome was absent on the Danubian *limes* and local political élites, Severinus included, seemed to have more frequent audiences with barbarian leaders than contacts with their own imperial authorities. Severinus' peregrinations along the Danubian frontier, recounted in a biography written by Eugippius, illustrate different ways of coping with growing insecurity on a frontier that was gradually abandoned by Roman forces and harassed by small tribes roaming the area.[108] The Roman outposts he visited experienced different stages of geopolitical grief from denial and delusion to, in the best case, an attempt at indigenous security provision.

The locals, as well as Severinus, were keenly aware that the frontier was not secure. The tangible presence of the empire was disappearing, and the towns were losing their main security providers. "So long as the Roman

[106] Jordanes, *The Gothic History*, Charles Christopher Mierow, ed. (Princeton, NJ: Princeton University Press, 1915), #259, 125.
[107] Peter Brown, *The Rise of Western Christendom* (Blackwell Publishing, 2003), 123.
[108] Eugippius, *The Life of Saint Severinus*, trans. by George W. Robinson (Cambridge, MA: Harvard University Press, 1914).

dominion lasted, soldiers were maintained in many towns at the public expense to guard the boundary wall. When this custom ceased, the squadrons of soldiers and the boundary wall were blotted out together."[109] But the recognition that imperial forces were not what they used to be was gradual. In fact, the slow withdrawal of Roman troops did not seem to have had a shocking impact on the locals, who perhaps did not notice immediately that their security required the presence of armed men. It is not unusual that few consider how security and deterrence are maintained while peace reigns.

One of the most visible Roman strongholds at Batavis (modern-day Passau) remained manned by soldiers. It was a military base more than a town; located on the confluence of two important rivers, the Danube and the Inn, it occupied important strategic real estate that most likely was deemed more valuable than other towns east of it. It was a remnant of a string of military outposts, and the soldiers based there appeared to be severed from the bulk of the legions located in the rear. At some point, "some soldiers of this troop had gone to Italy to fetch the final pay to their comrades."[110] They did not travel far, however, because the barbarians marauding in the area brutally killed them. For a while no one was aware of this massacre, but "one day, as Saint Severinus was reading in his cell, he suddenly closed the book and began to sigh greatly and to weep. He ordered the bystanders to run out with haste to the river, which he declared was in that hour besprinkled with human blood; and straightway word was brought that the bodies of the soldiers mentioned above had been brought to land by the current of the river."[111]

Such a shocking scene could not but generate consternation and despair. The role of these few Roman soldiers was first and foremost one of reassuring the local imperial subjects. They could not have defended the small towns in case of a prolonged barbarian assault, and certainly could not protect every village from small raids. They did not maintain the safety of the surrounding areas, leaving it open to small but frequent barbarian incursions – and as the violent end of the few soldiers heading to obtain the overdue pay indicates, they could not even protect their own forces. Finally, these scarce imperial forces certainly did not serve as a "tripwire" because it was unlikely that, in case of a barbarian attack on them, Roman legions would have marched north in retaliation. In brief, they did not deter the barbarians. But they were there to reassure the locals. They were good enough to reassure, even if not good enough to deter and defend.

[109] Eugippius, chapter 20, 69.   [110] Eugippius, 69.   [111] Eugippius, 69–70.

As Severinus witnessed, after the reassuring presence of imperial might had vanished, the local response did not include calls for defense or stronger walls. Rather, the populations of the frontier towns were in a state of disbelief and self-delusion. As Roman power waned, the locals comforted themselves with the delusion that the threats did not exist or, if they did, that the menace was not great. Perhaps the enemies would seek other targets. Perhaps the walls would suffice. Perhaps the barbarians liked peace and commerce as much as they did. Perhaps they would just go away. Perhaps they would peacefully blend in. The list of possible justifications for this delusion was as long as it was wrong. The result was that there were no attempts to rise as a unified region and provide security on the frontier. The locals "never tried to ambush [the barbarians], or to sink their boats as they crossed the Danube, or to launch punitive raids across the great river into the territory of those who were tormenting them."[112]

Severinus must have been aware that unifying the region without the Roman Empire was impossible. But individual cities may have indicated at least a modicum of interest in establishing some security. In the first town he visited, Asturis, Severinus warned the population that the enemy was indeed near and dangerous. They should repent, he told them. They should pray and fast, and they should unite by abandoning the search for the selfish fulfillment of material desires. Of course, as was to be expected from a complacent and materially satisfied polity, Severinus was laughed out of town. People who are deluded – and do not see higher reasons for their own existence – will gladly justify their material self-satisfaction. Severinus left "in haste from a stubborn town that shall swiftly perish."[113] And perish Asturis did. Other contemporaries of Severinus, such as Salvian in Gaul, observed a similar pattern of denial: The collapsing order was ignored and Romans were insouciantly continuing their life of enjoyment as if the barbarians were not a mortal threat. As Robert Markus put it, paraphrasing Salvian, "Laughing, the Roman people goes to its death."[114]

In the next town, Comagenis, Severinus was more successful in arousing the locals from complacency. Because one man escaped from the beleaguered Asturis bringing the terrible news of its demise, the people of Comagenis could no longer ignore the hard fact that the barbarians were nearby and were poised to destroy. They finally recognized that

---

[112] Thompson, "Britain, A.D. 406–410," 313–314.   [113] Eugippius, 30.
[114] Robert A. Markus, *The End of Ancient Christianity* (New York, NY: Cambridge University Press, 1990), 173.

security was a creation of force, not a self-sustaining reality that did not require arms and cohesion.

But even before the technical question of how to defend themselves, the locals needed a reason to do it. They needed what Roman troops, however scant, had provided before: some reassurance. And this was Severinus' greatest contribution: He reassured the local populations, albeit in ways that were different from those of frontier Roman forces. Severinus supplied the surviving towns with a firm motivation to resist and defend themselves, a reassurance that defense was worthwhile. With his presence the frontier "castles felt no danger. The trusty cuirass of fasting, and praiseworthy humility of heart, with the aid of the prophet [Severinus], had armed them boldly against the fierceness of the enemy."[115]

There was a nascent desire among some of the towns to provide for their own security, a sign of the decentralization of security. Security, these frontier towns realized, was not guaranteed by imperial forces, but needed to be underwritten by themselves. The problem at this stage is that the passage from delusion and panic to the desire to produce indigenous defense is not automatic. Before the "how" and the "where" of defending oneself, it is necessary to have a clear and firm answer to the "why." A polity can have all the technical marvels, logistical supplies, and tactical skills, but without a strong motivation to defend itself they will all be useless. A *castellum* can be architecturally pleasing and surrounded by thick walls, but if the people inside it do not know who they are and why they should fight, it is as undefended as a wide open field.

In one of the Danubian towns, the local commander Mamertinus, a future bishop, was concerned that the forces at his disposal were insufficient. Mamertinus told Severinus: "I have soldiers, a very few. But I dare not contend with such a host of enemies. However, if thou commandest it, venerable father, though we lack the aid of weapons yet we believe that through thy prayers we shall be victorious."[116] Material capabilities are important, indeed essential; yet motivation and morale is even more so. Severinus' role was to stiffen their spines. "Even if thy soldiers are unarmed, they shall now be armed from the enemy. For neither numbers nor fleshly courage is required, when everything proves that God is our champion."[117] Mamertinus' troops went out, found some of the barbarians, attacked, and succeeded in routing them while obtaining a stash of their abandoned weapons. This example is telling because individual cities most likely developed methods to enhance their security, for

[115] Eugippius, 76.   [116] Eugippius, 35.   [117] Eugippius, 35.

instance, by keeping scouts outside of town to alert their populations of an impending attack.[118]

There was, of course, no guarantee that a more assertive local leader could end the barbarian pressure. Success and survival are never certain. That is why local authority, and Severinus in particular, had more contacts with the barbarian warlords than with imperial authorities. Those warlords were near, and a fragile *modus vivendi* was often established, exchanging money for the protection of a barbarian chief. But this was a temporary solution and it frequently failed. It was "an accommodation made in a context of violence, and between parties in a very unequal and tense power relationship."[119] Severinus, in fact, had to negotiate releases of Romans kidnapped and enslaved by some ambitious and greedy barbarian.

A few years after Severinus' death the Danubian frontier was abandoned, and most of the Roman elites swiftly moved south, leaving the lower classes to fend for themselves. Eugippius, Severinus' biographer, emigrated to Italy, settling near Naples, as the abbot of a monastery frequented by the last Western Roman emperor, Romulus Augustulus, who ended his days in comfortable exile. Those who had the means abandoned the crumbling imperial frontier in favor of the relative security of Italy.

The story of Severinus indicates that, even in the clearest moments of danger, security decentralization was not guaranteed. Lacking leadership, locals did not take security provision seriously and in many cases marched toward catastrophe. Moreover, the persistence of the barbarian threat meant that the best one could do at the most exposed frontier locations was to mitigate the risks. The frontier settlements could not eliminate their barbarian enemies, but they could protect their immediate surroundings from small raids, negotiate the release of captured fellow citizens, and bring swift succor to a targeted area. In this form, security decentralization is a strategy of threat mitigation, limiting the damage inflicted by barbarian groups.

5.4   The Local Search for Security

The three stories of Augustine, Sidonius and Severinus illustrate the pressures and imperatives of security decentralization when barbarians target a region of the empire. Because of military weakness, leadership

---

[118] Heather, 413.
[119] Bryan Ward-Perkins, *The Fall of Rome and the End of Civilization* (New York, NY: Oxford University Press, 2006), 20.

ineptitude, or the sheer operational difficulty of dealing with the barbarian threat, a political entity may be unable to provide security and order. The areas most directly affected by the resulting instability are likely to search for alternative ways of protecting themselves. They have a variety of strategic options, ranging from accommodating the aggressors and accepting protection from them to renewed efforts to draw in more support from imperial forces. Irrespective of the particular path that the threatened area or city may undertake, one of the most immediate outcomes of regional insecurity is the rise of local leaders who are more attuned to the needs of their populations and swifter in their decisions.

Local leaders – in the case of the late Roman Empire, bishops and clergy – gain in importance because the threat is localized and does not immediately and clearly warrant the involvement of the entire imperial security apparatus. As the sway of imperial authority diminishes and the protection of the regions under barbarian threat is deemed either nugatory or ancillary, the beleaguered districts look for new leaders who can offer social cohesion, spiritual strength, material succor, and a diplomatic voice to make their case at the court of their emperor or in the camps of the enemy. Security can no longer be outsourced to the empire, to its forces, and to its generals. It has to be provided locally, and in this endeavor leadership is crucial. The legitimacy and appeal of these local leaders stem from their firm preference for their own region and for its inhabitants over wider concerns of the empire.

The position of these local leaders was unenviable. The bishops and saints of this chapter had to negotiate in their minds as well as in practice between the desire to maintain the empire, or at least their connection to it, and the needs of their local communities – two sets of demands that sometimes were congruent but with an intensification of barbarian frontier attacks became gradually less so. The story of the three saints is a story of a gradual narrowing of horizons, a retreat to the smaller confines of North Africa, of Clermont-Ferrand in Auvergne, of a few Danubian villages. And as these regions, cities, and villages collapse, the role of the bishops and of other leaders slowly changes too: There is less of a need for a leader of a well-delimited area and more of one attached to an ethnic group or, in the case of a bishop, tasked to evangelize a people.[120]

---

[120] Ugo Dovere, "La Figura del Vescovo tra la Fine del Mondo Antico e l'Avvento dei Nuovi Popoli Europei," *Archivum Historiae Pontificiae*, Vol. 41 (2003), 37–38.

6 Settlements, Local Forces, Fortifications, and Altering the Environment

This whole thing is one confounded humbug. 1000 such expeditions would have no tendency to subdue those hostile Indians, we have only made them mad, like sticking a long stick into a hornets nets.[1]

US Army Capt. Leonard Aldrich, 1864

Like all events in history, the gradual devolution of power in the Western Roman Empire, described in the preceding chapter, was not inevitable. It is, of course, nugatory to ponder what alternative strategies may have been employed by Roman imperial authorities to save the Western part of the empire, but the fact that barbarians overrun Europe and North Africa in this case does not suggest that they were always victorious. How polities and settled communities responded to the barbarian threat mattered to the outcome of the confrontation. It is true that, as examined in Chapters 2 and 3, the traditional tools of statecraft, from large military expeditions to commercial interactions, were not effective in dealing with barbarians.[2] At best, these means redirected barbarian attacks elsewhere; at worst, they merely postponed them.

But polities adopted a combination of other approaches targeting the strengths of barbarian groups. First, the construction of frontier fortifications combined with the development of local forces tried to stabilize the immediate frontier separating the polity from the barbarians. Second, great powers from Rome to the United States saw the high mobility of the barbarian tribes as a key source of their threatening power, and sought to limit it by settling them down. Finally, often the long-term strategy was to alter the environment that allowed barbarian groups to prosper. The empty or ungovernable spaces – the steppes, the deserts, and the difficult to conquer forests – had to be dominated through technology and the

---
[1] Cited in Paul Beck, *Columns of Vengeance* (Norman, OK: University of Oklahoma Press, 2013), 247.
[2] On commercial relations with nomadic tribes, see, for instance, Khodarkovsky, 26–28 (for Russian and the steppe tribes); Frederick Mote, *Imperial China, 900–1800* (Cambridge, MA: Harvard University Press, 1999), 692–693 (on Ming China's relations with the Mongols).

gradual expansion of state institutions, thereby limiting the area where barbarians could move unhindered. None of these strategies was a sureproof method to defeat the barbarians – and, in fact, they seem to have had as many successes as failures. But they addressed some of the facets of the barbarian threat, and as such, they could contribute to mitigate, if not eliminate, the threat.

6.1 Frontier Fortifications and Local Forces

Fortifications, manned by local forces, were perhaps the most immediate response to barbarian incursions. The human mind seeks solutions to a problem through inventiveness and technology, and fortifications, or more broadly the hardening of the potential targets and of the vectors of barbarian attacks, are an example of this tendency. In the late Roman Empire, for example, there was an effort to solve or at a minimum to mitigate the damages of barbarian incursions through the erection of forts that were expected to control the flow of enemy groups.

One of the most innovative policy proposals came in the twilight of the empire. A late fourth-century text *De Rebus Bellicis*, written by an anonymous author, paints a dire picture of the Roman Empire, surrounded by barbarians and weakened by fiscal burdens and manpower shortages. The underlying argument of the text is the need to shore up imperial defenses through technological innovations that would require less manpower. The writer describes several fantastic weapon platforms, such as a special chariot or a large ship propelled by animals, that arguably could have destroyed hostile forces with a smaller involvement of Roman manpower. As he writes, the emperor "will double the strength of [his] invincible army when [he has] equipped it with these mechanical inventions, countering the raids of [his] enemies not by sheer strength alone but also by mechanical ingenuity."[3] One such technological advance that, according to the author, would have multiplied Roman power and strengthened the empire's defenses was a line of fortifications to be erected along the imperial frontiers in Europe. This fortified line would be composed of forts placed at equal intervals of about a mile, "with watches and pickets kept in them so that the peaceful provinces may be surrounded by a belt of defences, and so remain unimpaired and at peace."[4] Moreover, and perhaps most interestingly, these forces and forts would be paid by local landowners, rather than from imperial coffers. The author was probably

---

[3] In E. A. Thompson, *A Roman Reformer and Inventor* (London: Oxford University Press, 1952), XVII:6, 120.
[4] In Thompson, XX:1, 123.

not one of the frontier landowners and was happy to suggest to the emperor that these individuals would carry the imperial fiscal burden of security provision. But he may also have seen an interest among that frontier population to step up their own efforts and contributions in order to protect their lands from the destructive but localized barbarian raids. And he delineated the key principle at work: A localized threat may require a local response and may be best addressed by a local response.

The detailed suggestions of *De Rebus Bellicis* were never implemented: The mechanization of the Roman army did not happen and a massive fortified *limes* was not built exactly as the anonymous author advised. In fact, the idea of a preclusive defense could only work if barbarian raids were rare and somewhat predictable, in which case a frontier barrier could buy some time to mass an army to reinforce the attacked location. But when the raids increased in number and occurred on many fronts or on a longer border, it was impossible to hold a frontier line: Reinforcements could not move quickly enough and a central army would simply prove insufficient to plug every targeted spot. Not surprisingly, in periods of higher barbarian activity, the frontier widened: Instead of being a defensive line that blocked hostile raids, it turned into a larger frontier region where the initial impetus of a raid could be absorbed, waited out, and perhaps repelled once a defensive force was organized. A symptom of such a situation was visible in the late Roman period, between the third and sixth centuries, when many towns and small settlements inside the empire erected walls while at the same time shrinking in size to make themselves more defensible. This development was due to the abandonment of the concept of a "preclusive defense" against barbarian raids, a situation replicated again in the Byzantine empire from the seventh century on when imperial lands faced the expanding Arab Muslim forces on the southern frontier. The attempts of Byzantium's imperial forces to block the raiding parties by controlling passes and other strategic locations proved to be futile because of the unpredictability and mobility of the enemy as well as the topography of that frontier, which did not present clear natural barriers.

Preclusive defense carried an additional risk: Were the fortified perimeter of the frontier to be broken by the barbarian forces, the internal provinces would have been effectively unarmed, as the bulk of resources and manpower was devoted to the protection of the border.[5] Defenses had to be organized inside imperial territories, trading space for the time to organize a military response. But this meant that a band of territory

---

[5] Walter E. Kaegi, *Byzantium and the Early Islamic Conquests* (Cambridge: Cambridge University Press, 1992), 60.

along the frontier was constantly exposed to Arab raids, leading either to depopulation or to a gradual development of local forces under the command of provincial leaders and of fortified settlements where the population could rapidly retreat and weather the barbarian raid.[6]

The ineffectiveness of a fortified frontline that could sustain a preclusive defense meant therefore that the most vulnerable cities and populated areas sought the protection of walls. The walling of cities, however, was often accompanied by a defensive attitude that placed too much value on physical barriers as opposed to a more armed and offensive posture. In many cases, from Byzantium to the Spanish empire in North America, the empire lacked sufficient resources and manpower to maintain a stable frontier, and, as mentioned in previous chapters, barbarians were notoriously difficult to deter in the first place. The inability to conduct (or the failure of) offensive operations or even of a mobile defense-in-depth strategy forced either a withdrawal or the building of walled cities. Walls were a recognition of weakness, not a statement of confidence. In the case of Byzantium facing Arab attacks in Syria and Palestine, for instance, "there was a propensity to passive resistance, to seek the security of walled towns instead of trying to establish an effective defensive line in the field, and to seek to purchase peaceful terms instead of attempting a violent but unpropitious armed resistance."[7] The outcome of such passivity was often a series of negotiated surrenders of isolated walled outposts of the empire, unwilling to incur the costs inflicted by regular barbarian raids and not expecting a strong imperial response in their defense.

A similar threat combined with an equally stretched reservoir of imperial resources presented itself between the late sixteenth and eighteenth centuries along the North American frontier of the Spanish empire. After the easy conquest of the sedentary Aztecs, the Spaniards faced a new threat from less sedentary indigenous tribes that engaged in hit-and-run raiding. In response to this menace on its northern frontier, in 1582 the Spaniards begun to build a line of small outposts, each manned by a handful of men (up to a dozen) in order to protect the routes between their various settlements and mining communities. In the end these forts proved to be unsuccessful in this particular task because the manpower located there was insufficient to guarantee security to the roads, but the idea of *presidios* was not abandoned. In the succeeding decades, the frontier continued to present a serious security threat. A series of studies (the *Reglamento* of 1729, the *Reglamento* of 1772) proposed to establish a

---

[6] John Haldon, *Warfare, State and Society in the Byzantine World, 565–1204* (London: UCL Press, 1999), 60–77, 249–250.
[7] Kaegi, 47 and 50.

line of *presidios* that would block the raids from the northern tribes, protecting the Spanish lands in the south. Similarly to the Byzantine situation vis-à-vis the Arab threat, these studies and resulting proposals were symptomatic of a defensive mindset because the *presidios* were "erected after the essentially offensive pattern of the Spanish conquest had run its course, when the primary function of the military had become defense, to protect occupied territory rather than to overrun additional lands."[8] And they were built expressly to face the Indian threat, rather than European rivals whose artillery would have easily destroyed the cheaply constructed forts.

The *presidios* alone were poor barriers to raids, quick and small projections of power that avoided any type of obstacle that would slow them down. They were more successful, however, when they were combined with small forces capable of equally rapid responses to the Indian raids. The *presidios* offered such forces a string of lily pads where they could seek brief shelter and resupply, and from where they could organize lightning forays to defend a community that had been attacked or to harass the Indian enemy. The Spaniards learned that the best way to project power inside Indian territories was to field small and light formations that required little logistical support and thus were able to reinforce quickly the frontier locations that were under attack or to pursue the raiding party. For this purpose, the most apt soldiers did not come from the regular imperial army, set up in any case to fight against rival great powers, but from local populations. The frontier formations of the *presidios* were "hard-bitten, home-grown *vaqueros* who were at ease in the saddle, inured to the harsh and lonely terrain in which they served, and accustomed to the cruel and unconventional tactics of Indian warfare."[9] Able to ride horses for days on end, requiring little food and logistical support, with a great knowledge of the local topography, these frontier men had both the skills and the incentives to protect their region from the raiding tribes. Their method of fighting but also their social status (in the last yeas of the eighteenth century, less than half of the officers of these frontier formations were able to read and write) often led to tensions with the imperial administrators and the military commanders. And these tensions were exacerbated by the different strategic interest: Central authorities were often more concerned with rival great powers, such as

---

[8] Max L. Moorhead, *The Presidio* (Norman, OK: University of Oklahoma Press, 1975), 5. See also, James M. Daniel, "The Spanish Frontier in West Texas and Northern Mexico," *The Southwestern Historical Quarterly*, Vol. 71, No. 4 (April 1968), 481–495); Robert S. Weddle, *After the Massacre: The Violent Legacy of the San Sabá Mission* (Lubbock, TX: Texas Tech University Press, 2007), xvi.
[9] Moorhead, 178.

Great Britain, while local officers and their troops had their eyes focused on the *presidio* line threatened by Indian groups. It is not surprising, therefore, that in the 1770s the frontier commander, Teodoro de Croix, managed to convince local citizens to pay for the frontier troops needed to man the *presidios* and to provide a modicum of security.[10] What the Roman author of *De Rebus Bellicis* had suggested centuries earlier but failed to put into practice was implemented at least in part in the North American imperial territories of Spain.

As described in Chapter 3, the barbarian threat was often peculiar because it did not exercise constant pressure on the frontiers of the settled polities. It was sporadic or impermanent. This meant that the targeted state rarely felt justified to put its security forces on a constant war footing, especially when other great powers were also menacing along some other front. Moreover, the problem of imperial defense on two fronts with the barbarians and a "peer rival" forced authorities to sequence their responses, prioritizing the allocation of resources and manpower. The threat of a peer rival called for long-term security commitments, in the form of large military formations armed with heavy artillery (at least after the "gunpowder revolution") and well-fortified bases. Barbarian threats arose as fast as they disappeared, and central authorities could hardly justify investing a lot of attention and resources to such a transient (albeit often persistent) security problem. Hence, a spike in barbarian raiding demanded an equally rapid increase in local security provision. The temporary nature of a lot of these security arrangements put a premium again on the ability of local citizens to organize formations capable of repelling an attack and, if necessary, of pursuing the barbarian enemy. For instance, in the early nineteenth century along the Texas frontier, Indian raids forced local settlers to establish their own methods of providing security. When a threat arose, "the Texans banded together under a local leader and went forth to war. When the expedition was over, the organization broke up and the men returned to their homes and farms. These early experiences taught the Texans how to act in emergencies, gave them training, developed their fighting technique, and brought forth by degrees leaders who were qualified to meet the foe, Mexican or Indian."[11] The barbarian threat was neither permanent nor large enough to warrant a more centralized effort, putting the burden of organizing a defense on individual ingenuity and local efforts.

---

[10] Moorhead, 83.
[11] Walter Prescott Webb, *The Texas Rangers* (Austin, TX: University of Texas, 1995, original 1935), 19.

The ability of a polity to field local forces quickly is a crucial asset for countering the barbarian menace. Historian Ray Allen Billington, for example, explains why the Spanish empire had a difficult time, and ultimately failed, to mitigate and solve the security problem stemming from the Indian tribes along their North American frontiers. The centralized nature of the empire set up a system in which settlers were sent to the frontier in order to benefit and enrich the state, represented by imperial authorities physically present in the capital. Therefore, the local populations settled on the frontier had an incentive to survive, but not necessarily to defend the larger imperial enterprise. As most of them did not benefit personally from mining or agricultural activities, the insecurity or loss of those territories mattered to them only in so far as their own life may have been affected, but they were equally content to abandon them. On the contrary, the Anglo-American "frontier technique" reflected a more individualistic culture, in which individuals and their small groups expanded and moved westward in search of land, money, or religious peace. The result was that these individuals had a strong incentive to provide for their own security, without waiting for the organizing hand of a central authority. As Billington writes,

Developed over the course of centuries by cocksure pioneers, this emphasized the role of the individual in the subjugation of nation, giving him free rein to exploit the new land for his own benefit. The frontier philosophy of Spain, on the other hand, subordinated the individual to the state; the pioneer's principal function was not to enrich himself but to help create a strong nation and a powerful church.[12]

Another example of local forces developing along a frontier in response to raiding was in the Balkans, the region separating the Ottoman lands from Venetian and later Habsburg territories. The Ottoman method of warfare was similar, especially early on in the history of this empire, to barbarian attacks: Irregular formations would attack a region not by invading and occupying it but by weakening and depopulating it through a series of plundering raids. These raids were brief, individually small, but persistent and in the long run they could devastate the targeted lands. The Ottomans had developed a concept of "permanent war," maintaining low-level but constant pressure on the territories of their northern neighbors.[13] Once the raids had weakened the resistance of the population, Ottoman imperial

---

[12] Ray Allen Billington, *The Far Western Frontier* (New York, NY: Harper & Row, 1956), 1. On the difference between the Spanish and the British frontiers in North America, see also J. H. Elliott, *Empires of the Atlantic World* (New Haven, CT: Yale University Press, 2006), 272–273.

[13] Gunther Erich Rothenberg, *The Austrian Military Border in Croatia, 1522–1747* (Urbana, IL: The University of Illinois Press, 1960), 11.

forces would invade with a large army and impose new political control over the wasteland. As a sixteenth-century historian, Johann Turmair (also called Aventinus), put it, "the Turks take whole counties bit by bit, not in one campaign but by steady nibbling."[14] The Turkish threat was one of permanent war, of relentless pressure on the border, requiring a defensive posture of constant readiness. The raiding Ottoman bands would appear quickly, avoiding a response from the imperial forces, creating "a state of constant insecurity along the frontier. The countryside lived in terror. Southern Croatia was a land of sudden death, where no man's life was safe outside the larger settlements."[15]

The distant capital, either in Venice or Vienna, was not very interested in expending tight funds or limited manpower on a threat that was considered to be local and small, leaving frontier security in the hands of local landowners and refugees. Central authorities had also few incentives to incur costs, and to ask imperial forces to sacrifice, for what many considered a far away and unimportant front. Large mercenary forces that could be raised only after sufficient funding was appropriated were not appropriate for such frontier warfare.[16] Fixed fortifications were not very useful in protecting the frontier against the rapid descent of small, armed Ottoman bands on horses. As a result, the targeted populations had to arm themselves and organize their own groups that would provide security. The defense of this frontier demanded forces that had a strong motivation to be constantly ready, to be willing to incur sacrifices, to be a society in arms.[17] As a local historian, Valvasor, recounted, "whenever a man was working in the fields, he always carried his arms with him and kept a saddle horse beside his plow. When the Turks approached he immediately mounted to give combat, or if their number was too large, to ride and give the alarm."[18]

That type of peasant, capable of dropping the plough, mounting a steed, and charging a small raiding party, had to be of a sturdy stock, accustomed to violence and individual initiative.[19] The "Uskoks" fit the

---

[14] Gunther E. Rothenberg, "Aventinus and the Defense of the Empire against the Turks," *Studies in the Renaissance*, Vol. 10 (1963), 65.
[15] Rothenberg, *The Austrian Military Border in Croatia*, 40.
[16] Rothenberg, "Aventinus," 65.
[17] Stevka Šmitran, *Gli uscocchi* (Venice: Marsilio Editori, 2008), 42.
[18] Quoted in Rothenberg, *The Austrian Military Border in Croatia*, 40.
[19] Walter Prescott Webb, in his classic history of the Plains, describes how a man from the Western frontier in the nineteenth century must have looked to an easterner, unhabituated to a life of constant danger: "He lives on horseback, as do the Bedouins; he fights on horseback, as did the knights of chivalry; he goes armed with a strange new weapons which he uses ambidextrously and precisely; he swears like a trooper, drinks like a fish, wears clothes like an actor, and fights like a devil. He is gracious to ladies, reserved toward strangers, generous to his friends, and brutal to his enemies. He is a cowboy, a typical Westerner." Webb, 496.

bill in the sixteenth century along the Croatian frontier of the Habsburg Empire. The term "Uskok" described a fugitive or a runaway, and was applied to refugees who escaped lands targeted by Ottoman raids and coalesced in bands that would in turn raid the territories from which they had fled that were under Ottoman control. In most cases, these Uskoks formed small groups for brief periods of time with the express purpose of defending their families and, if possible, of seeking revenge on the attacking Ottomans.[20] As Ferdinand I put it to a Venetian ambassador in 1553, "Only these people [the Uskoks] seem suited to guard the borders, being courageous and willing to suffer; which neither Germans, nor men of any other nation could do, but only these, who are able to fight for many days with only a single loaf of bread per man."[21]

The defensive operations were organized and executed by the "Uskoks" themselves, with little input from the Habsburg capital. The Uskoks chose their own leaders, planned their own defensive or offensive actions, and conducted them without the approval of Habsburg (and in some cases Venetian) authorities.[22] The Uskoks even killed imperial representatives (in 1601, an Austrian commissioner) in response to an assertion of central power that they considered out of line and unacceptable.[23] Their operational independence often led to further political tensions when either Venice or Vienna sought some diplomatic overture or moment of peace with the Sultan while the Uskoks were happy to continue their counterraids either in revenge for past slights or in search of booty. Imperial authorities had a hard time exercising constant and direct control over these local bands of Uskoks because this would have required the stationing of territorial forces and the establishment of costly bases in order to keep those frontier territories protected from the Ottoman expansion, a military posture that they had been unwilling to seek in the first place. The local appeal of the Uskoks stemmed from their ability to fend off Ottoman attacks; central imperial authorities would have to compete in security provision in order to undermine the local legitimacy of the Uskoks. And even then, the more traditional defensive posture of a great power based on large formations and fixed garrisons would not have been as effective as the loose, ad hoc, and hardy Uskok groups who could mobilize quickly because they were local and had a direct interest in protecting their own territories.

[20] Catherine Wendy Bracewell, *The Uskoks of Senj* (Ithaca, NY: Cornell University Press, 1992), 38.
[21] Quoted in Bracewell, 97.   [22] Bracewell, 44.
[23] Philip Longworth, "The Senj Uskoks Reconsidered," *The Slavonic and East European Review*, Vol. 57, No. 3 (July 1979), 355.

Of course, when the Western powers were at war with the Ottomans, they were eager to enlist the local frontier forces to conduct offensive operations. The Habsburgs, in particular, were more than happy to use Uskok forces because of their ability to supply themselves through raids, lifting the logistical and fiscal burden away from an already strained Austrian system.[24] An ancillary benefit for the Habsburgs was that the Uskoks, in the early seventeenth century, began also to attack Venetian possessions, a target of opportunity that arose because of the growing weakness of *La Serenissima* and the peace between it and the Ottomans. The Uskoks extended their raiding to the sea, hitting Venetians ships laden with commercial goods and engaging in a war with Venice for almost eighty years.[25] But as the Uskoks turned their attention away from the Ottomans and from the defense of the land frontier, Vienna sought a *rapprochement* with Venice (the 1617 Treaty of Madrid) and eliminated these frontier forces by the 1620s.[26] Moreover, by the end of the seventeenth century, the Ottoman threat became more traditional, with large formations and heavy artillery, and loose bands of Uskoks were insufficient to defend the frontier against it.

The defense of the frontier against raiding – the barbarian way of warfare – required the affected polity to abandon some direct control over the targeted area. The particular security conditions empowered local actors to organize their own military forces and to go on a permanent war footing as demanded by the nature of the threat. There were strong incentives to adapt and mimic the barbarian enemy that was effective at creating localized and relatively small but consistent problems. The result was that the border with barbarians gave rise to frontier societies that were capable of defending themselves and even raiding in turn, but frequently with only loose links to the imperial authorities of which they were an extension. Frontier forces, the defenders of empires against barbarians, were often most similar to the tribes and groups they opposed than to the settled and civilized lands they protected.

If a barbarian threat is returning to our strategic landscape, the lesson from the past is that hardening targets (building walls and fortifications) must go hand in hand with the development of small capabilities that provide local and thus speedy security. This naturally puts a burden on populations that perhaps have not been accustomed to thinking about their own security, and it can strain the cohesion of a polity that will need

---

[24] Bracewell, 95.   [25] Šmitran, 48 and 67–70; Longworth, 362.
[26] Gunther E. Rothenberg, "Venice and the Uskoks of Senj: 1537–1618," *The Journal of Modern History*, Vol. 33, No. 2 (June 1961), 155–156; Frederic C. Lane, *Venice: A Maritime Republic* (Baltimore, MD: The Johns Hopkins University Press, 1973), 398–400; Bracewell, 290–295.

to relinquish some authority and prerogatives to the most affected regions. To succeed without letting centrifugal forces take over, the polity must have structural and cultural characteristics that allow a large degree of decentralization. A culture that favors local and individual initiative and a political system that has built-in subsidiarity and some form of federalism are the most likely to succeed.

6.2 Strategy of Sedentarization: Settling Barbarians Down

Another approach pursued by states and empires when dealing with barbarians was to address more directly one of the sources of their strength, their mobility. The lack of attachment to a particular location and the resulting high mobility of barbarians created fears among settled populations. Groups of people on the move were a symptom of instability if they were escaping turmoil elsewhere, but were also themselves a source of volatility as they raided and attacked populations in their path or vicinity. Niccolò Machiavelli observed in his *Discourses* that the most dangerous wars, and the greatest fears, are "when an entire people, with all its families, removes from a place, necessitated by either famine or war, and goes to seek a new seat and a new province, not to command it like those above [conflicts of imperial expansion] but to possess it all individually, and expel or kill the ancient inhabitants of it. This was is very cruel and very frightful." The conflict is not merely a rivalry over who commands a slice of real estate (a conflict "to eliminate only those who command"), but it becomes a clash of annihilation ("these populations must eliminate everyone, since they wish to live on what others were living on").[27]

More broadly, population mobility is antithetical to the statist way of thinking: Polities, and modern states in particular, provide order by, among other means, constraining the movement of people. Only by having people attached to a location can a state tax them and control them.

An early example of sedentarization is presented by Julius Caesar at the beginning of his *De Bello Gallico*.[28] In 58 BC, the Helvetii, a tribe living in the Alps, burnt their villages and fields, abandoned their territory, and moved *en masse* westward, toward Gaul. This migration involved the entire population and all of its belongings. From then on, the Helvetii

---

[27] Niccolò Machiavelli, *Discourses*, trans. Harvey Mansfield and Nathan Tarcov (Chicago, IL: The University of Chicago Press, 1998), II:8, 143.
[28] For the description of this episode, see Caesar, *The Conquest of Gaul* (New York, NY: Penguin, 1982), Book I:1–29, 28–42; Adrian Goldsworthy, *Caesar: Life of a Colossus* (New Haven, CT: Yale University Press, 2006), 205–223.

had nothing to defend except themselves, and hence, devoted all their resources and manpower to attacking their neighboring tribes. For the Roman Empire, this situation was a serious and surprising menace, and Julius Caesar as the proconsul in the neighboring region had the duty to respond to it.[29] The migrating Helvetii were pushing on tribes that were allied with Rome, and thus created a threat to the imperial structure of alliances (of course, Julius Caesar had also the additional incentive to pick a fight with somebody for personal aggrandizement). However, this moving army could not be brought to heel through diplomacy or deterrence because the Helvetii, having destroyed all their villages and burnt their fields, were relatively immune to threats. Moreover, the Romans expected that the territory abandoned by the Helvetii would lure distant and potentially even more hostile tribes, bringing them closer to the imperial frontier. In brief, the mobility of the Helvetii, and their sudden nonterritorial nature, created a complex threat that required a swift but difficult and costly military response.

Roman forces, led by Julius Caesar, rushed to prevent the Helvetii from devastating the land of Rome's allies. After a strenuous campaign, which required the raising of several new legions, Caesar's soldiers defeated the moving tribe in a vicious battle.[30] The remnants of the Helvetii and their allies were forced to surrender, in part because they had lost all support from neutral tribes, which Caesar threatened with complete destruction were they to continue helping the migrant group. Roman legions could compel these settled tribes by promising them a rapid and devastating punishment if they helped the migrating group – and thereby they limited indirectly the mobility of the Helvetii. They fixed them in a place, so to speak, and then could apply the full might of the Roman military. Once the Helvetii were defeated, however, Julius Caesar followed this "action, glorious in itself ... with another yet more noble": he gathered all those who survived the battle and brought them back to the lands they had abandoned, instead of killing or selling them in slavery.[31] The Helvetii had to rebuild their villages, while the neighboring tribes were ordered to provide them with food and necessary supplies to resettle. It was an ancient case of state-building. The rationale for this policy was that the main threat was the mobility of the Helvetii tribe, and it was strategically more beneficial to root it back in a well-defined territory. Caesar also did

---

[29] Matthias Gelzer, *Caesar: Politician and Statesman* (Cambridge, MA: Harvard University Press, 1968), 103 and also footnote #3.
[30] For the battle, see J.C. Fuller, *Julius Caesar* (New Brunswick, NJ: Rutgers University Press, 1965), 105–106.
[31] Plutarch, "Caesar," in *Plutarch's Lives* (New York, NY: The Modern Library, 2001), Dryden translation, Vol. II, 212.

"not want the country they had abandoned to remain uninhabited, lest the Germans across the Rhine might be" tempted to move closer to Roman lands.[32]

The story of the Helvetii, even if embellished by Julius Caesar seeking political support back in Rome, is a telling example of the challenges and the fears that a mass movement of people created for an empire. It was necessary to use military force to defeat this particular group, but short of total annihilation they could be deprived of their mobility only through a resettlement. They had to be sedentarized again.

Centuries later, when the imperial frontiers of Rome were assaulted by a different type of barbarian tribes that were moving westward in Europe, Roman authorities also sought to settle them. The threat of these tribes was not just that they raided Roman *oppida* with impunity but they could not be controlled, deterred, or even defeated on the battlefield that they avoided. One approach pursued by Rome in the fourth to fifth centuries was to try to settle some of these tribes. To do so, Roman authorities implemented a longstanding policy of *hospitalitas*, essentially military billeting.[33] Usually, this was done on the frontier to protect against other barbarians, but later, as in the case of the Visigoths in Aquitania in the early fifth century AD, deep inside the empire, an event that was "a momentous stage in that process of compromise between the Roman Empire and the Germans which had been going on for many years."[34] Most empires, from Rome to Ming China, tried to settle individuals from nomadic tribes, with the objective of augmenting their own manpower while draining that of the tribal groups. In their new setting, separated from their clans and ethnic communities, these individuals were isolated, and sooner or later assimilated into the local population.[35] However, this brought slow and marginal results visible in a timespan of generations rather than a few years, and only mass sedentarization, a much more difficult endeavor, could mitigate the nomadic threat under certain conditions.

There were therefore vast differences in the ways in which sedentarization was implemented. Sedentarization encompassed a broad array of policies, ranging from Roman *hospitalitas* and the political incorporation of individual members of nomadic groups to the encouragement of a

---

[32] Caesar, I:28, p. 42.
[33] On *hospitalitas*, see Hagith Sivan, "On Foederati, *Hospitalitas*, and the Settlement of the Goths in A.D. 418," *American Journal of Philology*, Vol. 108, No. 4 (Winter, 1987), 759–772; C. R. Whittaker, *Frontiers of the Roman Empire* (Baltimore, MD: The Johns Hopkins University Press, 1994), 188–191.
[34] Bury, Vol. 1, 205. See also E. A. Thompson, *Romans and Barbarians* (Madison, WI: The University of Wisconsin Press, 1982), 23–37.
[35] Khazanov, 199.

centralized leadership and outright forced settlement of entire tribes. This strategy aimed to minimize the greatest source of danger presented by nomadic groups, their mobility, and to curb their offensive capabilities. Furthermore, in the long run, it aspired to alter the social structure of the nomadic tribes, centralizing and dividing them, while at the same time encouraging a fundamental change in how these groups behaved. The goal was to make the nomads into "territorial" entities, working under the expectation that dealing with states or settled communities was easier than facing mobile and dispersed groups.[36]

In brief, sedentarization had three objectives: to establish permanence for the barbarian group, to incite internal divisions, and to create targets.

The first purpose of sedentarizing barbarians was to instill temporal and geographic permanence. By itself it was not a solution to the barbarian threat because it merely limited one of their strengths, their mobility, and did not make them necessarily into friendly strategic actors. But the impermanence of the barbarian enemy, and the associated high mobility, generated enormous uncertainty and fear. By settling them, Rome, for instance, created "more stable barbarian governments exercising prescribed power over territories sanctioned by Rome."[37] Once such a barbarian group was settled, traditional tools of statecraft – deterrence, diplomacy, and use of force – could be employed against it with greater success.

The second purpose of sedentarization was to alter the structure and the nature of the barbarian group in question. It was a form of assimilation, of trying to make barbarians more like the settled populations of the empire or state. By giving barbarians a stake in a territory, it fixed them to a place and created new dynamics inside them. For instance, some historians suggest that the Roman settlement of the Visigoths in Aquitania in the early fifth century was a strategic success. One writes that "[b]y being collectively endowed with a more than adequate slice of state revenue, the barbarians were given an excellent inducement for sustaining the existing order in public, as well as private, economic relations."[38] Another historian even argues that the settled Visigoths turned into order-creating forces inside an empire that was wracked by internal rebellions and discontent caused by mismanagement. He writes

---

[36] There was also a fiscal reason for settling nomads. States wanted to increase their tax base, and also the manpower available to them, and it is very difficult to extract resources in a consistent fashion from mobile groups who, unlike settled peasants or urban dwellers, are immune to state pressures and administration. By forcing nomads to live in a fixed place, states had an easier time taxing and controlling the population.

[37] Thomas S. Burns, *Rome and the Barbarians, 100 BC- AD 400* (Baltimore, MD: The Johns Hopkins University, 2003), 183, see also 173.

[38] Walter Goffart, *Barbarians and Romans* (Princeton, NJ: Princeton University Press, 1980), 226.

At one stroke they converted wandering and hostile masses of barbarians into settled and on the whole contented communities of agriculturalists; they broke the alliance of the invading barbarians with the restless elements of the Roman countryside; and they provided themselves with an effective force which would defend southern Gaul from the uprisings of the indomitable slaves and their allies who had causes so much damage earlier in the fifth century.[39]

Such an outcome could be achieved because sedentarization had two broad effects on the barbarian group. First, it resulted in a growing centralization of the group. Decentralized networks of tribes are excellent at harassing settled communities and avoiding a head-on confrontation with state armies, but are less suitable for administering a piece of land. The economies of sedentary groups are more complex, requiring specialization, which in turn calls for a more effective management of commercial exchanges, division of land, and property rights. And this tended to be better administered through, what Joseph Strayer called, "impersonal, relatively permanent political institutions."[40] Loyalty to the family and clan is then gradually replaced by loyalty to these institutions, the authority of which slowly encompasses all those living in the given territory rather than one tribe or kin-group. In other words, sedentarization led to the gradual establishment of a territorially based and enduring political entity, fixed in space and persistent in time.

A slightly different way of describing this effect of sedentarization is by pointing out that with territory comes responsibility. The nomadic leader could no longer sustain himself by raiding a neighboring community, but had to manage the land, maintain stability, and provide the public goods, from security to food and wealth, that the population under him demanded. Fixing a group to a piece of real estate instills, therefore, a degree of responsibility. Gianfranco Poggi, writing on the rise of the modern state, makes a similar point when he argues that

feudalism rooted in the land ... a warrior class that had often come from afar and had strong nomadic tendencies. To this class feudalism attributed powers that went beyond those of a purely military nature, and in the exercise of which these warriors slowly but progressively learned to consider criteria of equity, to respect local traditions, to protect the weak, and to practice responsibility.[41]

---

[39] E. A. Thompson, "The Settlement of the Barbarians in Southern Gaul," *The Journal of Roman Studies*, Vol. 46, Parts 1 and 2 (1956), 74.

[40] Joseph Strayer, *On the Medieval Origins of the Modern State* (Princeton, NJ: Princeton University Press, 2005), 6.

[41] Gianfranco Poggi, *The Development of the Modern State* (Stanford, CA: Stanford University Press, 1978), 32. For a different argument, pointing to the personal ties, rather than territory, as a key feature of feudalism, see also Hendrik Spruyt, *The Sovereign State and Its Competitors* (Princeton, NJ: Princeton University Press, 1994), 36–42.

The second related effect of sedentarization on the internal structure of barbarians was the creation of elites or individuals inside the barbarian group that had an incentive to protect their newly acquired lands, rather than in plundering. This led to the rise of deep divisions inside the nomadic, now settled, community. In many cases, such divisions were so profound that they led to violent infighting and to an alliance between a splinter nomadic group and its former enemy, the state. These divisions were largely caused by what Friedrich Kratochwil defined as the "ascendancy of wealth over mobility."[42] When settled, nomadic groups experienced social differentiation through the creation of élites that greatly benefited from the new status and developed wealth through commerce and land ownership, thereby losing any desire and incentive to revert to an itinerant lifestyle. These élites begin to value the protection and maintenance of their own land more than some other, more adventuresome, objective, whether plundering wealthy imperial lands or seeking the outright destruction of the neighboring state. This logic was at work in the case of another highly mobile, nonterritorial group of warriors: the Crusaders. When in the early twelfth century the crusaders established a territorial foothold in the Holy Land – that is, when they "settled" or became "sedentary" – a profound split occurred between those who remained in the newly conquered territories and those who came from Europe in search of glory by fighting against the Muslims. The former, burdened by the defense of their strongholds and eager to maintain what they had, were more inclined to negotiate with the Muslim and Arab leaders around them. This was especially the case of the second generation of crusaders, already born in the Holy Land. The latter group, on the other hand, was less interested in managing the lands of the crusaders and showed their impatience at the possibility of political compromises with the Muslims. Their objective was to fight Muslims; the source of their glory (and, if possible, booty) was not in building and holding defensive positions but in projecting power further into hostile lands. The result was that "a gulf opened between the new crusaders, who arrived from the West to fight Muslims, and the local residents, who would have to live with the Muslims after the pilgrims returned home" – a gulf that weakened the power of the crusaders.[43] The change in the mission of the group, away from a purely offensive strategy, led to resentment of some factions and individuals, a deep division that sapped some of the group's power.

---

[42] Friedrich Kratochwil, "Of Systems, Boundaries, and Territoriality: An Inquiry into the Formation of the State System," *World Politics*, Vol. 39, No. 1 (October 1986), 30.

[43] Thomas F. Madden, *A Concise History of the Crusades* (Lanham, MD: Rowman & Littlefield Publishers, 1999), 48.

In some cases, the policy of sedentarization was pursued together with the elevation of some individuals to a position of authority inside the barbarian group. It was a diplomatic effort to interfere in the internal dynamics of a hostile group by engineering the rise of a particular leader through material benefits (e.g. an exclusive trade deal) or military advantages (e.g. by arming him and his retinue). Russia's approach toward the Central Asian steppe tribes in the nineteenth century is a case in point. The strategy of Russia was "to endow the position of khan [a tribal leader] with stronger authority by elevating him over the influence of his own people and forging direct links between a khan and Russian authority."[44] This policy changed, and was ultimately abandoned, in the early 1800s "when the Kazakhs of the Lesser and Middle Hordes had been directly incorporated into the imperial administrative and political institutions, and the position of khan became superfluous."[45] A similar approach was followed in North America by both Spanish and then American authorities that "insisted that the Indians produce leaders with whom they could negotiate ... United States commissioners took to appointing such spokesmen arbitrarily when the tribes were unable to agree upon a paramount chief. Federal officials were impatient with the diffused democracy of the Indians and demanded a responsible leadership."[46]

As a result, the nomadic tribe became internally divided not along clan or family lines, but on the basis of who benefited from territorial settlement and who continued to prefer the old way of life. Such a division weakened the unity of the nomadic group, creating new sources of legitimacy that were difficult to overcome by strong leadership. It effectively created two or more groups – the settled vs. the migrant – with completely different aspirations and objectives.

In some cases, this allowed the empire to coopt barbarian groups or individuals to their own side, and use them against hostile tribes. Byzantium, for instance, relied in the seventh century on some Arab tribes on its frontier to supply manpower to defend the empire. This was made necessary by a chronic lack of resources and manpower that constantly bedeviled the empire, but it had the additional benefit that the semi-friendly Arab tribes had a superior knowledge of the local topography and the tactics used by the hostile Arabs beyond the imperial frontiers.[47] In a more recent example, in the mid-nineteenth century when the US Army was facing Indian tribes in the West, it was eager to employ other

---

[44] Khodarkovsky, 33. A similar policy was pursued by Rome. See Burns, 346.
[45] Khodarkovsky, 34.
[46] T. R. Fehrenbach, *Comanches* (New York, NY: Anchor Books, 2003; original 1974), 367.
[47] Kaegi, 52.

Indians as scouts but also because of the psychological impact it had on hostile groups. As an officer put it in 1866,

> To polish a diamond there is nothing like its own dust. It is the same with these fellows. Nothing breaks them up like turning their own people against them. They don't fear the white soldiers, whom they easily surpass in the peculiar style of warfare which they force upon us, but put upon their trail an enemy of their own blood, an enemy as tireless, as foxy, and as stealthy and familiar with the country as they themselves, and it breaks them all up. It is not merely a question of catching them better with Indians, but of a broader and more enduring aim – their disintegration.[48]

Finally, on top of instilling permanence and internal divisions, the third purpose of sedentarization was target creation. By becoming fixed in a place and by deriving its livelihood from a specific area – or by becoming incorporated into a society, the nomadic group became also a target to threats and incentives. It had something valuable – land, villages, perhaps even agriculture, or participation in a society – that could not be moved and easily restored in some other location. Now the state could threaten to destroy or conquer these newly acquired possessions of the barbarian group, making the settled tribe susceptible to coercive measures. The factions or the leaders of the barbarian group that had an interest in protecting their territory and the wealth they derived from it were more likely to engage their proximate empire or state in negotiations than raiding. The result was that deterrence and diplomacy were more likely to succeed, and were they to fail, the state was more adept at waging a war of conquest against the now settled tribe. The traditional tools of statecraft became more effective. As Kratochwil writes, commenting on the interactions between China and newly settled Mongol tribes, the "development of territoriality ... made a more fixed relationship with China necessary."[49] The "territorialization" of the nomadic tribe stabilizes its relationship with the neighboring states because it allows for a more effective working of threats and inducements.

Arguably, the settled nomads could leave and revert to their previous nomadic ways, thereby restoring their main strategic asset, their mobility. The case of the Alans, whose settlement on Roman lands in the late fourth century caused serious upheavals, is a case of a group that had a difficult time adjusting to a different lifestyle. The Alans were probably incapable of adapting to the new settled lifestyle, as "agriculture was an art almost

---

[48] Robert M. Utley, *Frontier Regulars* (Lincoln, NE: University of Nebraska Press, 1973, 1984 edition), 54. For the use of Apache scouts by the US Army, see also Robert N. Watt, "Raiders of a Lost Art? Apache War and Society," *Small Wars and Insurgencies*, Vol. 13, No. 3 (Autumn 2002), 21.

[49] Kratochwil, 30.

completely outside the range of their experience."[50] Unsurprisingly, they ended up clashing with the local Roman landowners, crushing them. Nevertheless, many tribes, once settled and a generation or so passed, changed so profoundly that few of their members entertained the idea of abandoning their sedentary lifestyle.

In the end, the expectation was that a nomadic group that assumed some traits of a settled community would slowly wither away, decreasing the threat it presented to the polity and its settled communities. As Khazanov writes, sedentarization, whether forced or voluntary, "is frequently linked to the specific disintegration of a nomadic society and an essential transformation in its social organization."[51] Such disintegration did not annihilate the nomadic group, but it took away those key characteristics – mobility, dispersion, and decentralization – that gave nomads considerable military advantages, allowing them to inflict surprising defeats upon states and empires. It weakened them as a warrior force, and forced them to behave more like a state.

It was not a policy that solved all the security problems stemming from the presence of hostile barbarians. In particular, the changes associated with sedentarization affected the capabilities, and not necessarily the objectives, of the barbarian groups. It limited the ability of the barbarians to attack at will in unexpected places, retreat and disperse to remote locations, and avoid frontal fights with punitive expeditions sent by states. But settled barbarians often continued to nourish hostile intentions against their neighboring states or empires, especially if their motivation was religious in nature and therefore not amenable to compromise. Sedentarization, that is, did not create friends.

There are many examples of sedentarization gone awry. The danger was that settling nomads or migrant groups allowed them to build well-fortified bases from which they could then project power, receiving a steady flow of resources and wealth from their newly acquired lands. Militarily, especially in the case of migrant groups, it also freed them from conducting raids with their entire populations in tow, diminishing the strain on their logistics. In fact, despite the positive spin of some historians, the fourth to fifth-century settlement of several Germanic tribes inside the Roman Empire was not an unmitigated success. On the contrary, it weakened the empire even further, and it certainly made local populations deeply unhappy and resentful. While it limited the mobility of the barbarian groups and altered their social structure, the settlement also let them grow to the point that they presented an even more challenging threat to the empire, ultimately replacing its authority and tearing its

[50] E. A. Thompson, *Romans and Barbarians*, 27.   [51] Khazanov, 199.

Western portion apart.[52] Another case of a successful transformation of a nomadic group into a powerful state that threatened its neighbors was the Ottoman Empire.[53]

Similarly, a milder form of sedentarization consisting of policies aimed at establishing a centralized and friendly leadership among barbarians, making them more stable and settled, had also its drawbacks. As a historian observes, "on the one hand, the more power a barbarian chief had, the more stable was his hold over his followers, and the more he could deliver to Rome. On the other, the more power the confederacy had, the greater the threat it posed to the frontier and, ultimately, to Rome."[54] Favoring one leader to bring internal divisions and to have an accountable counterpart with whom to negotiate could easily backfire and undermine the potential benefits.

Sedentarization as a strategy, therefore, carries considerable dangers, and is never a panacea to the persistent threat of barbarian tribes. If it leads to the creation of a sanctuary, it simply strengthens the barbarian group by giving it resources and a base from which it can operate. However, if it is done under the shadow of war, it may in the course of time lead to the changes mentioned earlier, and be overall a positive strategy. Sedentarization must be accompanied by a credible threat to evict, defeat, and devastate the settled barbarians. The underlying idea is that barbarians groups who settle down are then more vulnerable to threats and, if necessary, to the actual use of force. As a result, they become more amenable to seek political solutions through negotiations, rather than trying to achieve their goals through relentless raids.

6.3 Altering Environment

The most difficult and long-term strategy adopted by some polities toward barbarians was to alter the environment that allowed for their existence. As described in Chapter 1, the presence of ungoverned spaces, inside and outside of states, established favorable conditions for the rise of non-state forms of societal organization: more mobile, less hierarchical, and less concerned with territorial administration. To remove the

---

[52] Averil Cameron, *The Mediterranean World in Late Antiquity, AD 395–600* (London: Routledge, 1993), 38–40. See also Thomas F. X. Noble, ed., *From Roman Provinces to Medieval Kingdoms* (New York, NY: Routledge, 2006); J. B. Bury, *The Invasions of Europe by the Barbarians* (New York, NY: W. W. Norton & Co., 1967); Peter Heather, *The Fall of the Roman Empire* (London: Pan Macmillan, 2006); Bryan Ward-Perkins, *The Fall of Rome* (New York, NY: Oxford University Press, 2006).
[53] See also Karen Barkey, *Bandits and Bureaucrats* (Ithaca, NY: Cornell University Press, 1994).
[54] Burns, 347.

barbarian threat, it was necessary to change the space that favored the lifestyle of these groups and that gave them an advantage over settled communities. Instead of targeting directly the groups, the strategy was to modify the conditions that made them possible and lethal.

Writing in 1895 about the challenges facing French forces in Indo-China, French General Albert Duchemin observed that the rebels prospered because of a favorable environment and could not be defeated merely by the use of force. Under pressure, the rebels, or as they were called, "pirates," would merely move farther away and continue to attack French colonial outposts. Duchemin writes that that the

> pirate is a plant which grows only on certain grounds ... The most efficient method is to render the ground unsuitable to him ... There are no pirates in completely organized countries. To pluck wild plants is not sufficient: one must plough the conquered soil, enclose it, and then sow it with the good grain, which is the only means to make it unsuitable to the tares. The same happens on the land desolated by piracy: armed occupation, with or without armed combat, ploughs it; the establishment of a military belt encloses and isolates it; finally the reconstitution and equipment of the population, the installation of markets and cultures, the construction of roads, sow the good grain and make the conquered region unsuitable to the pirate, if it is not the latter himself who, transformed, cooperates in this evolutionary process.[55]

To make the environment, the wider strategic landscape, "unsuitable" to the barbarians was obviously exceedingly difficult. The filling of ungoverned or empty spaces was a hard, perhaps impossible, task in premodern history, as the reach of even powerful empires was curtailed by logistical limitations. The tyranny of distance sapped any long projection of power that relied exclusively on human strength. Legions could march far but it took time and consumed their forces, and in the end, they could not sustain themselves for long periods of time in inhospitable and hostile areas. Even when horses were adopted by imperial forces, they were often not bred to subsist on grass alone and hence were not terribly useful after a few days spent on the Central Asia steppes or on the North American Plains. A US Army colonel commented in the mid-nineteenth century after an expedition chasing Indians:

> After the fourth day's march of a mixed command, the horse does not march faster than the foot soldier, and after the seventh day, the foot soldier begins to outmarch the horse, and from that time on the foot soldier has to end his march earlier and earlier each day, to enable the cavalry to reach the camp the same day at all.[56]

[55] Quoted in Jean Gottman, "Bugeaud, Galliéni, Lyautey: The Development of French Colonial Warfare," in Edward Mead Earle, ed., *Makers of Modern Strategy* (Princeton, NJ: Princeton University Press, 1943), 242.
[56] Utley, 49.

Altering Environment

The environment – deserts, steppes, prairies, heavily forested areas, or more broadly, difficult-to-reach places – could not be altered overnight. But those who faced barbarian groups quickly recognized the advantages that the topography and climate bestowed upon their enemies and that, correspondingly, weakened their own capabilities. Clashing with the Plains Indians, for example, quickly demonstrated to the American forces that their enemies had two key advantages that stemmed from the environment: specially bred horses and the buffalo. The rapid spread of horses in North America, initially introduced by the Spaniards in the seventeenth century, conferred an enormous advantage to those Indians who adopted them. By the early eighteenth century, the Comanches and the Kiowas were already on horses, quickly overpowering other tribes and presenting a serious threat to the Spanish and American settlers. "On foot [a Plains Indian] would have presented no great obstacle to the white settler; mounted he became a fearsome antagonist and a formidable opponent even for trained cavalry."[57] The Comanches, in particular, became a powerful group that mastered the horse and married it to the conditions of the Plains. Most the horses were stolen from Spanish and then American settlers in New Mexico and Texas, but were bred to be resilient, requiring only grass and a little water to sustain themselves. Horses gave Comanches great mobility, which in turn allowed them to engage in quick and distant raids – the Plains type of warfare – and to improve their diet by hunting distant buffalos. The buffalo was "indispensable to the way of life of the Southern Plains Indians."[58] Not particularly alert, this large animal was easy to hunt once a herd was found: A group could kill several hundred animals in a short hunt, a quantity of meat that was sufficient to feed a large tribe for weeks.

By the mid-nineteenth century, it became evident for American commanders in the Plains that in order to weaken, and ultimately defeat, their opponents, they had to deprive them of the source of their advantages, namely buffalos and horses. The former fed the tribes, while the latter gave them great mobility.[59] During the Civil War, buffalos were hunted by US forces and their contractors to feed the Army, but these hunts were

---

[57] William H. Leckie, *The Military Conquest of the Southern Plains* (Norman, OK: University of Oklahoma Press, 1963), 8.
[58] Leckie, 6. Also, Webb, 44–45.
[59] In fact, early on, the US military learned that the only way to engage the Plains Indians militarily was during the winter, when the tribes were hunkered down in camps, too weak to organize large attacks. The US Army on the other hand could project power on the plains thanks to its logistical skills and capabilities. These winter campaigns brought some successes, as the Indians were less dispersed than during the summer and thus presented a bigger and more fixed target. Allan R. Millett and Peter Maslowski, *For the Common Defense* (New York, NY: The Free Press, 1994), 254.

insufficient to deprive the Indians of their food sources. The discovery of a new way of turning buffalo hides into leather in 1871 (combined with the expansion of the railroads that allowed the shipping of the hides to processing places and then to the markets) created an incentive to hunt these animals on a mass scale. Expeditions were organized and over the course of a few years the buffalo herds of the Plains had been exterminated. An ecologically sustainable rate of hunting allowed for approximately 280,000 animals to be killed, more than enough for the Indians to feed themselves. But an average hunter could take down more than 100 animals per day because grazing buffalos will not become frightened by a shot, thus allowing repeated hits before a herd would move away.[60] Millions of buffalos had been shot between 1872 and 1876, most of them only for their hides, leaving the carcasses to rot. According to some estimates, 3.5 million buffalos were killed in two years, and only 150,000 of them by Indians.[61] By 1876, the southern herd was eliminated, leaving only a few thousand buffalos in the northern plains. General Phil Sheridan, when he was the commander of the Southwest, reportedly encouraged the massacre of the buffalo herds as a strategy to pacify the Indians: "Let them kill, skin and sell until the buffalo is exterminated, as it is the only way to bring lasting peace and allow civilization to advance."[62]

The Army also targeted horses. A man without a horse on the plains was a dead man, and the Comanches without horses were powerless.[63] In one of the last major military engagements between the US Army and the Prairie Indians, the 1874 battle of Palo Duro Canyon, the 4th US Cavalry led by "Bad Hand" Mackenzie surprised a group of Kiowas and Comanches and quickly routed them. The short battle caused very few casualties (only three Indians were killed) but the US forces caught almost all of the horses of these hostile groups. Almost 2,000 of them were quickly killed, leaving a pile of bones that allegedly was visible decades later until some entrepreneurial individual sold it as fertilizer.[64] As a soldier under Mackenzie put it, killing all the horses "was the surest method of crippling the Indians and compelling them to go into and stay

---

[60] On buffalo hunting, see Randolph B. Marcy, *The Prairie Traveler: A Hand-book for Overland Expeditions* (New York, NY: Harper & Brothers, 1861), 238–241.
[61] Leckie, 186; Utley, 213; Hämäläinen, 336; Russell F. Weigley, *The American Way of War* (Bloomington, IN: Indiana University Press, 1973), 160; Andrew Isenberg, *The Destruction of the Bison* (New York, NY: Cambridge University Press, 2000); James L. Haley, *The Buffalo War* (Garden City, NY: Doubleday & Co., 1976), 24–30.
[62] Quoted in Leckie, 187; Carolyn Merchant, *American Environmental History: An Introduction* (New York, NY: Columbia University Press, 2007), 20.
[63] Marcy, 213.
[64] Leckie, 222. The best description of the battle is in Haley, chapter 12, 169–183.

upon their reservations which they had fled from ... They were such valuable property that they were held in higher esteem than their squaws."[65] The Indians were defeated not on a traditional military battlefield, in a clash of soldier against soldier. They lost because their lifestyle, and thus their military advantages, were no longer possible.[66] A similar story can be told about the Central Asian steppe barbarians in the seventeenth century. The gradual change of the conditions prevalent on the steppes through the introduction of different methods of cultivation altered the lifestyle of the indigenous tribes. As a Russian historian put it, the "plow, not the sword, won the steppe, and the chicken prevailed over the horse."[67]

The extension of the railroad network across the North American prairie contributed even further to the altering of this environment. In a way analogous to the effect on the Eurasian continental states, the railroad unified the North American continent, filling the space that until then had remained impervious to state control.[68] The penetration of the railroad on the Plains meant that the settlers could move in faster and greater numbers, their products could be delivered to the eastern (and increasingly, western) markets with great speed, and the entire lifestyle that the plains had fostered over the previous centuries had been altered. General William Tecumseh Sherman, in his post-Civil War capacity as Commanding General of the US Army in charge of securing the Western states, observed that

> the great Pacific Railroads ... for better or worse, have settled the fate of the buffalo and Indian forever. There have been wars and conflicts since with these Indians ... but they have been the dying struggles of a singular race of brave men fighting against destiny, each less and less violent, till now the wild game is gone, the whites too numerous and powerful; so that the Indian question has become one of sentiment and charity, but not of war.[69]

Walter Prescott Webb, in his magisterial history of the Plains, suggests that other technological inventions, namely, the six-shooter, barbed wire,

---

[65] Robert G. Carter, *On the Border with Mackenzie* (Austin, TX: Texas State Historical Association, 2007; originally published in *c.* 1935), 495.
[66] Pekka Hämäläinen, *The Comanche Empire*, 339.
[67] Edward Louis Keenan, Jr., "Muscovy and Kazan: Some Introductory Remarks on the Patterns of Steppe Diplomacy," *Slavic Review*, Vol. 26, No. 4 (December 1967), 557.
[68] Margaret Sprout, "Mahan: Evangelist of Sea Power," in Edward Mead Earle, ed. *Makers of Modern Strategy* (Princeton, NJ: Princeton University Press, 1943), 424; Edward Mead Earle, "Adam Smith, Alexander Hamilton, Friedrich List: The Economic Foundations of Military Power," in ibid., 148–152; Paul M. Kennedy, *The Rise of the Anglo-German Antagonism, 1860–1914* (London: Ashfield Press, 1980), 44.
[69] William Tecumseh Sherman, *Memoirs of General W. T. Sherman* (New York, NY: The Library of America, 1990), 926.

and the windmill well, tamed and civilized the prairie.[70] But stressing the importance of these tools does not deny the role of other means and factors, such as the railroad and more broadly the process of industrialization that gradually led to the conquest of spaces until then out of reach for the administrative state. Moreover, the effect of the means mentioned by Webb was similar: they removed the conditions that allowed barbarian tribes to be strategic actors. Barbarians were a product, and a lethal one, of specific conditions that had hindered the expansion of state or imperial control. When the soldiers and pioneers streaming from the settled communities adopted technologies that allowed them to master the difficult environment and topography, the spaces that until then remained outside of state reach and thus fostered the presence of barbarians were gradually "filled."

Barbarians, whether in North America or in the Central Asian steppes, arose and lived from the nature that surrounded them. As French historian René Grousset noted, the steppe archers, the barbarians that for thirteen centuries had terrorized Europe and Russia, were the "spontaneous creation of the soil itself."[71] That soil had to be altered, changed, and even destroyed in order for the barbarians to lose their social cohesion and their capacity to project power.[72] The barbarians could avoid battles with trained and well-supplied imperial forces for centuries but could not withstand the industrial advances of the various powers in Eurasia, and then North American, from the sixteenth century on. "The cannonade with which Ivan the Terrible scattered the last heirs of the Golden Horde, and with which the K'ang-his emperor of China frightened the Kalmucks, marked the end of a period of world history."[73]

It is, of course, questionable whether such large-scale and long-term changes in the landscape or environment could have been – or can be in the future – an outcome of a conscious strategy. The vanishing of the spaces and conditions that made barbarians strategic actors capable of competing with states was after all a product of deep trends: the industrialization of economies, the expansion of the railroad, and the fielding of mass armies capable of increasingly greater firepower. The nineteenth

---

[70] See Webb, on the six-shooter (167–179), barbed wire (295–318), windmill well (333–348).

[71] René Grousset, *The Empire of the Steppes* (New Brunswick, NJ: Rutgers University Press, 1970), xi.

[72] T. R. Fehrenbach writes: "Almost all North American Indians, whether true savages or high barbarians, lived in a fragile symbiosis with the native wilderness. Europeans, out of a process that went back to the prehistoric deforestation of Greece and Italy, were compelled to advance their causes and civilization by remaking nature." Fehrenbach, *Comanches*, 268.

[73] Grousset, xi.

century was perhaps the culmination of trends that had begun in the fifteenth and sixteenth centuries, and the side effect of them was the conquest of the last vast spaces (e.g. Central Asian steppes, the American prairie) where remnants of barbarian groups survived. Without such deep historical forces at work, no state could have formulated and implemented a strategy of altering the environment to favor its own strengths and undermine those of the barbarian enemies. Nonetheless, in the limits imposed by the times, past empires and polities tried to extend their reach through the constructions of roads, the encouragement of colonial settlements, or the control over military technology in order to shape the environment and the ungoverned spaces. Such an approach, parallel to what often is termed now as "draining the swamp," required a persistent and farsighted leadership, a feat that was rarely attainable. As with all the other strategies, this one too mitigated and did not resolve the barbarian problem.

There was no one solution to the challenges presented by barbarians. In many ways, barbarians were a problem without a solution, and hence the core challenge was that there was naturally no clear strategy of how to deal with them. All the strategies described here – fortifications and local forces, sedentarization, and altering the environment – were at best long-term approaches to mitigate the barbarian threat. They addressed one particular aspect of the barbarian groups, namely their mobility and resulting ability to strike quickly along a lengthy frontier and in places often unprotected and unaccustomed to war. Traditional military solutions, such as territorial occupation, set piece battles, or large campaigns, were not as successful in preventing barbarian raids or defeating the enemy. The conflict between states and barbarians was therefore unsettling and terrifying, in large measure because it required a different mindset putting a premium on long-term approaches. Given the uncertainty of success of long-term policies, it was impossible to insulate the populations of the targeted states (or, to be more precise, the frontier populations located along the possible vectors of barbarian attacks) from the insecurity generated by the barbarian raids. This meant that the local populations could not subcontract their own security to a distant army and had to accept the costs of frontier instability by contributing both financially and personally to local security provision and obtaining some benefits such as greater autonomy or possession of land. A barbarian threat pushes the frontier, and all of its insecurity and instability, deep inside the territory of the targeted polity.

7 Conclusion
Sidewalks and Two Fronts

Throughout history, in diverse regions and to different degrees, barbarians presented a persistent menace to settled communities and polities of various size and nature. The latter had tactical advantages because they could usually defeat barbarians in a direct military clash: The barbarian groups rarely had the manpower, the discipline, and the technology necessary to win in a set-piece battle. But states had strategic disadvantages because they were less suited to confront multiple, geographically diffused, individually small, and yet destabilizing attacks – the barbarians' preferred military approach. Furthermore, for the most part, the main threat to states has been – and continues to be – other states, creating thus a dual security environment: one front with a rival peer competitor and a second front with barbarian groups. In turn, both the two-front challenge and the nature of the barbarian threat put a premium on local defenses and local forces, the first and perhaps most effective responders to a barbarian assault.

Barbarians were not invincible, but they presented serious challenges that required states and empires to adapt. And that adaptation did not come easily to most polities because it required some level of decentralization, arming populations that were usually disarmed and unaccustomed to defending themselves or giving more authority over the use of force to frontier communities. Whatever the particular form decentralization took, it was always a process fraught with danger because it opened up the possibility of a gradual splintering of the polity. Moreover, such an adaptation put the burden of defense on populations that in many cases lacked the skills and capabilities to protect themselves. In modern times in particular, security provision has been the domain of centralized state authorities and their military apparatuses. Driven in large measure by industrial necessities, security has been subcontracted to the state, capable of organizing, outfitting, and managing a large and lethal military. Only such an entity could compete with other similarly organized polities. Citizens of modern states are therefore accustomed to outsourcing the provision of civil order to local authorities (e.g. the police force) and the provision of security from external threats to their own state's military forces. Security is, at the various levels of the threat, something that is supplied to them and requires little, or no, civilian, popular participation. The citizenry is a consumer, not a provider, of security.

To a degree, a similar dynamic existed in the premodern period too, as, for example, large armies or navies required discipline that only lengthy training and practice could build and resources that only well-organized city states or empires could supply and manage. The population at large was therefore involved only marginally in security provision: Its contribution was material (e.g. food, housing), pecuniary (e.g. taxes), or in manpower (e.g. volunteers or conscripts). Populations certainly experienced the effects of security failures, often in catastrophic ways when, for instance, the walls of besieged city were breeched by a rival power or when hostile armies marched through the countryside slashing, burning, and eating on their way. But these were instances of insecurity that did not create incentives to give power to the affected populations; most often such a devolution of power would have come too late to do any good. The failure to deter or to defeat the army of a rival power would not have been necessarily ameliorated by arming the population writ large. There are few instances of guerilla warfare in premodern times, as populations switched their allegiance (and taxpaying duties) from one potentate to another with great celerity. By and large, therefore, polities were reluctant to relinquish security provision to local authorities, preferring to have their populations unarmed: The risks of arming them outweighed the potential benefits in case of a breakdown of security.

The barbarian threat created different conditions and incentives from those established only by the presence of other hostile polities or peer rivals. With barbarians attacking along a lengthy frontier and often deep inside the allegedly secure state territory, security provision could not be easily subcontracted to the state and its well-organized, well-supplied, and large but not ubiquitous armies. A local, relatively small threat often did not justify the involvement of the entire state national security apparatus, which in any case was not well suited to deal with it. Local communities had to take security in their own hands, and instead of being merely consumers, they had to become also suppliers of security. Another way to put this is that the presence of a barbarian threat called for the subsidiarity of security provision.

The principle of subsidiarity suggests that tasks ought to be assigned to the lowest competent authority capable of performing them. Accordingly, individuals, or their closest social groupings (e.g. families, friends, tribes, villages, cities), should not be deprived of the possibility of action in spheres in which they have competence and in tasks which they can fulfill more efficiently. In the realm of security provision, ancient and modern polities alike have arrogated to themselves the duty and the right to be the principal security suppliers – and rightly so, as interstate competition is too deadly for local communities or small groups of individuals to counter effectively. Facing a peer rival, the most efficient defense is through a similar state, the only actor capable of fulfilling the task of security provision.

But under some circumstances, security may be best provided by lower societal groups that have a clearer interest and incentive to do it and may be better suited to the task at hand. Subsidiarity, in other words, is not a principle that should be applied exclusively to nonsecurity issues ranging from education to law enforcement – a tendency that is justified when the main and only security menace was posed by other states, with all of their industrial capability, economic resources, and manpower. With the barbarian threat, the conditions are different. The rapidity, surprising locations, and circumscribed nature of barbarian attacks make the immediate targets the first and most competent responders. Sub-state groupings, local communities, and even individuals play an important role in responding to barbarian attacks, mitigating their effects, and protecting their own interests and lives. These local actors should be encouraged to consider security provision as their own task, and should be empowered to develop the skills and capabilities necessary to counter the enemy.

A centralized provision of security, where the state manages the resources and controls the immediate responses to the threats, is likely to fail when facing barbarian threats. At a minimum it is likely to fail the communities and locations immediately targeted by the barbarians, diminishing its own legitimacy while at the same time doing little to foster order. When the failure of security is localized and relatively small, the most effective and most necessary response is likely to be local.

An illustrative analogy is the role of sidewalks famously described by Jane Jacobs in her book, *The Death and Life of Great American Cities*. As she put it, the security of a neighborhood depends in large measure not on the presence of a large number of police officers, but on the watchful eye of a local storekeeper, a barber, or the old lady taking her daily walk. A safe sidewalk is the outcome not of a well-oiled state bureaucracy, but of "an intricate, almost unconscious, network of voluntary controls and standards among the people themselves, and enforced by the people themselves ... No amount of police can enforce civilization where the normal, casual enforcement of it has broken down."[1] These "eyes on the

---

[1] Jane Jacobs, *The Death and Life of Great American Cities* (New York, NY: Vintage Books, 1992), 31–32.

Conclusion

street" – the "natural proprietors of the street" – know how to distinguish a break in the pattern of the normal conditions of regular daily life.[2] Their watchful oversight of their immediate surroundings by itself is a source of security and stability, because the mere knowledge of their presence can serve as a deterrent to miscreants. This requires a number of individuals who consider the public space, the sidewalk, as part of their own responsibility, rather than a place under the authority and control of some higher power (e.g. the police force or other state authorities that, no matter how numerous, cannot be always present). In the case of a vibrant community, this means a large number of people walking around, for business or pleasure: "the sidewalk must have users on it fairly continuously, both to add to the number of effective eyes on the street and to induce the people in buildings along the street to watch the sidewalks in sufficient numbers."[3] Simply by their frequent presence and loitering, individuals protect the public space of the sidewalk: Foot traffic discourages crime. A vibrant sidewalk life creates a space where neighbors can meet and establish a community that is self-policing.

The simple argument made by Jacobs was proven to be correct, in particular when the sidewalks emptied and people retreated to their private spaces because of poor urban developments. But there is a larger point too. The sidewalk is shorthand for the idea that security is a result of actions of individuals occurring without a coordination imposed and managed by a centralized authority. A barber from the neighborhood or the retired gentleman on his daily stroll did not, and will not, singlehandedly provide security from the occasional attack, but are better suited at noticing a potential threat. A threatening individual, melted into the civilian population, is most likely to be found by watchful eyes of locals, rather than through a centralized bureaucracy.

In the case of barbarian attacks, the point is that state authorities and forces may not be present at the relevant locations on the threatened frontier. In fact, barbarians struck usually where there was no large army to oppose them and sought soft targets that could be raided quickly and with impunity. The state, therefore, needs the active involvement of local populations – of the sidewalks, so to speak – to prevent, disrupt, and defend against small barbarian attacks. The possibility of ubiquitous assaults leads to the necessity of ubiquitous security provision, something that a centralized state cannot do.

The nature of the barbarian threat is such that states have by necessity and by fact a permeable frontier. Even the most potent polity cannot

---

[2] Jacobs, 35.   [3] Jacobs, 35.

protect the entire length of a frontier because its resources are limited. Moreover, extending its forces along a frontier is risky because the enemy can amass at one point and through a surprising attack break through those defenses, opening the interior to devastation, especially if there are no highly mobile forces in the rear. Preclusive defense, in other words, is difficult to implement when facing barbarians. The expectation, therefore, should be that barbarians will strike inside the territory of the state, at sudden times and unforeseen places. Barbarians slip through frontier defenses. The interior of states is thus open to attacks, forcing the local populations to take action: In the past this often meant seeking refuge in fortified cities and being armed. Frontier populations have to rely on themselves first and foremost, rather than expect their polities to guarantee their security.

If my argument presented in Chapter 3 is correct, namely that barbarians are a recurrent threat in history, then local responses to the new barbarians may also be needed. The best way to harden targets against barbarian raids is to make the local population aware of their responsibilities as security providers. The nature of violent non-state actors, whether in their Islamist or other permutations, forces states to play catch up: The attacks occur in unexpected places through surprising methods, finding soft targets that the state will try to harden only after the attack. These modern barbarians, like those of the past, are parasitical entities because they benefit from existing technologies and order provided by states; they do not have to expend enormous resources to produce new tools of violence, only with new ideas of how to use them. Hardware is less important than the software. The advantage that modern states possess is their ability to develop, produce, and manage large and sophisticated hardware and organizations that underwrite their own security. Barbarians avoid this state advantage, and in fact, use some aspects of it (e.g. latest technologies) to strike with rapidity and surprise.

States respond to such attacks by activating their military might. Such *post hoc* security provision is necessary but is also characterized by a delay with which centralized authorities respond to such rapid and unforeseeable attacks. Like the imperial armies of the past, today's state forces come to the targeted area and populations after the attack and respond against the barbarian aggressors after the initial assault. Reprisals are, of course, needed to punish the attackers and disrupt potential future attacks, but do little to assuage the fears of the targeted populations. As a result, the citizens need to take security provision seriously, not simply by subcontracting it to the highest political authority – the state and military forces – but by playing an active role in it. A modest recognition of this necessity can be seen in the ubiquitous public signs advising

Conclusion

passers-by to "say something if you see something." Because the potential threat is small and thus difficult to notice in its stages of preparation (unlike, say, a conventional attack by a hostile state, which requires large and visible arrangements), the national security apparatus of a state may not be capable of preventing it. The population therefore must take active measures to provide for its own security, not to supplant but to supplement what a state may do at the same time. Subsidiarity does not mean, in fact, that the lowest competent authority is alone in fulfilling the particular task at hand, but only that it is the primary actor with the other, higher authorities backing it. It is the same in the case of security: Individuals and local communities are the primary providers of their own security in the case of barbarian attacks – the first responders – while the empires with their legions or modern states with their armies and intelligence structures follow close behind in a variety of ways.

Violent non-state actors find the holes in the security provided by states, and force the targeted populations to seek local solutions. There is thus a natural process of decentralization of security provision, as I described in Chapters 4 and 5. If the state cannot protect vulnerable populations at the frontier, they will organize themselves to do that. Some may be more successful than others, and the decentralization of security can be risky. The state may lose some of its legitimacy and authority, leading to centrifugal tendencies that can weaken it. Moreover, it is not easy to reactivate in a group of people a sense of urgency and recognition of the need to provide for their own physical security: Rearming a population accustomed to think of security as something delivered by a specialized professional force at the safe distance of a state border, or even beyond, requires patience and training.

Security subsidiarity is certainly risky and problematic but also necessary for three reasons. First, the greatest danger to a state in the end is another state. It is important to remember that Julius Caesar faced a graver threat from his rival Pompey with his legions than from an Ambiorix with his Eburones or a Vercingetorix with his Gallic tribes. In more recent times, the stability of the United States was rocked more by the Civil War than by all the conflicts with the Western Indians, and a few days of industrial firefights on the European battlefields of World War I or World War II killed more people than years of frontier conflict with barbarian groups. The clash between states, especially industrialized ones, creates more devastation and casualties than skirmishes with barbarian tribes.

The barbarian threat therefore should not be overestimated. The rise of barbarians on a frontier usually meant that the state faced a dual threat: barbarians on one side, peer rivals on the other. The two-front challenge was particularly problematic because it demanded not only large resources that needed to be allocated to protect against these threats but also two different approaches. As described in the preceding chapters, frontier warfare with barbarians was very different from a clash of imperial armies. What was useful to deter and, if needed, to defeat a fellow state, was not necessarily suitable to oppose and eliminate a barbarian enemy.

Frontier warfare against barbarians requires the participation of small local forces, drawn in large measure from the targeted populations. This seems to be the most effective way also to limit the drainage of state resources, or to avoid their allocation away from the primary long-term challenge of hostile states. If security is subcontracted in its totality, on both fronts, to the national security apparatus of the state, it is likely to be ineffective in the case of geographically diffused and individually small attacks – and it will drain the state's capacity to deter and compete with peer rivals. Not every security threat is best addressed by the full might of the state.

Second, related to the previous reason, security subsidiarity and the resulting decentralization may be a happy medium between the two risks associated with assessing the barbarian threat. Barbarians are in fact often either underestimated or overestimated as a menace. They are overestimated because they present surprising problems, shocking the targeted population with suddenness and brutality. They become an enemy that is larger in the imagination of the potential targets than in their actual ability on the battlefield; after all, they rarely can bring down an entire state in one sweeping invasion. As a result of overestimation, the entire state apparatus is directed to address this threat, to the detriment of other fronts. The war against the barbarians becomes the main preoccupation rather than one of the many. On the other side of the spectrum, it is also easy to underestimate the barbarian menace as nothing more than a small frontier challenge or a criminal problem, rather than a threat to the national security of the state. Particularly if the capital of the targeted polity is far away from the barbarian threat, the enemy raids are distant geographically and intellectually, and the frontier regions may end up being effectively left to fend for themselves. The risk here is that the affected regions and populations lose faith in the ability of their polity to secure them, leading to devolution of power and splintering of the state.

By embracing security subsidiarity, it may be possible to avoid swinging between an overly centralized response to the barbarian threat and a perilous insouciance to it. A population that is alert and prepared to respond may be the happy medium, offering a counterbalance to the tendencies of over- or underestimating the barbarian enemy.

Conclusion

The third reason why security subsidiarity may be beneficial is that if the perusal of past conflicts with barbarians offers one lesson, it is that the barbarian threat is a long-term problem, rather than a short blip. It is often a generational challenge that compels the state in question to have a supportive population. Barbarians arise out of a series of conditions (described in Chapters 1 and 3) that are linked to deep and lengthy trends, which cannot be quickly altered through policies pursued by states. For instance, the presence of territories difficult to control or the wide availability of lethal technologies are conditions that a state cannot change with great speed, regardless of its power. A strategy to alter those trends is also not something that states in the past seemed to have pursued consistently. The policy of states is geared to alter the behavior of other actors through the panoply of means at their disposal, including the application of force or the threat of violence. The target is rarely to alter fundamentally the wider environment that makes barbarians lethal actors – in part because it is a task too far for one state or one administration. In premodern times, it was something that polities rarely seemed to pursue with consistency, a recognition of the difficulty, if not futility, of altering the strategic environment in order to undermine the power of barbarians. Only in the late eighteenth and nineteenth century, Russia and the United States engaged in policies that aimed through sheer industrial might at expanding state reach to ungovernable spaces.

But the point here is that the violence of barbarian–state relations lasts longer than interstate wars, and rarely seems to end with a treaty or peace agreement. The length of these conflicts, therefore, requires a serious commitment of the affected populations. Like other forms of low-intensity wars, the competition is at the level of nerves, commitment, and will, rather than resources. Indeed, the military posture and strategy of the barbarians are set up to go around the advantages of their targets. Wealth, resources, and massed firepower and large well-supplied armies are some of these advantages of states that the barbarians avoid. States therefore have to learn how to adapt to this asymmetric competition, lengthening the timeframe of the conflict. In the end, a conflict with barbarians was more a condition to manage rather than a problem to solve. Such a long conflict cannot be sustained without the active participation of the population, especially when some segments of that population are targeted while most of them remain vulnerable but unaffected.

The return of the barbarian menace is not inevitable, of course, and we can hope that the challenges premodern polities faced will remain a relic of the distant past. But events of the past decade indicate differently. States are not the only strategic actors, and non-state groups, mostly of Islamist persuasion, are lethal, mirroring the ancient barbarian threat.

Undoubtedly, the Islamist tint of these groups is particular and does not find exact parallels with premodern groups: so does their global reach and lethality, which are made possible by modern day technologies that they parasitically use. Differences abound. But there are also many similarities, pointing to the recurrent nature of this type of threat. And if we are seeing a return of barbarian threats, then we will also have to expect a greater involvement in security provision by the population at large. Subcontracting security to higher authorities, the state, may not be the most effective approach to dealing with barbarians. The political and social order is best protected from barbarian attacks not only by the larger polity – under whatever form it may be, empire, city or modern nation state – but also by a vigilant people, aware of the responsibility to provide their own security.

Index

A2/AD, anti-access/area denial, 114
Adrianople, battle of, 23, 33, 70, 76, 134, 137
Aeschylus, 35
Aetius, 167
Alans, 58, 159, 201
Alaric, 54, 56, 136, 141
Algeria, 64, 66
Al-Qaeda, 13, 96, 98, 105, 109, 110, 111, 118
Ambiorix, 61, 128, 129, 215
Ambrose, Saint, 133, 155, 161
American Plains. *See* North American Plains
Ammianus Marcellinus, 23, 56, 58, 70, 80
Ancient Greece, 2, 9, 74
Andreski, Stanislav, 29, 30, 36, 80
Aquitania, 134, 176, 196, 197
Aristotle, 49
Arminius, 26, 69, 125
Athens, 78
Attila, 58, 77, 178
Augustine, Saint, 140, 148, 149, 154, 155, 156, 157, 158, 159, 160, 161, 162, 163, 164, 165, 166, 167, 168, 173, 177, 182
Augustus, Octavian, 21, 125, 147, 155
Aurelian wall, 141
Avitus, emperor, 169, 170, 172

Basilius, bishop of Aix, 175
Batavis, 179
Bean, Richard, 21
Billington, Ray Allen, 63, 190,
Bloch, Marc, 32, 33, 48, 59, 76
Boniface, 154, 159, 162, 163, 164, 165, 166, 167, 168
Braudel, Fernand, 21
Brodie, Bernard, 15, 72, 90
Brown, Peter, 24, 43, 50, 140, 147, 148, 178

Brunt, P. A., 29, 31, 35, 144, 145
Bury, J. B., 14, 21, 58, 143, 168, 196, 203
Byzantium, 28, 46, 59, 76, 101, 118, 141, 144, 149, 150, 151, 186, 187, 200

Canossa, 43
Carduchi, 37
Carolingian empire, 145
Carthage, 155, 167
Central Asia, 24, 27, 58, 97, 204
Chalons, battle of, 58
Clausewitz, 46
Claval, Paul, 39
Clearchus, 40
Clermont, 147, 168, 170, 171, 174, 175, 176, 177, 183
clientela, 31
Comanches, 10, 12, 22, 43, 47, 50, 53, 61, 63, 67, 69, 200, 205, 206, 208
comitatenses, 149
Commodus, emperor, 77, 78
Congress of Vienna, 78, 111
Crusaders, 101, 199
Crusades, 45, 199
cyber mobilization, 101

Danube, 52, 76, 77, 84, 127, 132, 134, 135, 136, 141, 154, 177, 178, 179, 180
Dawson, Christopher, 45, 73
de Croix, Teodoro, 189
De Rebus Bellicis, 185, 186, 189
decentralization, 11, 52, 98, 100, 122, 123, 125, 128, 130, 131, 132, 135, 138, 144, 145, 147, 148, 150, 151, 152, 153, 154, 155, 167, 168, 170, 177, 181, 182, 194, 202, 210, 215, 216
decolonization, 3, 15, 19, 41, 107
deterrence, 10, 13, 19, 48, 60, 65, 66, 67, 69, 70, 71, 72, 74, 80, 81, 84, 88, 91, 108, 112, 114, 115, 116, 117, 121, 152, 179, 195, 197, 201

219

220　Index

diplomacy, 7, 10, 13, 18, 19, 46, 48, 60, 67, 72, 73, 74, 75, 78, 79, 80, 81, 83, 84, 88, 108, 109, 110, 111, 112, 117, 121, 137, 195, 197, 201
Duby, Georges, 21, 32, 33, 34
Duchemin, Albert, 204

Eburones, 61, 128, 129, 215
Eckstein, Arthur, 4, 18, 75, 78, 82
Eugippius, 178, 179, 180, 181, 182
Euric, 169, 175

Finley, M. I., 82
Freedman, Lawrence, 68
Fritigern, 55

Gat, Azar, 31, 33, 44, 46, 67, 72, 83
Gaul, 20, 31, 38, 41, 47, 51, 52, 60, 61, 63, 125, 128, 129, 136, 140, 143, 145, 146, 147, 150, 154, 155, 168, 169, 170, 171, 172, 173, 174, 175, 176, 177, 180, 194, 198
Geiseric, 171
Genghis Khan, 56
Genseric, 158
Germania, 35, 38, 39, 84
ghazis, 30, 34, 45
Gibbon, Edward, 133, 149, 158, 159, 171, 172,
Gilpin, Robert, 27
gladius, 24, 26
glory, 23, 33, 44, 46, 47, 50, 54, 69, 70, 76, 78, 81, 82, 83, 103, 136, 157, 164, 166, 169, 199
Golden Horde, 208
Goths, 21, 23, 32, 50, 52, 54, 70, 136, 137, 147, 169, 174, 196
Graecus, bishop of Marsilia, 176
greek fire, 28
Gregory of Tours, 147, 175
Grousset, René, 24, 35, 41, 208,
guerilla warfare, 22, 51, 152, 211
Guicciardini, Francesco, 15, 16
Guilmartin, John, 45, 83
gunpowder revolution, 95, 189

Hadrian's Wall, 70, 71
Hadrianople, battle of, 60
Hale, J. R., 44, 45
Hamas, 92, 111
Helvetii, 40, 51, 194, 195, 196
Hezbollah, 98, 105, 113, 115, 116, 118
Hippo, 154, 155, 162, 164, 167, 168
Hoag, Malcolm, 95, 96
Hobbes, Thomas, 6

Holy Roman Empire, 5, 89
hospitalitas, 196,
Howard, Michael, 69, 70, 87, 123
hubris, 44
Huns, 10, 21, 27, 35, 51, 52, 53, 54, 55, 56, 58, 70, 76, 77, 135, 137

IEDs, 93, 96
incastellamento, 141
Ivan the Terrible, 208

Jacobs, Jane, 212, 213,
Jerome, Saint, 54, 136, 157
Jones, A.H.M., 37, 144, 146
Jugurtha, 34
Julius Caesar, 2, 31, 38, 40, 41, 51, 60, 61, 63, 65, 125, 128, 129, 170, 194, 195, 196, 215
Julius Nepos, emperor, 175

Kazan, 16, 38, 81, 207
Khazanov, Anatoly, 57, 58, 59, 71, 196, 202
Kiowas, 205, 206
Knorr, Klaus, 112
Krasner, Stephen, 3, 14, 17
Kratochwil, Friedrich, 42, 199, 201

Late Antiquity, 27, 29, 50, 52, 54, 86, 119, 134, 136, 142, 147, 149, 151, 203
Lattimore, Owen, 64, 71
limes, 24, 134, 156, 178, 186
limitanei, 149
Livonia, 84
Lukacs, John, 87

Machiavelli, Niccoló, 2, 115, 116, 163, 194
Mackenzie, Ranald S., 36, 61, 206, 207
MacMullen, Ramsay, 23, 31, 37, 44, 124, 129, 140, 141, 142, 144
Mamertinus, 181
Marcus Aurelius, emperor, 77
Markey, Daniel, 44
Markus, Robert, 4, 41, 42, 156, 158, 163, 164, 165, 180
Marrou, Henri, 148, 155, 157
Maurice, Byzantine emperor, 53, 61, 70
McNeill, William, 27, 28, 59, 71, 95, 148
Melos, 55
Middle Ages, 2, 5, 7, 13, 14, 17, 21, 29, 32, 73, 86, 89, 97, 118, 123
Ming, 21, 25, 27, 54, 60, 71, 80, 81, 184, 196
Mongols, 28, 35, 50, 51, 53, 55, 56, 59, 60, 64, 71, 184
Mons Graupius, battle of, 51, 60
Muscovite Russia, 16, 38, 39, 81

Index

Nasrallah, Hassan, 105
Nestorians, 45
Nicholson, Harold, 76
Noricum, 52, 136, 154, 177, 178
North Africa, 29, 64, 125, 127, 129, 134, 136, 150, 154, 155, 156, 158, 159, 162, 163, 164, 166, 167, 183, 184
North American Plains, 37, 54, 97, 204

Octavian. *See* Augustus
Octavian Augustus, 31
oppida, 141, 196
Orosius, 140

Pannonia, 76, 142
Parry, J. H., 84
Parthia, 26, 84
Parthian empire, 83
Pax Nicephori, 78
Peace of Callias, 78
Peace of Nicias, 78
Peloponnesian war, 82
Piganiol, André, 133, 134
Pirenne, Henri, 24
Plains Indians, 27, 47, 67, 82, 205
Plutarch, 47, 195
Poggi, Gianfranco, 32, 124, 198
polis, 49
Polybius, 132, 133
Pompey, 61, 215
Possidius, 148, 159, 160, 164, 167
presidios, 187, 188
prestige, 33, 42, 43, 44, 51, 82, 103
Procopius, 159, 167
Pueblo tribes, 25

raids, 27, 33, 34, 47, 51, 52, 54, 55, 61, 64, 70, 76, 81, 84, 116, 134, 135, 137, 144, 145, 147, 150, 177, 178, 179, 180, 182, 185, 186, 187, 188, 189, 190, 192, 193, 202, 203, 205, 209, 214, 216
Rhine, 24, 38, 41, 52, 63, 84, 128, 129, 132, 134, 135, 136, 141, 143, 196
Romulus Augustulus, emperor, 148, 176, 182
Roy, Oliver, 10, 104
Rumsfeld, Donald, 115

Sallust, 34, 156
Salvian, 180
Santa Cruz de San Saba, 63

Santa Fe Trail, 62
Saracens, 59
Schelling, Thomas, 46, 65, 66, 83,
Scott, James, 39
Scott, James C., 39, 42
Severinus, Saint, 154, 155, 177, 178, 179, 180, 181, 182,
Sheridan, Phil, 206
Sherman. William Tecumseh, 207,
Shubik, Martin, 90, 91
Sidonius, 140, 147, 148, 150, 155, 168, 169, 170, 171, 172, 173, 174, 175, 176, 177, 182
Sidonius, Apollinaris, 154
Sienkiewicz, Henryk, 48
Spain, 17, 24, 29, 91, 98, 134, 141, 143, 145, 146, 150, 158, 160, 189, 190
Sparta, 78
Spruyt, Hendrick, 17, 32, 198
Stalin, 42
stirrup, 29
Strayer, Joseph, 20, 78, 79, 198
subsidiarity, 194, 211, 212, 215, 216, 217

Tacfarinas, 39, 125, 126, 127, 129
Tacitus, 35, 38, 39, 51, 60, 61, 69, 84, 125, 126, 127, 139
Tamerlane, 55
Tatars, 16
Teschke, Benno, 32, 83
Teutonburg, battle of, 25, 33, 60, 69, 125
Thagaste, 155
Theodosius, Code of, 23, 170
Thucydides, 2, 4, 6, 44, 55, 56, 65
Tiberius, emperor, 20
Tilly, Charles, 15, 19, 20, 29, 57, 122
Tocqueville, Alexis de, 64
Tu-Mu, battle of, 33, 60, 71
Turmair, Johann (Aventinus), 191

UAVs, 92, 96
Uskoks, 21, 191, 192, 193

Valens, emperor, 60, 70
Valentinian III, emperor, 145
Vandal, 136, 145, 150, 159, 160, 163, 168
Vandals, 29, 52, 56, 134, 154, 158, 159, 160, 161, 162, 165, 167
Varus, 25, 60, 125

Venice, 21, 30, 191, 192, 193
Vercingetorix, 2, 61, 170, 215
Vitellius, 127

Ward-Perkins, Bryan, 21, 70, 133, 135, 137, 138, 145, 146, 182, 203
Webb, Walter Prescott, 47, 67, 82, 125, 189, 191, 205, 207, 208

Westphalia, 14, 17
Westphalia, Peace of, 14
Wight, Martin, 15, 16, 75, 111

Xenophon, 33, 37, 39, 40

Zosimus, 140, 141, 149